An Approach to Environmental Psychology

KU-162-954

The MIT Press
Cambridge, Massachusetts, and London, England

An Approach to Environmental Psychology

Albert Mehrabian and James A. Russell

Copyright © 1974 by
The Massachusetts Institute of Technology

All rights reserved. No part of this book may be reproduced in any form or by any
means, electronic or mechanical, including photocopying, recording, or by any information storage and retrieval system, without permission in writing from the publisher.

This book was set in IBM Press Roman
by Allen Wayne, Waltham, Inc.,
printed on Mohawk Neotext Offset
and bound in G.S.B. S/535/9 "Black"
by The Colonial Press, Inc.
in the United States of America

Library of Congress Cataloging in Publication Data

Mehrabian, Albert.
 An approach to environmental psychology.
 Bibliograpy: p.
 1. Emotions. 2. Man–Influence of environment. I. Russell, James A., joint
author. II. Title. [DNLM: 1. Emotions. 2. Environment. 3. Psychology,
Experimental. 4. Social environment. BF353 M498a 1974] BF531.M43
152.4 73-16437 ISBN 0-262-13090-4

This book is dedicated to
my brother Robert
A.M.
my mother and my grandmother Meme
J.R.

Contents

Preface

Despite the rapidly increasing interest in environmental psychology, a theory, or even a definition, of the field has been lacking. This volume represents a preliminary effort to identify the relevant variables and their relationships within a coherent framework. Reliable and valid measures for the pertinent variables are developed, and then the major hypotheses of our theory are tested. As our title suggests, the proposed framework represents only one of the many possible theoretical approaches to environmental psychology. Nevertheless, its success in subsuming the diversity of experimental findings and the validity of its predictions (as confirmed by our own preliminary experiments) motivated us to write this volume.

Our framework centers on the use of human emotional responses to environments as intervening variables linking the environment to the variety of behaviors it elicits. Evidence suggests that there are three basic emotional responses (pleasure, arousal, and dominance), combinations of which can be used to describe adequately any emotional state (e.g., anxiety). By considering their impacts on these basic emotional dimensions, the effects of diverse stimulus components within or across sense modalities (e.g., color, pitch, texture, temperature) can be readily compared. However, the complex and changing combinations of multimodal stimulation that are encountered in everyday environments cannot be readily related to the emotional response dimensions through separate enumeration of the effects of each stimulus dimension (e.g., what are the combined effects of all the colors, sounds, and changing configurations of shapes in a setting on the emotional reactions to it?). We, therefore, rely on an additional concept, information rate, to compare the effects of different environments, each with stimulation in many sense modalities. Information rate is a direct correlate of the emotional response of arousal and is therefore an important variable in environmental studies. Its use also allows the inclusion, within a coherent framework, of familiar descriptors of environments such as novelty, complexity, meaningfulness, harmony, distance, naturalness, and scale.

A series of hypotheses, reviewed in the final chapters, relates the emotional response variables to a diversity of behaviors, such as physical approach, performance, affiliation, and verbally or nonverbally expressed preference. These behaviors are more generally subsumed under the concept of approach-avoidance, a dependent measure of central importance in our studies. For instance, one major hypothesis that emerges from our review is that approach-avoidance is an inverted-U-shaped function of the arousal level elicited by a situation. The results of our own studies support this inverted-U hypothesis while providing detailed information on the circumstances in which it needs to be modified, for instance, as a function of the personality of the subject or the specific behaviors involved.

In using emotional responses to environments as basic intervening variables, we are readily able to conceptualize the role of individual difference variables in the environment-approach behavior relationships. Individual differences such as trait anxiety, sex, or extroversion are viewed as having characteristic emotional components (e.g., an anxious person characteristically feels displeasure, is highly aroused, and is submissive). We experimentally specify the characteristic emotional correlates of various individual difference dimensions that have been of central importance in studies of environmental psychology. In this way, we show how these characteristic emotions, together with the emotion-eliciting qualities of situations, mediate the approach-avoidance behaviors to various situations. Similarly, we conceptualize the effects of drug use, alcohol, or environmental pollutants on emotional state, thereby providing some guidelines to the study of the effects of such chemicals on the preference for or the avoidance of various environments.

Our approach to environmental psychology, then, seeks a broad overview to summarize the salient aspects of the man-environment interaction. In a field that has often relied on a diversity of ad hoc or borrowed concepts and measures, our theoretical position leads us to the selection of a few central concepts. We hope this approach will facilitate research, identify the neglected areas in this emerging field, and provide preliminary guidelines for everyday design problems.

We are most grateful to Lena Chow for her untiring assistance in the preparation of the numerous drafts of this volume. We also wish to thank the following journals and publishers for permission to reprint material in this book: *Perceptual and Motor Skills* (Chapter 2); *Environment and Behavior* (part of Chapter 3); and Wadsworth Publishing Company (part of Chapter 7).

Albert Mehrabian and
James A. Russell,
University of California,
Los Angeles

An Approach to Environmental Psychology

1 A Conceptual Framework

There has been an increasing concern with the physical and social environment and its effects on man. Congestion, pollution, and the undisciplined spread of cities, for example, are becoming major influences on human feelings, social interactions, the ability to work, and general physical and psychological well-being. This volume deals with these concerns, which are grouped under the rubric of environmental psychology. We have attempted to present an integrated framework that provides a broad overview of the environment and that outlines the major variables that occur in most situations. With these variables, we have described the impact of environments in terms of their immediate effects on everyday activities as well as their cumulative effects on human affective and attitudinal orientations and behaviors.

The concerns of the environmental psychologist are diverse, as is evident from some of the questions that he may be asked. How can this community center attract people? How can a classroom help a child learn? What kinds of architecture are more likely to generate warm and friendly feelings among the occupants? He may also be asked to make predictions about the impacts of proposed or anticipated environments that have yet to come into existence (e.g., a city designed by Soleri, 1969). Because of the diversity of its concerns and the lack of any definition or theory, previous research in environmental psychology has involved heterogeneous contents and methods, ranging from physiological studies with different animal populations to audio recordings of subjective impressions of pedestrians walking through city streets. For this field to develop and become useful, its loosely interconnected and unspecified set of concerns must be integrated, and its unique principles must somehow be distinguished from other areas of psychology.

Proshansky, Ittelson, and Rivlin (1970a) undertook the first important step in this direction with their pioneering survey of studies in environmental psychology. However, a survey of such diverse interests and findings leaves a number of problems unresolved. One must determine how to analyze and integrate findings from such heterogeneous studies as: the effects of temperature changes on "freshness" (Bedford, 1961); the annoying effects of sonic booms (Kryter, 1966a; 1966b); the effects of redecorated hospital rooms or wards (Proshansky, Ittelson, and Rivlin, 1970c; Sommer, 1969, pp. 83–87); color preferences (Guilford, 1939); differences in performance on manipulative and inspection tasks under tungsten and fluorescent lighting

(Lion, 1964); the psychology of art (Hogg, 1969c; Ross, 1938; Valentine, 1968); and the effects of complex versus simple stimuli on arousal and preference (Berlyne, 1960; Wohlwill, 1968).

The analysis and integration of these heterogeneous studies are further hindered by their frequent lack of experimental controls. For instance, subjects in Burnham and Grimm's (1969) study evaluated the appropriateness of various bricks for different kinds of buildings. Winick and Holt (1961) explored the emotional response of their patients to various arrangements of a set of chairs differing in color and shape. Seaton (1968, p. 10) included a report that dyads in a particular restaurant tended to select small tables, whereas individuals who were alone chose large tables. Markus (1967) found that workers in a particular office had a greater preference for windows with "meaningful" views. Ittelson, Proshansky, and Rivlin (1970) redecorated an entire room in one hospital ward and sought to relate this change to variations in social, isolated-active, and isolated-passive behaviors, All these studies involved changes in a whole host of variables that were left unaccounted for. For example, how many variables are changed when an entire room is redecorated? Particular objects, buildings, or combinations of persons and physical settings constitute a complex of variables. Therefore, it is not possible to relate a particular behavioral change to a specific experimental stimulus. The lack of appropriate experimental controls in some of these studies is partly due to the absence of a conceptual framework. Such a framework would indicate which variables are relevant (or irrelevant), which ones should be explored, and which ones need to be controlled.

Even where rigorous experimental designs have been used and reliable results have been obtained, a conceptual framework is necessary to connect the diverse findings. The endless listings of relations among specific physical variables (e.g., noise, temperature, color) and specific behavioral variables (e.g., galvanic skin response, performance on a vigilance task, exploration, or semantic differential responses) must somehow be integrated to provide a concise statement of the major experimental findings. Such a statement, in turn, would serve to identify those areas in which study has been neglected or those in which excessive attention has produced redundant results. Since it enables the identification of interactions among stimulus effects, a conceptual framework helps resolve inconsistencies obtained from different studies. It is also helpful in designing economical experiments by suggesting all the possible dependent measures that can be included within a given design with little additional cost to the experimenter, with the advantage of enabling tests of more hypotheses.

An additional important contribution of the conceptual framework is that its generality allows the extrapolation, from available findings, of solutions for practical and everyday design problems that have not been the object of specific experiments.

Definition

An additional problem encountered in a field lacking an adequate conceptual framework is the definition of the phenomena under study. Proshansky, Ittelson, and Rivlin (1970a) discussed the problem of defining environmental psychology and suggested that the definition of any field can be one of two general types: a conceptual definition (a theory), or an operational definition (a survey of what environmental psychologists do). Their book constitutes such a survey, and they indicated that they could give no conceptual definition: "The simple fact is that as yet there is no adequate theory, or even the beginnings of a theory, of environmental psychology on which such a definition might be based [p. 5]."

One difficulty in formulating a definition is distinguishing environmental psychology from the study of psychology per se (Wohlwill, 1970). After all, psychology in large part deals with the relationship between stimulus and response; and any stimulus in a psychological theory or experiment constitutes a part of the environment. Thus, the stimulus-response approach to psychology and the traditional boundaries between the various established areas of psychology are of little help in defining environmental psychology as a unique field. Because of the lack of a definition for this field, it is not surprising that researchers have often chosen very specific topics for study, relying on an implicit consensus to determine which problems are relevant. Our approach to this field is, of course, based in part on this consensus, which can be briefly summarized as follows.

One area of concern has been the effects of the physical environment on emotional responses of the persons within it. In many ways, this area is unique to environmental psychology and encompasses much of the work in this field, including many of the socially significant effects of the physical environment. Some of the earliest studies, for example, sought to relate

physical stimuli to anxiety, comfort, and fatigue, or more generally and recently, to the emotions of pleasure and arousal.

This line of inquiry then led to questions about the preference or avoidance
of certain settings and the implications of such preferences for various activities, such as problem solving and work performance. For example, studies
in the field of human engineering attempted to relate work efficiency to
physical stimuli, such as lighting level, background noise, room temperature,
or the arrangement of objects on the workbench.[1]

Another major concern for environmental psychologists has been the effects of spatial arrangements of objects and persons on social interaction.
How does the physical environment, as defined or modified by individuals,
influence the frequency and quality of social interactions? This line of research included studies of the effects of territoriality, crowding, urban renewal, and immediacy or proxemics (e.g., physical distance) on attitudes and
social interaction. It has been found, for instance, that the spatial arrangement of residences affects the frequency of social interaction and the formation of social groups, as well as prejudicial attitudes.[2]

Some investigators have studied both the emotional and the social interaction effects of a physical situation. In studies of hospital environments,
patients' recovery rates, social behavior, and sense of well-being have been
discussed as functions of spatial arrangements of the patients, architecture,
room decorations, and furniture arrangements.[3] There has also been an
increasing concern with the effects of architecture and interior design on
individual and social behavior in normal populations.[4]

These basic concerns in environmental psychology may be conveniently
summarized as (1) the direct impact of physical stimuli on human emotions
and (2) the effect of the physical stimuli on a variety of behaviors, such as
work performance or social interaction.

The areas of interest just outlined should be distinguished from Barker's
(1960; 1965) studies of "ecological psychology," which is a method of
studying the spatial and temporal distributions of behavior. This method
centers around the identification of "behavioral settings," which are units
of specific locations and times with identifiable patterns of behavior that
are independent of the particular people involved. Concerned essentially
with the identification of the frequency and location of types of behavior,
ecological psychology is an observational method and does not involve the

manipulation of experimental variables to explore their effects on various dependent measures. In contrast, the major concerns of environmental psychology do not specify a method; rather, they deal with the causal influences of physical variables on emotions and behavior, using whatever methods may be best suited to a particular problem.

Although the two sets of concerns we have summarized provided our preliminary definition of environmental psychology, we consider such a definition inadequate. In an analysis of the general issues involved in defining any field, Burke (1962, Chapter 2) pointed out that a survey definition, being a simple list of what is to be included, incorrectly presupposes that all the elements are known and that the number of elements is finite. Such a definition, then, excludes all the yet unexplored areas of the field and is therefore inadequate. The field of environmental psychology must ultimately be defined in terms of a conceptual framework: a set of concepts that summarize diverse phenomena and principles that describe the relations among these concepts. The set of concepts and principles may then be applied in an unlimited number of ways to the particular problems that are encountered. In turn, the adequacy of the conceptual framework, such as the one proposed in this volume, is assessed by the reliability and validity of the basic concepts plus the validity and generality of the hypothesized interrelations (Mehrabian, 1968, Chapter 1).

The Description of Environments

Another preliminary task in any study of environments is the selection of useful environmental descriptors, that is, the stimulus variables or categories. According to Craik (1970a), "The feasibility of an environmental psychology rests upon confidence that an adequate taxonomy of dimensions, and eventually a system of metrics, can be developed for the ordinary physical environment [p. 15]." We would add to this prerequisite that the taxonomy of dimensions must include a minimal number of basic concepts, various combinations of which would adequately define almost all of the concepts that an environmental psychologist might require. In other words, the basic taxonomy must be parsimonious to provide the kind of conceptual economy that is an inherent goal of science and to provide practical solutions to actual design problems.

A number of alternative sets of stimulus categories have been used in environmental studies. The most common, but least parsimonious, approach has been the use of the everyday language of specific events and entities. For instance, a classroom may be described in terms of various objects in it (desk, chair, and amount of lighting) and the relations among such objects (e.g., a circular desk arrangement). This approach is exemplified by Craik's (1970b) concept of "environmental displays." These are "units of the everyday physical environment, of which buildings, urban scenes, and forest glades are instances [p. 647]." Further examples of such descriptors are: a flower, a tool, the Grand Canyon, and Manhattan Island. In another study, Craik (1970a) collected even more concepts of this type: lake, church, rock, railroad tracks, valley, dirt, traffic, walls, door, room, and corner.

It is evident that such a list of descriptors can be extended indefinitely and, consequently, does not permit any integration of the concepts. Moreover, each term in the list is so vaguely defined that the host of variables it encompasses remains unspecified. Thus there can be no comparison among environments described by these concepts, and it is impossible to analyze behavioral changes as functions of changes in environments so described. Even with the technique of "behavior maps" (Ittelson, Rivlin, and Proshansky, 1970), which employs a more limited set of categories based on physical locations such as bedroom, kitchen, and closet, the total list of categories is still left indefinite, and each category includes a large number of unspecified variables.

A possible alternative approach is to use terms already defined by a scientific discipline. Craik (1970a) suggested that the descriptors used by geographers and environmental designers could be useful. As we shall see, one drawback of sampling from the lexicon of a professional group outside psychology is that descriptors that are well suited to the problems of that group may not be representative of the concerns of environmental psychologists. For instance, in Chapter 4 we present the results of the factor analyses of a set of environmental descriptors proposed by Kasmar (1970) taken from architectural and design journals. The descriptors were highly redundant, and most of them measured evaluative attitudes. In addition, they referred mainly to visual sources of stimulation and thus did not include adequate representation of stimulation in other modalities. Furthermore, this long list of descriptors failed to account for the presence of other people as an important part of the environment.

The sense modality variables such as those for color, sound, temperature, and texture, which have been identified in studies of perception, provide the best alternative proposed to date. Much of the research in environmental psychology has relied on these variables, and they provide a useful base for further study. Chapter 4 is devoted to a review of this literature. However, the list of sense modality variables is still quite long and cumbersome. For instance, color involves three independent dimensions; thermal stimulation involves at least five. Furthermore, everyday environments include inter-related components with spatial and temporal variations in each of these dimensions.

To account for this variability over time and space, the concept of information rate is introduced in Chapter 5. Using this concept, we are able to subsume within the framework a variety of important concepts, such as complexity, novelty, crowding, and harmony. Nevertheless, the exact description of an everyday environment such as a shopping center in terms of the sense modality and information rate variables can still be difficult. To simplify analysis, we sought a small number of mediating variables. These variables were to be basic, immediate, and measurable reactions to all types of stimulation. In addition, they were, first, to relate directly to the stimulus variables (e.g., arousal is simply a direct correlate of information rate) and, second, to account for variations in other behaviors of concern, such as task performance and social interaction. Chapter 2 presents the rationale for selecting three emotional reactions—pleasure, arousal, and dominance—as the mediating variables.

Given this set of mediating variables, our strategy was as follows. First, systematic research helped specify the relationship between these three mediating emotional responses and the stimulus variables. As mentioned, Chapters 4 and 5 are devoted to this topic. The mediating variables, in turn, are related to the generic class of approach-avoidance behaviors; this topic is taken up in the final chapters.

Summary

Environmental psychology has been concerned with two major topics: the emotional impact of physical stimuli and the effect of physical stimuli on a variety of behaviors such as work performance or social interaction. A number of problems become evident in reviewing this research. An endless

list of dependent and independent variables have been employed, and thus
controlled experimentation has been hampered. What effects should the
experimenter control? What effects might interact with his independent
variables? Also, the results of research using so many different variables
and methods are difficult to integrate. The major conclusions are thus not
easily stated, and practical applications are not readily evident.

Figure 1.1 presents the framework proposed in this volume for studying
the problems of environmental psychology and outlines the important variables that occur in most situations. We propose the theory that physical or
social stimuli in the environment directly affect the emotional state of a
person, thereby influencing his behaviors in it. Three emotional response
variables (pleasure, arousal, and dominance) summarize the emotion-eliciting
qualities of environments and also serve as mediating variables in determining a variety of approach-avoidance behaviors such as physical approach,
work performance, exploration, and social interaction.

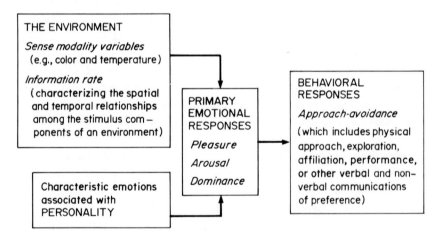

Figure 1.1. Outline of the proposed framework

Notes

1. The work of Berrien (1946), Fox (1967), McCormick (1957), Pressey (1921), Teichner
(1967), or Wells (1965a; 1965b; 1967) exemplifies this approach.

2. Work on territoriality is exemplified by the studies of Altman (1968), Altman and
Haythorn (1967), Altman, Taylor, and Wheeler (1971), Carpenter (1958), Lyman and

Scott (1967); on crowding, by Calhoun (1962a; 1962b; 1966; 1968), Christian (1961), Schmitt (1963); on urban renewal, by Chapin (1938), Fried (1963), Fried and Gleicher (1961), Gans (1962; 1968), Loring (1956), Rand (1969), Srivastava and Good (1969); and on the effects of physical distance on social interaction, by Blake, Rhead, Wedge, and Mouton (1956), Hall (1959; 1966), Sommer (1969), Van der Ryn and Silverstein (1967), Wilner, Walkley, and Cook (1955).

3. For example, see Bayes (1967), Goffman (1961), Ittelson, Proshansky, and Rivlin (1970), Izumi (1965), Proshansky, Ittelson, and Rivlin (1970b), Searles (1960), Spivack (1967; 1969), Srivastava and Good (1968).

4. For example, see Alexander, Hirshen, Ishikawa, Coffin, and Angel (1969), Alexander, Ishikawa, and Silverstein (1968), Gutman (1966), Hershberger (1969), Mehrabian and Diamond (1971a; 1971b), Mintz (1956), Osmond (1957; 1959; 1969), Van der Ryn and Silverstein (1967), Wilner, Walkley, Pinkerton, and Tayback (1962).

2 The Basic Emotional Impact of Environments [1]

In a general approach to understanding man's interaction with various environments, it is essential to identify those responses that are the immediate result of stimulation and that occur in varying degrees in all environments. Further, a systematic environmental psychology requires a parsimonious description of such responses. Perceptual responses do not yield a parsimonious list since it is necessary to consider several dimensions of response within each sense modality. We therefore turned to intermodality, responding in an effort to identify responses common to all types of stimuli, regardless of the sense modality stimulated.

Studies of synesthesia, physiological reactions, and the semantic differential show that there are basic response dimensions that cut across sense modalities. More specifically, this evidence shows that emotional (affective, connotative, feeling) reactions represent the common core of human response to all types of environments. This chapter presents the rationale and the supporting evidence for the selection of pleasure, arousal, and dominance as the three basic emotional reactions and includes the development of specific measures for them.

Evidence concerning Intermodality Responses

Whereas evidence of intermodality responses is available from a variety of experimental studies, it is also available in everyday observations. For example, relations among sensations from different modalities are often culturally prescribed. Note the commonly accepted thermal associations for various tastes (e.g., spicy foods are considered "hot") or the general opinion that reds, oranges, and yellows are "warm" colors whereas blues, greens, and violets are "cool." An interesting cultural variation is the Iranian system of thermal associations to various foods. All food and drink are categorized as either hot or cold in reference not to the temperature or spiciness but rather to the heavy or light feeling that results from eating or drinking. Yogurt and cucumber, for example, are cold foods; meats and more oily foods are hot. Furthermore, cold foods customarily are eaten during warm seasons, and hot foods are eaten during cold ones.

Synesthesia

Intermodality associations have also been demonstrated in experimental studies where stimulation in one sense was observed to affect perception in another. Effects related to such associations are experimental subjects' matching of stimuli corresponding to different modalities with above-chance accuracy. Along these lines, Hazzard (1930) asked subjects to describe 14 different odors and found that a large percentage of the adjectives used characterized stimulation in other modalities (e.g., light, bright, lively, heavy, rough). Intermodality associations may also be evident in actual perceptual experiences in one sense while another is being stimulated (e.g., visual imagery associated with auditory stimulation). Alternatively, perceptions in one modality may be modified, as in a change in the threshold value for that modality, by stimulation in another modality (e.g., Loveless, Brebner, and Hamilton, 1970).

Among earlier studies, intermodality associations were explored with "photistic visualizers," that is, persons who visualize tactile and auditory stimulations. Such persons were found to visualize exciting music in bright forms or sharp and angular figures, and slow music in rounder forms (Karwoski and Odbert, 1938; Karwoski, Odbert, and Osgood, 1942; Luria, 1969). In a randomly selected group, 18% of the subjects claimed to actually see the music that was played to them. This group differed significantly from the others in the complexity of colors they associated with each piece of music. Nevertheless, all subjects significantly agreed in associating color names and mood adjectives with the music (Odbert, Karwoski and Eckerson, 1942). In Uhlich's (1957) study, among 848 subjects, 14% of the male and 31% of the female subjects reported auditory-visual synesthetic experiences.

In one study employing randomly selected subjects, "pitch could be determined which was experienced as having the same brightness as the scent of fresh lilacs. . . . Similarity was experienced between the brightness of the scent of benzol, the brightness of a shade of grey, and the brightness of a pitch [von Hornbostel, 1931, pp. 518–519]." Holt-Hansen (1968) asked 16 subjects to identify the "pitch of fit" while drinking two different kinds of beer, by picking pure tones to correspond to each one. Working independently, subjects selected tones ranging from 510 to 520 cps for one beer, and tones ranging from 640 to 670 cps for the other.

Zietz (1931) found that tones of various frequencies had different effects on afterimages. For instance, afterimages flickered as a function of a "vibrating" tone's frequency. For low-frequency tones (200 cps), the afterimages were of darker, warmer, softer, and duller colors and vaguer contours. For tones of intermediate frequency (550 cps), afterimages had sharper contours and were in brighter, colder, clearer, and harder colors. For high-frequency tones (1100 cps), rounded afterimages were occasionally transformed into squarish forms. Zietz (1931) noted that the association was not necessarily one way—visual experiences could likewise influence audition. For instance, when the room was well lit, his subjects judged tones to be of higher frequency than when the room was dark. Zietz's (1931) study exemplified the methods and findings of early synesthetic studies. One explanation of the colored hearing phenomena was that some types of sounds and visual stimuli were associated because they aroused the same emotions (Langfeld, 1929).

Experiments with children also showed consistent associations between auditory and visual experiences. Simpson, Quinn, and Ausubel (1956) asked 995 elementary school children, grades 3 through 6, to tell what colors they thought of when they heard each of six tones. The children consistently reported certain color associations for tones of various frequencies (e.g., yellow and green in response to higher tones, red and orange in response to middle-pitch tones, and blue and violet for low-frequency tones). Further, the percent of reports of yellow as a function of tone frequency was a mirror image about the vertical for that of blue. Similarly, a plot of the percent report of red in response to various frequencies of tone was the mirror image for that obtained for reports of violet.

Other studies have explored the above-chance matching of various sets of stimuli (e.g., Scheerer and Lyons, 1957). In one extensive series, congruent and incongruent sets of line drawings of gestural symbols, colors, nonverbal sounds, and words referring to spatial positioning (e.g., near, far) were developed. Langer and Rosenberg (1964) and Rosenberg and Langer (1965) found that subjects matched line drawings of postures and gestures with certain color names (e.g., red, blue) and sound symbols (e.g., clack, mumble) with beyond-chance expectations. Rosenberg, Langer, and Stewart (1969), using a paired-associate learning paradigm, found that subjects learned congruent pairs (those matched by subjects in the earlier studies) of gestures and colors, and of postures and sounds, faster than incongruent pairs.

In one of the most thorough studies of synesthetic tendency, Osgood (1960) noted:

There is ample evidence for visual-verbal synesthesia within our own culture. As early as 1921, Lundholm (1921) reported data on the "feeling tones" of lines: that SAD was represented by large, downward-directed curves; that MERRY was represented by small, upward-directed lines; that GENTLE was represented by large, horizontally-directed curves, and so on. Poffenberger and Barrows (1924) confirmed and extended the relationships reported by Lundholm. Karwoski, Odbert, and Osgood (1942) were able to demonstrate similar relationships between word meanings and the synesthetic drawings of photistic visualizers. More recently, Scheerer and Lyons (1957), Hochberg and Brooks (1956), and McMurray (1958) have reported Western intracultural consistencies in relating line drawings and/or verbally defined visual dimensions to connotative meanings or feeling-tones. As far as I am aware, the present study is the first attempt to demonstrate that the visual-verbal synesthetic relationships characteristic of our own language/culture community are shared by peoples who speak different languages and enjoy different cultures— the Navajo, the Japanese, and the Mexican-Spanish living in the American Southwest. The over-all similarities in synesthetic tendencies across these groups are impressive—when the synesthetic relationships that are significant (.01 level) intraculturally are tested for cross-cultural agreement, approximately 90% of the relationships prove to be in the same direction. We can conclude with confidence then that the determinants of these synesthetic relations are shared by humans everywhere—to the extent that our sample of "everywhere" is representative. . . . The present study and others along the same line (Kumata, 1957; Kumata and Schramm, 1956; Suci, 1957; Triandis and Osgood, 1958) strongly support the position that, for certain aspects of cognitive behavior at least, "world view" may remain relatively stable despite differences in both language and culture. . . . The phenomena which seem to display generality across human groups regardless of language or culture are essentially connotative—the affective "feeling tones" of meaning which contribute to synesthesia, metaphor and the like. . . .

Finally, we may inquire into the reasons behind similarities in connotative systems despite language/culture differences. First, by virtue of being members of the human species, people are equipped biologically to react to situations in certain similar ways—with autonomic, emotional reactions to rewarding and punishing situations (evaluation), with strong or weak muscular tension to things offering great or little resistances (potency), and so on—and hence they can form connotative significances for perceived objects and their linguistic signs varying along the same basic dimensions. Such connotative reactions enter into a wide variety of meaningful situations, are therefore broadly generalized, and provide a basis for synesthetic and metaphorical transpositions. Beyond this shared connotative framework, there are many specific relations between human organisms and their generally similar environments whose stability can be the basis for synesthetic and metaphorical translations. These may be either innate to the species or developed by learning under similar conditions. An example of the former (innate) basis may be the common association of the red end of the spectrum with warmth and activity and the blue end with coldness and passivity. An example of the latter (acquired) basis may be the common association of visually large with auditorily loud—it is simply a characteristic of the physical world that as any noise-producing object approaches or is approached, increases in visual angle are correlated with increases in loudness. These "homotropisms" and experiential contingencies may be expressed in language but are independent of the structure of any particular language [pp. 166–168].

It is precisely these emotional-connotative associations that provide the basis for our present organization of the heterogeneous findings. Although some intermodality associations observed in synesthetic studies can be attributed to learned associations, there are more basic and transcultural affective reactions that account for most synesthetic associations.

Physiological Reactions

The existence of some basic response dimensions also becomes evident in physiological studies where certain effects are found to be common to stimulations in all the sense modalities. Studies of the physiological correlates of the experiences of pleasure and pain led to the identification of pleasure-pain centers in the midbrain. Electrical stimulation of areas of the hypothalamus and certain midbrain nuclei is pleasant, and stimulation of lower parts of the midline system is painful (Heath, 1954; 1963; 1964a; 1964b; Olds, 1956). There is, then, a well-defined physiological mechanism associated with the experience of pleasure-pain, and this mechanism is common to all the sensory modalities.

Lindsley (1951) postulated the concept of arousal as a basic response that is independent of the sense modality stimulated. This concept received considerable attention from other workers (e.g., Berlyne, 1960; Duffy, 1957; 1962) and was initially proposed to account for the intensity, but not the quality or direction, of a behavior. In the same vein, Hebb (1955) identified arousal with the concept of drive in the Hullian (1951; 1952) learning theory. Malmo (1959) most clearly defined this early conception of arousal of the entire organism as activation of the ascending reticular activating system (ARAS). Excitation of the ARAS was measured directly by EEG desynchronization, that is, fast EEG activity with concomitant decrease in alpha waves. Since the ARAS in turn excited other parts of the nervous system and was therefore responsible for the arousal of the entire organism, it was possible to look for other physiological and behavioral correlates of EEG desynchronization. Among these secondary measures, the most promising involved the sympathetic nervous system—GSR, rise in arterial blood pressure, and pupillary dilation. Respiratory activity, oxygen consumption, pulse rate, muscle tension, and thermal properties of the skin also provided indexes of behavioral activities. Although the latter indexes have rarely been used, they do relate to this conception of arousal.

In reviewing the concept of arousal in 1960, Berlyne wrote that this is "one of the variables that would have to be assigned a value if the psychological condition of a human being or higher animal at any particular time were to be adequately described. It is a measure of how wide awake the organism is, of how ready it is to react. The lower pole of the continuum is represented by sleep or coma, while the upper pole would be reached in states of frantic excitement [Berlyne, 1960, p. 48]." Similarly, Corcoran (1963a) defined arousal as the inverse of the probability of the subject falling asleep.

Research evidence challenged this unitary conception of arousal. The work of Lacey (1950) and Lacey, Bateman, and Van Lehn (1953) showed that there were individual differences in characteristic modes of arousal response and differential responsiveness of the GSR, pulse rate, or pupil dilation, for instance, to various categories of stimulation. Therefore, these various secondary indexes of arousal were not generally intercorrelated.

Additional work by Feldman and Waller (1962) showed that whereas "electrocortical" arousal depended on the reticular formation, "behavioral" arousal depended on the hypothalamus. Experimentally, these two aspects of arousal could be made to occur independently of one another (Bradley, 1958; Wikler, 1952). In addition, Lacey (1967) found a third, autonomic aspect of arousal that was functionally independent of the other two. The relative independence of these three aspects of arousal challenged the original conception of a unitary dimension of total organismic arousal.

In reviewing these studies Lacey (1967) stated that "the evidence shows that electrocortical arousal, autonomic arousal, and behavioral arousal may be considered to be *different forms* of arousal, each complex in itself . . . [and which] *in general* occur simultaneously. In other words, the assertions of activation and arousal theory seem to me to be true only in an actuarial sense. The limitations of our present knowledge make it impossible to say at present with what frequency and under what conditions these 'arousals' do occur together. This difficulty arises primarily, I think, because the representativeness of laboratory experiments is so limited [pp. 15–16]."

Although available physiological evidence fails to establish the exact nature of the arousal response(s), support is provided for the notion of basic cross-modality responding. Further, it is important to note that a combined index of several aspects of physiological arousal has been found to correlate highly with verbal self-reports of arousal state (Thayer, 1967; 1970). This finding

is important in the present context in establishing the link between a physiological arousal system and verbal reports of arousal.

The Semantic Differential

The physiological mechanisms reviewed support the idea that there are basic
reactions that cut across sense modality distinctions and distinguish pleasure
and arousal as two such dimensions. It is reassuring to find an entirely separate source of evidence that corroborates this conclusion. Work with the
semantic differential (Osgood, Suci, and Tannenbaum, 1957; Snider and
Osgood, 1969) helped to characterize human judgments of, or reactions to,
stimuli of any degree of complexity, regardless of the number of cues or the
modalities affected. These studies defined arousal (the activity factor that
was obtained from studies with this method) and pleasure (the evaluation
factor) as basic responses to stimuli, and also suggested a third dimension
(potency).

Initial work with the semantic differential was aimed at the denotation of
a limited set of factors that could be used to describe the meaning of concepts. Subsequent work with this same technique, however, revealed a far
greater generality of the identified factors. For instance, in one of the earlier
experiments by Tucker (1955), artists and nonartists judged various kinds of
paintings and rated them on semantic differential scales. The three factors
that characterized the various paintings were named activity (which included
high loadings from dynamic to static, active to passive, vibrant to still),
evaluation (which included high loadings from smooth to rough, profound
to superficial, meaningful to meaningless), and potency (which included high
loadings from hard to soft, strong to weak). Solomon's (1954) study of
judgments of sonar signals again yielded the same three factors: evaluation
(pleasant-unpleasant, good-bad, pleasing-annoying), potency (large-small,
heavy-light), and activity (busy-resting, violent-gentle).

Subsequent work by Osgood (1966) and other investigators reviewed by
Mehrabian (1970a; 1972a) provided evidence for a similar description of
social cues such as facial and vocal expressions, postures, and movements.
The results showed that implicit interpersonal cues that are most prevalent
in the social interaction process can be described in terms of three basic
dimensions that are similar to those obtained from earlier studies of verbal
cues by Osgood, Suci, and Tannenbaum (1957).

More specifically, for emotional reactions, a similar set of three basic dimensions was obtained by Bush (1973). She selected 264 adjectives to sample the entire domain of feeling responses and scaled these with a multi-dimensional scaling technique. Three dimensions resulted from the analysis and corresponded to the three factors of the semantic differential. These dimensions were named pleasantness-unpleasantness, level of activation, and level of aggression. Even though Bush (1973) named the third factor "aggression," she noted that, "Perhaps the only clear parallel between Dimension 3 and dimensions in other studies is to potency of the semantic differential. The difference between words high and low on the dimension seems to be arousal for defense and autonomy (e.g., outraged versus needed), which is interpersonal potency by most definitions [p. 55]."

To summarize, studies of intermodality associations, synesthesia, physiological responses to stimuli, and the semantic differential all suggest that there exists a limited set of basic emotional (connotative, affective, feeling) responses to all stimulus situations, independent of the sensory modality involved. Judgmental responses of evaluation and activity on the semantic differential are hypothesized to correspond to the emotional responses of pleasure and arousal, respectively. The judgmental response of potency corresponds to an emotional reaction that may be labeled dominance versus submissiveness, such that low stimulus potency elicits a feeling of dominance, and high stimulus potency elicits a submissive feeling. Variations in pleasure, arousal, and dominance constitute the common core of human emotional responses to all situations. Such affective responses, in turn, account for the phenomenon of synesthesia, in that stimuli involving different sense modalities may nevertheless elicit the same emotional responses.

Additional terms describing a diversity of emotional reactions to situations may be defined in terms of these three basic dimensions. Thus, for example, the feeling of boredom or fatigue may be described as one that is low on pleasure, arousal, and dominance. On the other hand, excitement may be characterized as an emotional state of high pleasure, arousal, and dominance. Anxiety and stress rate high on arousal, but low on pleasure and dominance. Relaxation, contentment, and comfort rate high on pleasure and dominance but low on arousal. These are tentative hypotheses intended to illustrate possible applications of the three basic emotional factors to the description of the many kinds of emotional reactions that are of interest to environmental psychologists.

The Three Emotional Dimensions

Pleasure

Pleasure-displeasure is a feeling state that can be assessed readily with self-report, such as semantic differential measures, or with behavioral indicators, such as smiles, laughter, and, in general, positive versus negative facial expressions. The latter can be reliably scored on a dimension of pleasantness, which is independent of both their aroused quality and dominance-submissiveness. Thus these cues provide an important behavioral index, particularly in social interaction (Mehrabian, 1972b).

Within the present conceptualization, pleasure is distinguished from preference, liking, positive reinforcement, or approach-avoidance. Although pleasure and these latter responses are correlated, a distinction is necessary since the latter responses are also determined by the arousing quality of a stimulus. For example, Day (1968a) found that the word "prefer" was correlated with the word "pleasing," but the two words related differently to "complexity" (a direct correlate of arousal). Day and Crawford (1969) found that "liking" was related to "pleasing" as well as "interesting" and "complexity"—the latter two are also correlates of arousal.

Arousal

In considering the problems that are associated with physiological measures of arousal, Berlyne (1967) commented, "All this need not worry us unduly, although it certainly calls for circumspection, as long as we regard arousal as a dimension and not as a phenomenon—not, that is, as a process that goes on in one location in the central nervous system [p. 12]."

Thus, even though there is insufficient knowledge of the relations between the primary and secondary physiological measures of arousal (especially over a variety of situations), Berlyne's (1960, p. 48) definition of arousal still has considerable heuristic value. Consistent with that definition, arousal is conceptualized here as a feeling state varying along a single dimension ranging from sleep to frantic excitement.

We employ the semantic differential method to measure arousal in our experiments reported in the chapters to follow. Our data, presented in the following section, have shown that by using verbal reports of subjects, a unitary and primary factor for characterizing a person's arousal level can be readily identified. Further, as already noted, there is evidence showing that a combination of physiological indexes of arousal is highly correlated with a verbal self-report measure of arousal state (Thayer, 1967; 1970). Thus, we shall define arousal as a feeling state that is most directly assessed by verbal report. However, in developing hypotheses from earlier literature, it will be necessary to refer to the various physiological measures of arousal since they have been used almost exclusively.

Several nonverbal measures have also been identified that are intercorrelated and essentially define a measure of responsiveness or arousal in social situations (Mehrabian, 1970a; 1972b, Appendix A). These are vocal activity (including positive as well as negative), facial activity (including positive and negative expressions), speech rate, and speech volume.

Dominance

Dominance-submissiveness is a feeling state that can be assessed from verbal reports using the semantic differential method. This dimension is the inverse of the judged potency of the environment. Behaviorally, dominance is measured in terms of postural relaxation (i.e., body lean and assymmetrical positioning of the limbs) and is independent of pleasure and arousal (e.g., Mehrabian, 1970a; 1972b).

Analogous concepts have been used by some investigators to describe the effects of environments. Spivack (1969) described different aspects of hospital environments in terms of the degree to which they restricted variability in patients' behaviors. Proshansky, Ittelson, and Rivlin (1970b) proposed "freedom of choice" as one dimension to describe hospital environments and related it to more familiar concepts such as privacy, territoriality, and crowding. Privacy and territoriality permit greater freedom of choice, whereas crowding can limit freedom. Proshansky, Ittelson, and Rivlin (1970b) suggested that crowding need not have negative connotations—when it limits freedom, it is negative, but when it does not limit freedom or even enhances a freer feeling (e.g., as in instances of deindividuation discussed by Festinger, Pepitone, and Newcomb, 1952), then it is preferred.

Since the way in which the concept of dominance is used in the present context is somewhat novel, some elaboration of its definition is appropriate. An individual's feeling of dominance in a situation is based on the extent to which he feels unrestricted or free to act in a variety of ways. This feeling can be hampered by settings that limit the forms of behavior and enhanced by settings that facilitate a greater variety of behaviors. For instance, an individual has greater freedom, and therefore a feeling of dominance, in his own territory (e.g., listening to music at home relative to doing so in a concert hall or reading the same book in his office rather than in a library). A kitchen or an office that is well stocked with a variety of tools facilitates more behaviors (and enhances a feeling of dominance) than one that is only sparsely equipped. Flexible interior decorations, such as movable room partitions, adjustable levels of lighting, or movable furniture allow many arrangements suited to a greater variety of activities. Thus, relative to others that are fixed and difficult to change, such flexible arrangements are conducive to a feeling of dominance.

Physical stimuli that are rated as more intense, more ordered, and more powerful on the semantic differential are associated with a submissive feeling for the person encountering them. For instance, an intense and/or large stimulus can constrain behavior by masking the contribution of other stimuli that might elicit other behaviors.

For social environments, once again the dominance of the participant can be described in terms of familiar concepts. Formal social situations constrain behavior more than informal ones. Thus, ceremonial occasions in which implicit homage is paid to a higher or more potent idea or entity (e.g., a religious meeting) are typically associated with well-defined forms of behavior which are judged acceptable and distinguished from other, unacceptable ones. For instance, a person has less freedom of choice (is less dominant) in the presence of others of higher status. Note the difference in the extent of behavioral freedom of a patient compared to that of a physician in a hospital ward. This is consistent with the general idea that there is an inverse relationship between a dominant feeling and the potency of the environment.

As will be seen, this dimension of emotional response has received little attention from investigators. There is a lack of data on how the physical aspects of a situation determine the feeling of dominance or on how dominance influences approach-avoidance behaviors. For this reason these comments are offered tentatively at this point and are only suggested by evidence from the semantic differential (Snider and Osgood, 1969).

Psychometric Properties

The three emotional dimensions are conceptualized as orthogonal, although in fact they sometimes exhibit small, but significant, correlations (e.g., Osgood, Suci, and Tannenbaum, 1957). Various studies have yielded sizable positive relationships between pleasure and arousal for specific sets of stimuli (e.g., Vitz, 1966b). Day (1968c) found that semantic differential ratings of "pleasingness" were negatively correlated with ratings of "complexity," that is, arousing quality. However, in an earlier study (Day, 1967a) no such correlation was found. Such findings are not inconsistent with the hypothesized independence of the three dimensions of emotional response, since dimensions that are independent across stimuli in general may nevertheless exhibit a variety of relations (linear or curvilinear) within particular sets of stimuli. Experimental findings reported later in this chapter directly test this hypothesized independence of the three emotional response dimensions across a wide range of situations.

The semantic differential further indicates that the three dimensions are bipolar; that is, pleasure extends along a single dimension from extreme displeasure to extreme pleasure, and similarly for arousal and dominance. This bipolarity has been challenged by Nowlis's (1965) research with the Mood Adjective Check List (MACL), which includes separate scales for pleasantness, unpleasantness, activation, deactivation, control, and lack of control. If the three scales of pleasantness, activation, and control were indeed bipolar, we would expect high, inverse correlations between the corresponding separate MACL scales. Nowlis (1965), however, found low, nonsignificant correlations in a large study in which subjects were asked to describe their present mood.

This apparent contradiction was explained by Bentler (1969). He hypothesized that the adjective checklist format (the type used in the MACL) suffers from a significant acquiescence bias, that is, the tendency on the part of some subjects to see all adjectives as self-descriptive. As in Nowlis's (1965) study, Bentler presented subjects with the scales of the semantic differential in a single adjective checklist format. Opposite ends of the same continuum (e.g., pleasantness and unpleasantness) were found to be uncorrelated. The expected high, inverse correlations did emerge, however, when the acquiescence bias was statistically controlled by partial correlation. Thus, if the acquiescence bias is statistically accounted for, it can be shown that the pleasure, arousal, and dominance dimensions are indeed bipolar.

Thus, the Nowlis (1965) MACL constitutes one verbal report measure of the three dimensions, provided that the acquiescence bias is statistically controlled. Verbal measures relating to pleasure and arousal were provided by Johnson and Myers (1967), who developed Thurstone-type scales of happiness, anger, fear, depression, and arousal. The latter scales have already been used in environmental studies (e.g., Radloff and Helmreich, 1968). Finally, our own studies described in this chapter provided direct verbal measures that were constructed to be free of acquiescence bias.

Development of Self-Report Measures of the Three Emotional Dimensions

Study 1. In our first step to develop verbal measures of the three emotional dimensions, the twenty-eight adjective pairs presented in Table 2.1 were written. Based on intuitive grounds, they represented a tentative set of descriptors for the three emotional dimensions. Forty verbally described situations (Numbers 1 through 40 in Appendix A) were also written to provide a diverse sample of physical settings that would elicit a large variety of emotional states. Although the situations were not systematically developed, their large number provided some assurance that they constituted a representative sample of environments.

In this first experiment, 134 University of California undergraduates served as subjects. Each of them was presented with a random selection of eight situations and was asked to describe how he would feel in each one by using the twenty-eight adjective pairs in Table 2.1. These items were randomly ordered, half of them were reversed in direction, and the entire set was presented to the subjects in a format similar to that shown in Appendix B. The accompanying instructions to the subjects were:

Read situation number —— [the situation identification number was written here] very carefully and then try to imagine yourself in it. Take about two minutes to really get into the mood of the situation; then rate your feelings in this situation with the adjective pairs below. Some of the pairs might seem unusual, but you'll probably feel more one way than the other. So, for each pair, put a check mark (Example: - - - -:- - -ˠ-:- - -) close to the adjective which you believe to describe your feelings better. The more appropriate that adjective seems, the closer you put your check mark to it.

The resulting 28 X 28 matrix of correlations was factor analyzed, and a principal component solution was obtained. There were four factors with eigenvalues exceeding unity, although the fourth factor consisted only of a single item. Oblique rotation of these factors yielded the loadings for the first three factors that are shown in Table 2.1. The various items have been arranged in Table 2.1 to facilitate the distinctions among the three sets of

Table 2.1. Rotated Factor Matrix of the Preliminary Set of Emotional Response Scales*

Emotional Response	Factor 1: Pleasure	Factor 2: Arousal	Factor 3: Dominance
Happy-unhappy	0.89	−0.01	0.07
Pleased-annoyed	0.89	−0.03	0.03
Satisfied-unsatisfied	0.86	−0.07	0.02
Contented-melancholic	0.83	−0.02	0.00
Hopeful-despairing	0.79	0.05	0.03
Relaxed-bored	0.80	0.06	−0.13
Comfortable-uncomfortable	0.85	−0.20	0.10
Excited-irritated	0.72	0.34	0.03
Secure-insecure	0.69	−0.25	0.23
Stimulated-relaxed	−0.16	0.82	0.07
Excited-calm	−0.20	0.80	0.03
Frenzied-sluggish	0.07	0.77	0.00
Jittery-dull	0.02	0.74	−0.13
Wide awake–sleepy	0.11	0.77	0.11
Aroused-unaroused	0.23	0.78	−0.07
Alert-peaceful	−0.34	0.70	0.13
Excited-soothed	−0.30	0.77	0.09
Vigilant-uninterested	0.38	0.66	−0.09
Irritated-depressed	0.08	0.16	−0.04
Controlling-controlled	0.16	−0.05	0.72
Powerful-overpowered	0.21	−0.10	0.71
In control–cared for	−0.12	0.08	0.69
Important-awed	−0.06	−0.15	0.64
Dominant-submissive	0.10	0.20	0.71
Autonomous-guided	−0.05	−0.04	0.62
Influential-reverent	−0.19	0.12	0.66
Domineering-helpless	0.33	−0.02	0.69
Daring-cautious	0.29	0.12	0.39
Percent variance	27	21	12

*The correlations used to compute this factor analysis were based on 1072 observations.

emotional responses. It is seen that the six highest loading items in each factor were adequate measures for that factor. Factor 1 (pleasure) accounted for 27%, Factor 2 (arousal) for 21%, and Factor 3 (dominance) for 12% of the total variance. Factor 1 correlated –0.02 with Factor 2 and 0.19 with Factor 3; Factor 2 correlated 0.05 with Factor 3.

Study 2. To improve the emotional descriptors a second study was performed. Additional situations were written to provide the complete list in Appendix A. On the basis of the results of the first study, the eighteen adjective pairs were selected from Table 2.1 that best measured the respective emotional dimensions. Five additional adjective pairs, designed to measure dominance, were written. This new set of twenty-three adjective pairs is presented in Table 2.2.

A new sample of 163 University of California undergraduates each rated approximately twenty situations that were randomly selected from Appendix A. They used the adjective pairs of Table 2.2, presented to them in a random order, with half the items within each of the three factors inverted to control response bias. The subjects were given the same instructions employed in the first study.

The resulting 23 X 23 matrix of correlations was factor analyzed, and a principal component solution was obtained. There were three factors with eigenvalues exceeding unity. Oblique rotation of these factors yielded the loadings shown in Table 2.2. As in the first study, the various items have been arranged in Table 2.2 to facilitate the distinctions among the three sets of emotional responses. Once again, it is seen that the first factor measured pleasure, the second, arousal, and the third, dominance. Factor 1 (pleasure) accounted for 32%, Factor 2 (arousal) for 17%, and Factor 3 (dominance) for 12% of the total variance. Factor 1 correlated 0.05 with Factor 2 and 0.26 with Factor 3; Factor 2 correlated 0.13 with Factor 3.

Study 3. This was an attempt to cross-validate the findings from the second study and employed the best six items for each dimension listed in Table 2.2. These eighteen items were randomly ordered, and three items within each of the three factors were inverted to control response bias. The subjects were 214 University of California undergraduates, each of whom rated a different subset of six situations selected from the list given in Appendix A.

The resulting 18 X 18 matrix of correlations was factor analyzed, and a principal component solution was obtained. Once again, there were three

Table 2.2. Rotated Factor Matrix of the Second Set of Emotional Response Scales*

Emotional Response	Factor 1: Pleasure	Factor 2: Arousal	Factor 3: Dominance
Happy-unhappy	0.88	−0.01	0.13
Pleased-annoyed	0.89	−0.06	0.08
Satisfied-unsatisfied	0.87	−0.02	0.11
Contented-melancholic	0.78	−0.01	0.13
Hopeful-despairing	0.71	0.04	0.19
Relaxed-bored	0.84	0.07	0.00
Stimulated-relaxed	−0.22	0.80	0.02
Excited-calm	−0.09	0.82	0.02
Frenzied-sluggish	0.01	0.79	0.02
Jittery-dull	0.02	0.70	−0.09
Wide awake-sleepy	0.15	0.79	0.05
Aroused-unaroused	0.21	0.77	−0.04
Controlling-controlled	0.06	−0.04	0.76
Dominant-submissive	0.06	0.15	0.75
Influential-influenced	0.06	−0.07	0.72
Important-awed	−0.05	−0.14	0.69
Autonomous-guided	0.08	−0.01	0.63
In control–cared for	−0.07	0.10	0.62
Powerful-overpowered	0.21	−0.10	0.64
Bold-cautious	0.29	0.10	0.45
Protecting-protected	−0.48	0.27	0.35
Free-restrained	0.72	0.04	0.26
Unimpressed-impressed	−0.70	−0.42	0.16
Percent variance	32	17	12

*The correlations used to compute this factor analysis were based on 3261 observations.

factors with eigenvalues exceeding unity. Oblique rotation of these factors yielded the loadings that are shown in Table 2.3. The factorial composition as noted in Table 2.3 provided support for the grouping of emotions given in Appendix B and in all respects was a satisfactory replication of the findings

Table 2.3. Rotated Factor Matrix of the Final Set of Emotional Response Scales*

Emotional Response	Factor 1: Pleasure	Factor 2: Arousal	Factor 3: Dominance
Happy-unhappy	0.92	0.01	0.01
Pleased-annoyed	0.91	−0.09	−0.02
Satisfied-unsatisfied	0.92	−0.04	−0.01
Contented-melancholic	0.85	0.01	0.02
Hopeful-despairing	0.79	0.02	0.09
Relaxed-bored	0.84	0.08	−0.05
Stimulated-relaxed	−0.29	0.75	0.05
Excited-calm	−0.11	0.82	0.01
Frenzied-sluggish	−0.04	0.80	0.05
Jittery-dull	0.04	0.77	−0.04
Wide awake-sleepy	0.24	0.79	0.00
Aroused-unaroused	0.06	0.80	−0.03
Controlling-controlled	0.11	−0.06	0.76
Dominant-submissive	−0.01	0.28	0.67
Influential-influenced	0.02	−0.01	0.79
Important-awed	0.00	0.02	0.46
Autonomous-guided	0.03	−0.09	0.69
In control–cared for	−0.12	−0.02	0.68
Percent variance	27	23	14

*The correlations used to compute this factor analysis were based on 1284 observations.

from the second study. Pleasure, arousal, and dominance accounted for 27%, 23%, and 14% of the total variance, respectively. The pleasure factor correlated −0.07 with arousal and 0.03 with the dominance factor; arousal correlated 0.18 with dominance.

Appendix B was thus based on the results from all three studies and includes the six best items for each of the three factors. These three scales constitute our measures of the three basic emotional dimensions and are used in the studies reported in the rest of this volume. To compute factor scores for a subject who rates his emotions in a situation using the scales of Appendix B, a simple and satisfactory approach is to sum his responses to all six items of each factor for that situation.

Discussion. Our review of the relevant literature showed that various combinations of pleasure, arousal, and dominance may adequately represent the diverse human emotional-connotative reactions to environments. The experimental data presented here were therefore not intended to replicate that evidence. Thus, no effort was made in our initial selection of emotional descriptors used in Study 1 to include a list of adjective pairs that would exhaustively describe the great diversity of human emotions. Rather, we proceeded directly to construct scales that would most directly and uniquely measure each of the three factors.

The hypothesized weak relations of the three emotional response dimensions were confirmed by the data. Across the three studies conducted, the inter-correlations ranged from –0.07 to 0.26. In two of the studies, however, there were significant positive correlations between pleasure and dominance. These low intercorrelations among the three emotional response dimensions provide support for our assertion that they constitute a parsimonious base for the description of the great diversity of emotional responses that occur in every-day situations.

The resulting three measures, given in Appendix B, can be used readily to assign exact coefficients to any emotional state (e.g., boredom) in terms of the three emotional response factors. For instance, subjects could be re-quested to rate these specific emotions on the eighteen scales of Appendix B. Separate factor scores of pleasure, arousal, and dominance can then be computed from each subject's ratings of a specific emotion. Finally, a mul-tiple regression analysis can be used to compute weighting coefficients and to write an equation in which a specific emotional state is expressed as a linear function of pleasure, arousal, and dominance.

The three emotional factors can also be used to categorize environments. Psychologists have traditionally grouped stimuli on the basis of the sense modalities that stimuli affect (e.g., temperature, sound intensity). However, the description of any ordinary environment would be extremely cumbersome in this way because of the multitude of dimensions involved, together with the temporal variations that occur along each of these dimensions. For in-stance, how many dimensions are needed to describe the environment of a person riding in an open sports car through the countryside, and how often would one need to assign new values to the person's experience in each of these dimensions? In contrast to the latter approach, the description of the same experiences in terms of emotional responses can be accomplished quite readily. The person in the sports car may be said to be in a highly arousing, pleasant, and dominance-eliciting environment.

Although this method for the description of environments is unusual, it should be noted that stimuli are generally response-defined (e.g., a stimulus is said to be reinforcing, stressful, or frustrating). Indeed, studies of perception distinguish stimuli on the basis of their differential impacts on the different sense organs. Our suggested alternative, then, is an extension of the response-defined approach to the description of stimuli or situations and has the advantage of providing a parsimonious set of environmental descriptors. Thus, the scales in Appendix B can be presented to subjects with the instructions that they rate their emotional reactions to a particular situation, and average reports of emotional reactions along each of the three factors of emotional response could then be used to describe that situation.

Summary

Available literature provides ample evidence that there are basic responses that are elicited by stimuli but that are independent of sense modality distinctions. Everyday observations of intermodality associations, studies of synesthesia and of physiological reactions to different stimuli, and semantic differential studies all showed evidence of such primary responses. Semantic differential studies, in particular, have shown that human judgments of diverse samples of stimuli can be characterized in terms of three dimensions: evaluation, activity, and potency. We have termed the corresponding emotional responses pleasure, arousal, and dominance. Simple self-report measures of these emotional reactions were developed by using questionnaire studies in which subjects described a variety of situations using semantic differential type scales.

Note
1. This chapter is reprinted with the permission of the publisher: Mehrabian, A., and Russell, J.A. The basic emotional impact of environments. *Perceptual and Motor Skills* *38* (1974): 283–301.

3 Personality and Internal Sources of Emotion

Persons enter a situation with different levels of emotion. Characteristic emotional levels associated with personality and temporary internal states (such as hunger- or drug-induced states) combine with the situation to determine the overall emotional response. It is then this overall emotional response that the person reports and that mediates other behaviors in the situation. Thus, baseline information about the emotional correlates of personality traits and the emotional correlates of internal states is needed to predict more accurately the effects of different environments on different kinds of people.

Just as various emotions may be defined in terms of pleasure, arousal, and dominance states, analogous definitions are hypothesized to apply to the characteristic levels of emotion associated with personality. Anxiety, for example, rates high on arousal, but low on pleasure and dominance. This definition is equally applicable to state and trait anxiety. Other personality traits that have been of central concern in environmental studies (e.g., extroversion, neuroticism, arousal-seeking tendency) can thus be defined in terms of the characteristic levels of pleasure, arousal, and dominance that are associated with each. Part of this chapter presents a method that can be used to obtain such definitions for (characteristic) emotions. Since internal states (such as fatigue or hunger) and drug-induced states also contribute to variations in levels of pleasure, arousal, and dominance, another section is devoted to the discussion of their effects.

The bulk of this chapter, however, deals with a dimension of personality that has been of considerable importance in studies of environmental psychology. Evidence to be presented in Chapter 6 shows that various approach behaviors to a situation (e.g., desire to explore, work, or affiliate) are maximized with increasing pleasantness of the situation and with an intermediate level of arousal. Thus, the pleasure state of an individual prior to his contact with a situation is not as important as his arousal state in determining his approach-avoidance reaction to that situation. In other words, no matter what level of pleasure he starts with, he is likely to prefer situations where pleasure is enhanced; however, depending on his initial level of arousal, the increment in arousal due to a situation may either be too much, too little, or just enough.

Thus, in addition to a person's characteristic level of arousal (i.e., trait arousal), a second personality trait essential to our framework is the individual's characteristically preferred arousal level. Indeed, the data to be presented show that there are consistent individual differences in arousal-seeking tendency. Accordingly, the first section in this chapter is devoted to the development of a questionnaire measure for this personality trait.

To avoid confusion in terminology, we shall make the distinction between trait emotions and state emotions (e.g., trait pleasure versus state pleasure). The *characteristic* levels of emotion associated with an individual's personality. (his temperament) are described in terms of trait pleasure, trait arousal, and trait dominance. Specific instructions for assessing these attributes with semantic differential scales are given in Appendix B. On the other hand, *momentary* feelings of an individual are described in terms of state pleasure, state arousal, and state dominance, that is, the three emotional dimensions defined in Chapter 2 and measured with the first set of instructions in Appendix B. This distinction between state and trait is analogous to Spiel- berger, Gorsuch, and Lushene's (1970) analysis of anxiety. In their discus- sions, "state anxiety" referred to the condition of an individual at a particular time, and "trait anxiety" referred to an enduring predisposition.

The Development of a Questionnaire Measure of Arousal-Seeking Tendency[1]
An individual's preference for an environment is closely related to his pre- ferred arousal level; some people characteristically prefer calm settings, whereas others actively seek to increase their arousal by selecting novel, complex, or unpredictable settings. Thus, a person's preferred arousal level is of central importance to our framework, and a reliable questionnaire meas- ure of arousal-seeking tendency is essential to our study of environmental psychology.

A number of personality measures relate to this trait. Extroversion has been defined by Eysenck (1967; 1970) to include an arousal-seeking com- ponent, and available research, to be mentioned later in this chapter, supports this view. Extroversion, however, also includes a variety of additional com- ponents, which confound the interpretation of obtained results; that is, when an extroversion scale is used to study the contribution of individual differences to preferences for environments, it is ambiguous whether arousal- seeking tendency or some other component accounts for the behavioral differences.

Similarly, experimental studies exploring reactions to stimuli differing in levels of complexity have often relied on measures of trait anxiety because the latter partially reflect characteristic (high) arousal levels (e.g., Day, 1967b). However, the concept and available measures of anxiety relate not only to characteristic arousal levels but also to other emotional dimensions (e.g., trait pleasure). Thus, the environmental preferences of the more anxious persons may be due either to their characteristically higher arousal levels or to their characteristic displeasure. Needed, therefore, is a measure of individual differences in arousal-seeking tendency that is independent of other dimensions.

Several existing personality scales tap components of arousal-seeking tendency, such as change seeking, sensation seeking, and stimulus seeking. The 95-item questionnaire of change seeking developed by Garlington and Shimota (1964) includes items such as "I prefer to spend most of my leisure hours with my family (–)," "I like to dabble in a number of different hobbies and interests (+)," and "Because I become bored easily, I need plenty of excitement, stimulation, and fun (+)." The signs within parentheses following each item indicate the direction of scoring.

Jackson's (1967) personality tests included a measure of change seeking. Some of the items on this measure were: "I like to have new things to eat from week to week (+)," "Most people have a hard time predicting how I will respond to something they may say to me (+)," "Changes in routine disturb me (-)," and "I would be satisfied to stay at the same job indefinitely (-)."

Zuckerman, Kolin, Price, and Zoob's (1964) measure of sensation seeking included items such as "I often wish I could be a mountain climber (+)," "I like some of the earthy body smells (+)," "I get bored seeing the same old faces (+)." This scale correlated positively with field independence, as measured by the Embedded Figures Test (Witkin, Dyk, Faterson, Goodenough, and Karp, 1962), and negatively with anxiety. In a recent validational study of this scale, Zuckerman, Schultz, and Hopkins (1967) found that high scorers volunteered more readily for sensory deprivation and hypnosis experiments (assumed to be more novel experiences and therefore more arousing).

McCarroll, Mitchell, Carpenter, and Anderson (1967) used the scales developed by Garlington and Shimota (1964), Penney and Reinehr (1966), and Zuckerman, Kolin, Price, and Zoob (1964) and found significant differences in the stimulus-seeking tendency of college students relative to high-school graduates about to enter college.

A TAT-based test of stimulus-seeking tendency was discussed by Maddi (1961). Performance tests of change-seeking behavior were also explored. Howard (1961) and Howard and Diesenhaus (1965) asked subjects to trace paths to the goal of a maze. The number of different routes a subject selected over five trials was used as a measure of change seeking. Domino (1965) provided test-retest and internal consistency estimates of reliability for the latter test and showed that persons scoring higher on the test had more varied social behaviors.

In our attempt to draw on the available studies and to develop a measure of arousal-seeking tendency, we aimed at incorporating most of the salient components of arousal seeking present in the measures noted and at eliminating unrelated or only tangentially related aspects. Our purpose was to develop a homogeneous measure of arousal-seeking tendency that we hoped would tap the most relevant components of this personality attribute. The research strategy represented a compromise between attempting to provide a general measure of this trait that would be relevant in most situations and achieving a homogeneous scale. It was recognized that a highly homogeneous scale may lack generality across diverse situations, whereas a scale that taps a variety of contents may have low homogeneity. To attain a compromise between these two extremes, we started with all the available measures that related to arousal-seeking tendency. A series of three questionnaire studies was carried out using three different samples of subjects to obtain the final scale given in Appendix C.

Study 1. An initial questionnaire was prepared that included most of the items from the measure of curiosity provided by Day (1971), the change-seeking measures of Garlington and Shimota (1964) and of Jackson (1967), the curiosity scale of Penney and McCann (1964), and the sensation-seeking scale of Zuckerman, Kolin, Price, and Zoob (1964). Items from the latter scale were rewritten to make them consistent with the format of the remaining ones. An additional thirty-four items were written to augment those selected and to tap areas of arousal-seeking tendency not represented. The total of 312 items thus obtained were randomly mixed with the Crowne and Marlowe (1960) social desirability scale. A group of 203 University of California undergraduates responded to the 312-item mixed questionnaire using a scale that ranged from −4 (very strong disagreement) to +4 (very strong agreement).

In a preliminary analysis of the subjects' responses, those items of the arousal-seeking questionnaire that were confounded ($r > 0.15$) by social desirability and those with low item-total correlations ($r < 0.2$) were elimimated. To help clarify what was being measured in the remaining items and to identify those theoretically relevant aspects of arousal-seeking tendency that were either disproportionately or inadequately represented, the items were factor analyzed, and a principal component solution was obtained. There were seventeen factors with eigenvalues exceeding 2.0. Oblique rotation of these factors yielded the groupings of items given in Table 3.1. An examination of these groupings shows that there was a considerable amount of redundancy within each factor (i.e., several items in each factor were quite similar in wording and content).

The following criteria were used in selecting items from each factor to form a second questionnaire: (1) item-total correlation in excess of 0.25, (2) high factor loadings, (3) item correlations with social desirability less than 0.10, (4) simple wording and style, and (5) no redundancy with other items from the same factor.

Study 2. The total of 125 items obtained from Study 1 were intermixed with the Crowne and Marlowe (1960) social desirability scale, the Jackson (1967) dominance and succorance scales, and the Mehrabian (1970c) measures of affiliative tendency and sensitivity to rejection. The random arrangement of the items from the various questionnaires served to minimize subjects' awareness of the traits being measured. A sample of 316 University of California undergraduates responded to this questionnaire. Again, they used a nine-point scale of agreement-disagreement.

In addition, subjects were asked to describe their characteristic emotions, using the scales of Appendix B. The following instructions were provided:

Each pair of words below describes a feeling dimension. Some of the pairs might seem unusual, but you may generally feel more one way than the other. So, for each pair, put a check mark (Example: - - - - -:- - ✓- -:- - -) to show how you feel IN GENERAL, that is, most of the time. Please take your time so as to arrive at a real characteristic description of your feelings.

Three adjective pairs designed to measure trait anxiety were added to the emotional dimensions of Appendix B. These were anxious–nonanxious, nervous–not nervous, and tense–at ease. Thus, it was possible also to compute characteristic levels, or trait values, for the pleasure, arousal, dominance, and anxiety of each subject.

Table 3.1. The Results of a Preliminary Factor Analysis of Arousal-Seeking
Questionnaires

	Item-Total Correlation	Item–Social Desirability Correlation
Factor 1		
For me planning one's activities well in advance is very likely to take most of the fun out of life.	0.44	−0.10
There are several areas in which I am prone to doing things quite unexpectedly.	0.34	−0.13
I like to experience novelty and change in my daily routine.	0.46	0.03
I like to plan out my activities in advance, and then follow the plan.	−0.45	−0.01
People view me as a quite unpredictable person.	0.35	−0.05
I prefer people who are emotionally expressive even if they are a bit unstable.	0.35	−0.06
When things get boring, I like to find some new and unfamiliar experience.	0.50	−0.07
I like continually changing activities.	0.57	0.02
I tend to act impulsively.	0.37	−0.13
Factor 2		
I like to look at pictures which are puzzling in some way.	0.36	0.00
A painting is more interesting to me if I can study it before having it interpreted.	0.37	−0.03
A painting which could represent many different things makes me think a lot more than an obvious one.	0.35	0.00
I like to touch and feel a sculpture.	0.37	0.05
I would be particularly attracted to an art display featuring many interpretations of a single theme.	0.35	−0.01
Factor 3		
It would take me a long time to adapt to living in a foreign country.	−0.34	−0.09
I would prefer to spend vacations in this country, where you *know* you can get a good holiday, than in foreign lands that are colorful and different.	−0.26	−0.02
I much prefer familiar people and places.	−0.48	−0.03
It would be fun to move to another town.	0.38	−0.12

Table 3.1   (continued)

	Item-Total Correlation	Item–Social Desirability Correlation
Factor 3		
I would not like to change to a new school.	−0.24	0.07
I would like the job of a foreign correspondent for a newspaper.	0.35	−0.10
I like a place better the more I am around it.	−0.21	−0.01
My likes and dislikes are the same from year to year.	−0.28	0.11
Factor 4		
When I was in school, I preferred to work on one subject until I had finished the assignment.	−0.26	0.00
I like to complete a single job or task at a time before taking on others.	−0.27	0.05
I like to work on several projects at the same time so I can change from one to another.	0.37	0.01
When I go on a trip, I like to plan my route and timetable fairly carefully.	−0.47	0.02
I don't like to sleep in any bed but my own.	−0.20	0.02
I feel a person just can't be too careful.	−0.29	0.04
In going places, eating, working, etc., I seem to go in a very deliberate, methodical fashion rather than rush from one thing to another.	−0.30	0.12
Factor 5		
I would be satisfied to stay at the same job indefinitely.	−0.40	0.12
I like to continue doing the same old things rather than to try new and different things.	−0.49	−0.09
I would be content to live in the same town for the rest of my life.	−0.36	0.09
In my job I appreciate constant change in the type of work to be done.	0.33	0.06
I am continually seeking new ideas and experiences.	0.50	0.10
I would not like to be hypnotized.	−0.30	0.11
I would rather stay at home than go out most of the time.	−0.32	0.00

Table 3.1   (continued)

	Item-Total Correlation	Item–Social Desirability Correlation
Factor 6		
Changes in routine disturb me.	−0.34	−0.15
I like to do routine work using a good piece of machinery or apparatus.	−0.22	−0.03
I feel that people should avoid behavior or situations that will call undue attention to themselves.	−0.30	−0.01
I don't like things to be uncertain and unpredictable.	−0.52	−0.02
I like a job that is steady enough for me to become expert at it rather than one that constantly challenges me.	−0.23	−0.02
I try never to do anything that others might think silly or foolish.	−0.27	−0.11
I like to have my life arranged so that it runs smoothly and without much change in my plans.	−0.47	−0.04
I don't like to change my plans once I have made them.	−0.28	−0.06
I prefer a routine way of life to an unpredictable one full of change.	−0.57	−0.04
I would prefer to be a steady and dependable worker than a brilliant but unstable one.	−0.36	0.10
I find a certain pleasure in routine kinds of work.	−0.19	0.02
Factor 7		
There are only a few kinds of food I like.	−0.28	0.01
I like to try kinds of food I haven't had before.	0.38	0.01
I like to eat the same kind of food most of the time.	−0.36	0.05
I like to try new foods that I have never tasted before, even though I may find that I don't like them.	0.45	−0.07
There are many kinds of food that I don't like.	−0.28	−0.02
I like to have new things to eat from week to week.	0.28	−0.02
I like to have just a few kinds of food at one meal.	−0.23	−0.01

Table 3.1   (continued)

	Item-Total Correlation	Item-Social Desirability Correlation
Factor 8		
I like to move about the country and to live in different places.	0.45	−0.08
I like to conform to custom and to avoid doing things that people I respect might consider unconventional.	−0.39	0.04
I prefer the clarity, symmetry of form, and harmony of colors in classical art to the "clashing" colors and irregular forms of modern paintings.	−0.21	0.00
I would be willing to give up some financial security to be able to change from one job to another if something interesting came along.	0.31	−0.06
In general, I would prefer a job with a modest salary, but guaranteed security rather than one with large, but uncertain earnings.	−0.27	0.04
I am well described as a meditative person, given to finding my own solutions instead of acting on conventional rules.	0.20	0.03
I have the wanderlust and am never happy unless I am roaming or traveling about.	0.35	−0.03
I get a lot of bright ideas about all sorts of things— too many to put into practice.	0.36	−0.11
I like to avoid situations where I am expected to do things in a conventional way.	0.41	−0.01
Factor 9		
I like music.	0.24	−0.04
I would like to visit another country.	0.27	−0.03
I play or would like to play a musical instrument.	0.23	−0.02
I like to travel and see the country.	0.38	−0.07
I like surprises.	0.40	0.00
I like to learn new words.	0.29	0.06
I like to have someone else pick out my new clothes for me.	−0.26	−0.06
I see no reason to change the color of my room once I have painted it.	−0.28	−0.10

Table 3.1   (continued)

	Item-Total Correlation	Item–Social Desirability Correlation
Factor 10		
I wonder why things like mushrooms are considered plants, since they aren't green like other plants.	0.24	−0.08
I like to look at rocks which are made of many kinds of minerals.	0.31	0.05
Whenever I visit a library, I want to ask about the filing system for classifying books.	0.23	0.01
I would like to watch geologists identify different kinds of minerals in rocks.	0.39	0.03
I try to think of new ways to interpret classical art.	0.35	0.11
It is fascinating to learn how mountains are created.	0.39	0.02
When I see an unusual plant, I wish a naturalist were around so I could ask him questions.	0.44	−0.08
I would like to ask a musical conductor what all his hand movements mean.	0.20	0.11
I would like to inspect a beaver's habitat.	0.33	−0.01
I like to reflect on the strange behavioral patterns of wildlife animals.	0.41	−0.07
Factor 11		
I would like to think up new ways to entertain patients in hospitals.	0.22	0.03
I would rather talk to people of different opinions than to people who agree with me.	0.35	0.11
I would like to ask a dietitian about some contradictory facts pertaining to fat and skinny people.	0.28	−0.02
I like to change the pictures on my walls frequently.	0.40	−0.01
When I choose a book to read, I look for an author with something new in his approach.	0.29	0.04
Factor 12		
If I hear something rustling in the grass, I have to see what it is.	0.36	−0.03
I like to dabble in a number of different hobbies and interests.	0.42	0.00
I have more than one hobby.	0.30	0.11
If I make a new friend, I like to ask him all sorts of questions.	0.32	−0.11

Table 3.1   (continued)

	Item-Total Correlation	Item–Social Desirability Correlation
Factor 12		
I like to go to stores with which I am quite familiar.	−0.32	−0.10
I like to find myself in new situations where I can explore all the possibilities.	0.53	−0.12
It's fun to go to town and just look around.	0.20	0.02
I would rather visit a park I have never seen before than one I knew well.	0.24	−0.02
Factor 13		
I am always looking for new routes to take on a trip.	0.42	0.14
I sometimes take different routes to a place I often go, just for variety's sake.	0.42	0.14
I prefer a guide when I am in a place I don't know well because I dislike getting lost.	−0.37	−0.04
I am invigorated by a brisk, cold day.	0.17	−0.05
In traveling abroad I would rather go on an organized tour than plan for myself the places I will visit.	−0.34	−0.02
My life is full of change because I make it so.	0.44	0.14
I like to go somewhere different nearly every day.	0.46	−0.04
Factor 14		
If I were reading a travel book, I would keep a map beside me.	0.18	−0.01
When I see a foreign car, I associate it with the country it is from.	0.20	0.00
If I find a word I don't understand, I try to figure out its meaning.	0.40	−0.02
If I come across a new word, I try to look it up in the dictionary.	0.19	0.00
When I hear a new song on the radio, I like to phone the station to get its name.	0.23	0.00
When I am waiting for my appointment in an office, I try to identify the occupations of the staff I can see.	0.36	−0.04
When I read conflicting reports about an incident in the newspaper, I like to find out what really happened.	0.29	−0.07

Table 3.1   (continued)

	Item–Total Correlation	Item–Social Desirability Correlation
Factor 15		
It is interesting to try to figure out how an unusual piece of machinery works.	0.18	0.02
When I see a complicated piece of machinery, I like to to ask someone how it works.	0.26	0.10
I like to tinker with complicated machinery.	0.21	0.04
It is fascinating to look at new machines.	0.24	−0.09
If I worked in a factory, I would like to find out everything that is going on.	0.32	0.07
If I saw some spectacular scientific feat on TV, it would make me want to ask many questions.	0.36	−0.01
Factor 16		
Parachute jumping is too dangerous for me.	−0.34	−0.09
I would like to learn to fly an airplane.	0.33	−0.15
I would like to hunt lions in Africa.	0.22	0.02
I enjoy doing "daring," foolhardy things "just for fun."	0.33	−0.06
I like a job that offers change, variety, and travel, even if it involves some danger.	0.53	0.00
I would like to take up the sport of water skiing.	0.29	−0.04
I sometimes do things just because others are afraid to do them.	0.35	−0.06
I sometimes like to do things that are a little frightening.	0.45	0.00
I would not want to be a mountain climber because it is such a risky sport.	−0.29	−0.11
I would like the type of work which would keep me constantly on the move.	0.31	0.00
Sometimes it is fun to be a little bit scared.	0.37	−0.08
Factor 17		
I like to have lots of activity around me.	0.29	−0.06
I enjoy lots of social activity.	0.21	−0.01
I like to go to parties and other affairs where there is lots of loud fun.	0.26	−0.07
I avoid busy, noisy places.	−0.19	0.00

Table 3.1   (continued)

	Item-Total Correlation	Item–Social Desirability Correlation
Factor 17		
l like being amidst a great deal of excitement and bustle.	0.32	−0.06
It's fun to go to places where there is a lot of noise.	0.21	−0.08
I seek out fun and enjoyment.	0.38	−0.03
I like to be the center of attention in a group.	0.24	−0.08
I am always glad to have someone visit me.	0.16	0.01
I like to eat in the homes of friends or relatives when I can.	0.26	−0.07

Responses to this second questionnaire of arousal-seeking tendency were analyzed, and item-total and item–social desirability correlations were obtained for each of the 125 items. All but one of the items correlated significantly with the total score on the questionnaire in the expected direction. This provided a preliminary cross-validation for the items.

Study 3. A third and final version of the scale was constructed by selecting the best items from this second, 125-item questionnaire. These were forty items with item-total correlations in excess of 0.40, and item–social desirability correlations below 0.10. This forty-item scale was administered to a third sample of 214 University of California undergraduates. Subjects also responded to the Eysenck and Eysenck (1968) measures of extroversion and neuroticism and the Mehrabian (1970c; 1972b, Appendix B) measures of affiliative tendency and sensitivity to rejection, and provided information about their characteristic (trait) emotions by using the scales of Appendix B. Seventy-eight of the subjects in this study (forty males and thirty-eight females) returned four to seven weeks later for a retest on the forty-item arousal-seeking scale and the trait measures of pleasure, arousal, and dominance.

The final forty-item questionnaire measure of arousal-seeking tendency is given in Appendix C where plus (+) and minus (−) signs preceding each item indicate the direction of scoring, and instructions to the subjects are given preceding the scale. A total score for the scale can be computed by first changing the sign of a subject's responses on the negative (−) items, and then obtaining an algebraic sum of all forty items of the scale.

Total scores for this forty-item scale correlated 0.96 with total scores based on the full set of 125 items in the second questionnaire. Thus, the shorter, final scale essentially measured the same attribute that was measured by the longer version.

For the forty-item scale, data obtained from the sample of 214 subjects in Study 3, as well as from a fourth sample of 202 subjects, yielded a mean of thirty-nine and a standard deviation of thirty-four, as reported in Appendix C.

Internal Structure

To explore the composition of the final scale, 530 subjects' responses to the forty items were factor analyzed, and a principal component solution was obtained. Oblique rotation of the first five factors yielded groups of items referring to similar sources of arousal. A primary group of items that measured "arousal from change" included twelve items, examples of which were: "I like to experience novelty and change in my daily routine (+)," "I like to go somewhere different nearly every day (+)," "My ideal home would be peaceful and quiet (–)."

The second factor, "arousal from unusual stimuli," consisted of eleven items, examples of which were: "I like to look at pictures which are puzzling in some way (+)," "It's unpleasant seeing people in strange, weird clothes (–)," and "Designs or patterns should be bold and exciting (+)."

The third factor, which consisted of nine items, measured "arousal from risk" and consisted of items such as "I wouldn't enjoy dangerous sports such as mountain climbing, airplane flying, or sky diving (–)." "I sometimes like to do things that are a little frightening (+)," or "I prefer friends who are reliable and predictable to those who are excitingly unpredictable (–)."

The fourth factor, which consisted of five items, measured "arousal from sensuality" and included items such as "I never notice textures (–)," "I like to run through heaps of fallen leaves (+)," or "I don't pay much attention to my surroundings (–)."

The fifth factor, which consisted of three items, measured "arousal from new environments" and included items such as "I would be content to live in the same town for the rest of my life (–)."

For each subject, a total score was computed on each of these five factors, and these factor scores were, in turn, intercorrelated. The correlations obtained, reported in Table 3.2, showed that all the factors were positively and significantly intercorrelated, with correlations that ranged from 0.27 to 0.65.

Table 3.2. Intercorrelations among the Various Factors of Arousal-Seeking Tendency*

	2	3	4	5
Factor 1 (Arousal from change)	0.60	0.65	0.44	0.53
Factor 2 (Arousal from unusual stimuli)		0.53	0.57	0.45
Factor 3 (Arousal from risk)			0.41	0.40
Factor 4 (Arousal from sensuality)				0.27
Factor 5 (Arousal from new environments)				

*Correlations in excess of 0.15 are significant at the 0.01 level.

Thus, these data showed that various factors of the scale in Appendix C
measured related aspects of a single personality trait.

Reliability

The reliability of the forty-item scale in Appendix C was assessed by computing the Kuder-Richardson (1937) reliability coefficient for the data obtained
in Study 3. The obtained reliability of 0.87 was adequate and was not surprising, considering the summary of factor correlations given in Table 3.2.
It will be recalled that seventy-eight subjects from Study 3 returned to provide test-retest data on some of the measures. For the four to seven week
test-retest interval, the reliability correlation obtained for the scale of
Appendix C was 0.88, which was also satisfactory.

Validity

The validity of the arousal-seeking tendency scale was tested, in part, in terms
of its hypothesized correlations with other personality measures. The first
hypothesis related arousal-seeking tendency to trait anxiety (or neuroticism).
Findings to be reviewed in the next section showed that persons who were
characteristically more anxious were also generally more aroused physiologically. Cattell (1966) noted: "Insofar as one can bridge from human to
animal concepts, [anxiety] may be identical with the concept of arousal or
activation [p. 37]." Thus, for people who are usually anxious, any additional
sources of arousal would be likely to raise their arousal level above the
optimum. Indeed, studies have shown that less anxious persons behaved in
a manner opposite to anxious ones when they were offered a choice of stimuli
varying in level of complexity. This evidence, reviewed in some detail in
Chapter 6, implies that there should be an inverse relationship between
arousal-seeking tendency and anxiety.

Arousal-seeking tendency was also hypothesized to correlate directly with
extroversion. This hypothesized relation follows from Eysenck's (1967,

1970) definition of extroversion as including an arousal-seeking (stimulus hunger) component. Investigators have found that extroverts do indeed seek arousal. Weisen (1965) found that extroverts, compared to introverts, pressed buttons more to obtain stimulation of colored lights and radio sounds. Conversely, introverts pressed more to turn off this stimulation when it was presented continuously. More recent studies, employing various sources of arousal, have confirmed these results (Davies, Hockey, and Taylor, 1969; Gale, 1969; Philipp and Wilde, 1970).

To explore these hypotheses, the 312-item arousal-seeking scale given to the subjects in Study 1 was rescored using only the items that had been retained in the final forty-item version of Appendix C. Scores were also available on the Crowne and Marlowe (1960) social desirability scale, the Eysenck and Eysenck (1968) extroversion and neuroticism scales, the Husek and Alexander (1963) semantic differential type measure of anxiety, the Mandler and Sarason (1952) test anxiety questionnaire, and the Spielberger, Gorsuch, and Lushene (1970) measures of trait and state anxiety. The subjects had described their characteristic feelings using the scales of Appendix B and three adjective pairs that measured anxiety: anxious–nonanxious, tense–at ease, and nervous–not nervous. Thus, their characteristic levels of pleasure, arousal, dominance, and anxiety were made available for analysis.

Intercorrelations among these measures are presented in Table 3.3. As expected, our arousal-seeking tendency scale correlated positively and significantly with extroversion. Also, it correlated inversely with all of the

Table 3.3   Intercorrelations among Five Measures of Anxiety, and Measures of Neuroticism, Extroversion, and Arousal-Seeking Tendency*

	1	2	3	4	5	6	7
1. Neuroticism (Eysenck and Eysenck)							
2. Anxiety (Husek and Alexander)	0.35						
3. Test anxiety (Mandler and Sarason)	0.38	0.25					
4. State anxiety (Spielberger et al.)	0.48	0.50	0.30				
5. Trait anxiety (Spielberger et al.)	0.70	0.40	0.43	0.60			
6. Trait anxiety (based on our semantic differential scales)	0.48	0.37	0.31	0.46	0.55		
7. Extroversion (Eysenck and Eysenck)	0.05	–0.07	–0.09	–0.10	–0.25	–0.16	
8. Arousal seeking (Appendix C)	–0.14	–0.10	–0.04	–0.16	–0.20	–0.15	0.29

*Correlations exceeding 0.14 are significant at the 0.05 level.

anxiety measures and the measure of neuroticism, although two of the correlations with anxiety were not significant at the 0.05 level. The low value of the inverse correlations with anxiety was encouraging, in that it showed that our arousal-seeking tendency scale was not simply another (inverse) measure of anxiety. Further, since the arousal-seeking tendency scale correlated only -0.10 with sex (male = 1, female = -1), the same set of norms should be equally applicable for male and female subjects.

Additional validational data were available from Study 2. As already noted, all but one of the item-total correlations of the 125-item scale were significant and in the expected direction. Also, correlations between the forty-item scale and other personality questionnaires administered in Study 2 provided further evidence. In particular, discriminant validity was demonstrated by low correlations with the Crowne and Marlowe (1960) social desirability scale ($r = 0.12$) and with the Jackson (1967) measure of succorance ($r = -0.09$). Also, a significant correlation of 0.30 ($p < 0.01$) was obtained between arousal-seeking tendency and trait arousal (based on the measure in Appendix B). This finding was in line with our expectations and provided one kind of construct validity.

For the data in Study 3, the arousal-seeking tendency scale of Appendix C correlated 0.34 ($p < 0.01$) with extroversion, but did not exhibit significant correlations with neuroticism or trait anxiety (as measured by the Spielberger, Gorsuch, and Lushene, 1970, scale). The arousal-seeking tendency scale correlated 0.37 ($p < 0.01$) with trait arousal (Appendix B); it also correlated 0.32 ($p < 0.01$) with affiliative tendency and -0.30 ($p < 0.01$) with sensitivity to rejection.

Emotional Correlates of Familiar Personality Attributes

In addition to arousal-seeking tendency, several other personality attributes also play a part in determining individual responses to the environment. A knowledge of the emotional correlates of these personality attributes is therefore helpful in predicting different persons' responses to various situations. For example, what is the relationship between level of maladjustment of hospitalized patients and their preferences for quiet versus lively surroundings? We would be able to answer such a question if we had information about the emotional correlates of neuroticism and if measures of the patients' neuroticism were available. With this type of problem in mind, we sought to describe the emotional correlates of personality scales within our three-dimensional framework for emotions.

Trait Pleasure, Trait Arousal, and Trait Dominance

The measures of pleasure, arousal, and dominance in Appendix B are equally applicable to state and trait emotions. Two kinds of reliability estimates were obtained for their use as trait measures. Data from Study 3 of the preceding section were used to compute the Kuder-Richardson (1937) reliability coefficients. These values were 0.81 for trait pleasure, 0.50 for trait arousal, and 0.72 for trait dominance. Test-retest data were also available from the seventy-eight subjects of Study 3 who returned to take the same measures four to seven weeks after the first testing session. The corresponding reliability correlations for test-retest were 0.72 for trait pleasure, 0.69 for trait arousal, and 0.77 for trait dominance.

Scales with only six items can be expected to show low reliability, and therefore these particular reliability values were reassuring. Thus, these trait measures are used here to delineate the characteristic emotional states associated with various personality attributes.

Data from the three studies of the preceding section were available to allow the description of the personality measures used in these studies as functions of trait pleasure, trait arousal, and trait dominance assessed by using the scales and the appropriate instructions in Appendix B. Study 1 had involved several anxiety and neuroticism measures including our own semantic differential measure based on three adjective pairs, our arousal-seeking tendency scale, and an extroversion scale, as well as the verbal report of the subject's traits of pleasure, arousal, and dominance (Appendix B). Each of the personality attributes was therefore expressed in a stepwise regression equation as a function of the three trait-emotion dimensions, and the results were summarized in the A equations of Table 3.4. At each successive step in each regression analysis, the 0.05 level of significance was used to decide whether any other terms could be added to the equation. To facilitate comparison of the relative magnitudes of the various effects, all the variables were normalized before the regression equations of that table were computed.

In a similar way, the data from the 316 subjects of Study 2 provided the results summarized in the B equations of Table 3.4. The third sample of 214 subjects in Study 3 provided the results given in the C equations of Table 3.4. Finally, a fourth sample of seventy-eight subjects provided the information

Table 3.4. The Expression of Various Personality Attributes and a Measure of State Anxiety in Terms of Characteristic Levels of Pleasure, Arousal, and Dominance*

1A.	Anxiety (Husek and Alexander)	$= -0.32 P + 0.14 A$	(0.36)
2A.	Test anxiety (Mandler and Sarason)	$= \qquad -0.30 D$	(0.30)
3A.	State anxiety (Spielberger et al.)	$= -0.40 P$	(0.40)
4A.	Trait anxiety (Spielberger et al.)	$= -0.45 P + 0.13 A - 0.26 D$	(0.64)
4C.	Trait anxiety (Spielberger et al.)	$= -0.62 P + 0.14 A - 0.30 D$	(0.73)
5A.	Trait anxiety (our semantic differential scales)	$= -0.52 P + 0.43 A - 0.11 D$	(0.71)
5B.	Trait anxiety (our semantic differential scales)	$= -0.44 P + 0.42 A - 0.16 D$	(0.58)
6A.	Neuroticism (Eysenck and Eysenck)	$= -0.27 P \qquad -0.21 D$	(0.43)
6C.	Neuroticism (Eysenck and Eysenck)	$= -0.39 P + 0.23 A - 0.34 D$	(0.56)
7A.	Extroversion (Eysenck and Eysenck)	$= +0.14 P \qquad +0.22 D$	(0.32)
7C.	Extroversion (Eysenck and Eysenck)	$= \qquad +0.23 A + 0.19 D$	(0.34)
8A.	Arousal-seeking tendency (our first version)	$= \qquad +0.13 A + 0.21 D$	(0.24)
8B.	Arousal-seeking tendency (Appendix C)	$= \qquad +0.24 A + 0.22 D$	(0.37)
8C.	Arousal-seeking tendency (Appendix C)	$= -0.13 P + 0.36 A + 0.15 D$	(0.41)
9B.	Dominance (Jackson)	$= \qquad +0.13 A + 0.54 D$	(0.59)
10B.	Succorance (Jackson)	$= \qquad +0.19 A - 0.39 D$	(0.40)
11B.	Affiliative tendency (Mehrabian)	$= +0.36 P + 0.17 A$	(0.39)
11C.	Affiliative tendency (Mehrabian)	$= +0.11 P + 0.41 A - 0.14 D$	(0.43)
12B.	Sensitivity to rejection (Mehrabian)	$= \qquad -0.11 A - 0.36 D$	(0.40)
12C.	Sensitivity to rejection (Mehrabian)	$= \qquad -0.45 D$	(0.45)
13D.	Empathic tendency (Mehrabian and Epstein)	$= \qquad +0.33 A$	(0.33)
14A.	Sex (male = 1, female = −1)	$= -0.28 P - 0.13 A + 0.28 D$	(0.32)
14C.	Sex (male = 1, female = −1)	$= -0.21 P - 0.22 A + 0.42 D$	(0.44)

*In the equations, P = trait pleasure, A = trait arousal, and D = trait dominance, as measured on the scales of Appendix B. The significance of the various terms in these equations was assessed at the 0.05 level. All variables were normalized to provide ready comparison of the relative magnitudes of the various effects. The number in parentheses to the right of each equation is the multiple correlation coefficient. The A equations were based on data of Study 1, the B equations were based on data of Study 2, and the C equations were based on the data of Study 3. Finally, the D equation was based on a fourth, separate sample of seventy-eight cases.

that related Mehrabian and Epstein's (1972) measure of empathic tendency
to arousal in equation 13D. The results from all four samples of subjects are
discussed later in this chapter.

Anxiety and Neuroticism

Spielberger, Lushene, and McAdoo (in press) defined the state of anxiety as
"unpleasant, consciously-perceived feelings of tension and apprehension, with
associated activation or arousal of the autonomic nervous system. It may be
noted that this conception is quite comparable in many respects to the conception of anxiety as an emotional state that was suggested by Freud (1936)
[p. 17]." Within our framework, the state of anxiety can be described as
one of low pleasure and low dominance, but high arousal. Similarly, the trait
of anxiety is characterized by the persistence of the anxious state and is
associated with frequent low pleasure, low dominance, and high arousal.

Evidence obtained with Spielberger, Gorsuch, and Lushene's (1970) measure of state anxiety showed an inverse relation between feelings of pleasure
and anxiety. Spielberger, Gorsuch, and Lushene (1970) reported that
subjects' state anxiety increased under threat of shock. Anxiety correlated
significantly with the number of problems the subject reported on the Mooney
Problem Checklist, College Form (Mooney and Gordon, 1950). When subjects
were given feedback of failure on a memory task, their state anxiety scores
increased over pretest scores. On the other hand, subjects who were told
that they had succeeded reported lower anxiety. Auerbach (1969) replicated
the latter finding using a word completion task. Finally, Sarason (1960)
concluded from his reviews of various trait-anxiety scales that more anxious
persons were more self-deprecatory and less content with themselves.

Considerable theoretical and empirical work has related anxiety to high
levels of arousal (e.g., Cattell, 1966; Farber, 1954; Maher, 1966; Malmo,
1957; Martin, 1961). An anxiety factor correlated with systolic pulse pressure, heart rate, respiration rate, basal and current metabolic rate, electrical
skin resistance, and a number of other physiological cues (Cattell, 1966, p.
33). DiMascio, Boyd, and Greenblatt (1957) found a significant correlation
between heart rate and rated tension. Martin (1961) reviewed evidence that
fear, anxiety, and anger were all states of physiological arousal; fear and
anxiety resembled an epinephrine reaction, whereas anger resembled a
norepinephrine reaction. Farber (1954) concluded from his review of a
large body of evidence that anxiety functions as a drive state (Hull, 1951),

that is, as an energizer. Malmo (1959) indicated that drive, in turn, could be equated with arousal. Indeed, Malmo (1957), using a large variety of measures, had found that patients classified as anxious had higher physiological indexes of arousal than normal persons. However, contradictory findings were reported by Silverman (1957). During rest sessions, subjects' anxiety was positively correlated with arousal, as measured by palmar skin conductance, but, under threat of shock, a negative correlation was obtained. Finally, evidence from clinical work provided corroboration for the hypothesis. Drugs that lowered physiological arousal were effective antianxiety treatments (Jarvik, 1969).

As noted in the preceding chapter, there is considerable difficulty in interpreting the various physiological measures of arousal, and self-report measures can provide a useful alternative. Fairly clear-cut results have been obtained in our studies, and the results are summarized in Table 3.4.

In exact agreement with our hypotheses, equations 4A, 5A, 5B, and 5C of Table 3.4 showed that persons who were characteristically anxious tended to feel unpleasant, submissive, and highly aroused. The Husek and Alexander (1963) semantic differential type measure was designed to measure state anxiety, as was the "state" measure of Spielberger, Gorsuch, and Lushene (1970). Both of these showed inverse relations to pleasure, but only one of them showed a direct relation to arousal (equations 1A and 3A). It is interesting to note that the results for these measures of state anxiety were not as supportive of the hypotheses as those for the measures of trait anxiety. The discrepancy in these findings is readily explained, since a person's feelings at a given moment are determined partially by the situation. As a result, reports of temporary feelings are not sufficiently representative of characteristic emotions. Indeed, the situation which the subjects were in (i.e., answering the questionnaires) was low in arousing quality.

The Mandler and Sarason (1952) test anxiety questionnaire was found to relate to only one of the hypothesized effects: It exhibited an inverse correlation with dominance. Rather than measuring subjects' characteristic levels of anxiety across a variety of situations, this questionnaire assesses their reactions only to situations where intellectual abilities are evaluated. Even though anxiety in these situations correlates with general levels of anxiety, this measure is not as appropriate as others that relate to a greater diversity of situations.

The findings summarized in Table 3.4 provided construct validity for the Spielberger, Gorsuch, and Lushene (1970) measure of trait anxiety. Construct validity was also provided for our own very simple measure of characteristic anxiety based on three adjective pairs.

As expected, the configuration of emotions for the neuroticism scale of Eysenck and Eysenck (1968) was similar to that for measures of trait anxiety. Neurotics, according to equations 6A and 6C in Table 3.4, characteristically feel unpleasant and submissive. This is not surprising, since their problems are, of course, unpleasant and are experienced as beyond their control (Mehrabian, 1970b, Chapter 2). It can also be seen in equation 6C, although not equation 6A, that neurotics are aroused. Thus, arousal is a weak emotional component of neuroticism.

Extroversion

The direct correlations of extroversion with pleasure and dominance in equation 7A, and with dominance in equation 7C, are consistent with predictions made by Mehrabian (1971a) and the definition of extroverts: such persons are friendly, outgoing, and capable of taking charge of social situations.

Equation 7A shows that there is no significant relation between extroversion and trait arousal. Equation 7C, however, shows a significant positive correlation between the two. This difference in findings and the generally low level of the effect can be explained as follows. Trait arousal is an average of a person's arousal state over a representative sample of situations. For any one of these situations, the arousal state of a person is, of course, in part determined by the arousing quality of the setting. High-arousal seekers are much more responsive to the arousing quality of the environment, such that their arousal level covaries directly with the latter. On the other hand, low-arousal seekers have a more moderate level of arousal in general, and, even though their arousal level also covaries with the arousing quality of the setting, this relationship is weaker. In terms of this hypothesis, high-arousal seekers should be more aroused than low-arousal seekers in arousing settings; however, for nonarousing settings, observed differences, if any, are likely to be reversed. Since extroversion is a correlate of arousal-seeking tendency, a corresponding, though weaker, difference in responsiveness to external stimuli should be observed between extroverts and introverts.

Dominance, Dependency, Affiliative Tendency, Sensitivity to Rejection, and Empathic Tendency

The information in the remaining equations not only provided construct validity for the various personality measures but also revealed the unique constellation of emotions associated with each of the traits. For example, Jackson's (1967) dominance scale correlated highly with characteristic level of dominance. It also correlated to a small degree with trait arousal, showing that dominant people are more aroused. Equation 10B showed that succorant (dependent) subjects also had a relatively high level of arousal, but were distinguished from dominant subjects by their general submissiveness. Subjects who were more sensitive to rejection tended to be primarily more submissive and, to a smaller degree, less aroused (equations 12B and 12C). This was consistent with many findings (e.g., Mehrabian and Ksionzky, 1973) that showed that such persons were less self-assured and more constricted in their social behavior. On the other hand, affiliative persons were found to feel pleasant and aroused, and, to a small extent, submissive (equations 11B and 11C).

Finally, the relationship between the measure of empathic tendency (Mehrabian and Epstein, 1972) and arousal was of considerable interest. This measure was devised specifically to assess characteristic emotional responsiveness to others. The constellation of factors in this measure showed that highly empathic individuals responded to others' pleasant as well as unpleasant experiences. On these grounds, it was expected that the measure would relate primarily to arousal, but not to pleasure or dominance. Equation 13D showed that this was indeed the case. It was encouraging to have been able to identify an aspect of personality that uniquely tapped this dimension of responsiveness to interpersonal stimuli and that was independent of the pleasant or unpleasant quality of the stimuli.

Hostility

Even though personality data were not available to express hostility in terms of the trait measures of pleasure, arousal, and dominance, some data from Study 3 were used to provide an analogous relationship. In Study 3 subjects read descriptions of various situations and rated their emotional states on the scales of Appendix B plus three scales designed to measure the feeling of hostility. These were aggressive–nonaggressive, hostile–not hostile, and angry–not angry. The aggressiveness ratings of all the subjects over the various situations correlated 0.45 with their hostility ratings and 0.46 with their ratings of anger; the ratings of hostility correlated 0.79 with those for anger. These intercorrelations justified the summing of responses to these three scales to obtain an estimate for each subject's feeling of hostility in each situation that was described to him. Since composite scores of his feelings of state pleasure, arousal, and dominance for each of these situations were also available for the subject, it was possible to do a regression analysis that yielded the following results for normalized variables:

Hostility = –0.74 pleasure state + 0.36 arousal state + 0.09 dominance state

Thus, the feeling of hostility can be described as being associated with displeasure, arousal, and dominance, in that order of importance. Further, since the multiple correlation coefficient for the regression equation is 0.87, the findings show that these basic emotions quite satisfactorily account for most of the variance in the feeling of hostility.

This equation was written for temporary emotional reactions. Nevertheless, it is likely that the general relationships (but not necessarily the specific coefficients) portrayed in the equation will hold for characteristic hostility (a personality trait) as a function of the trait measures of pleasure, arousal, and dominance (Mehrabian, 1971a, Chapter 4). However, to avoid possible misinterpretation of these findings, the equation was not included in Table 3.4.

The equations of Table 3.4 are only preliminary results and were presented to demonstrate the heuristic value of our three-dimensional approach to the characterization of trait emotions. Nevertheless, they illustrate how familiar concepts from diverse areas can be described succinctly as derivatives of the primary emotional dimensions. Further exploration of personality-related problems of environmental psychology would, of course, be facilitated by the construction or selection of reliable measures that relate only to each one of the characteristic (trait) emotions.

Emotional Correlates of Temporary Drive- and Drug-Induced States
Physiological events are correlated with emotional states. Internal, cyclical variations in hunger, thirst, sexuality, and sleep and noncyclical states such as fatigue, pain, or sickness all contribute to the emotional state of an

individual and are associated with well-defined feelings. These feelings can be conceptualized and measured in terms of our three emotional dimensions. Hunger or thirst, for instance, can be described as arousing, unpleasant, and associated with the feeling of submission; fatigue would be associated with lowered arousal, displeasure, and submission. In addition, drug-induced states may be similarly described in terms of pleasure, arousal, and dominance.

For example, Corcoran (1964) found that sleep deprivation lowered arousal (measured physiologically). Also, Weybrew (1967) surveyed the literature for evidence of physiological responses to sleep deprivation. His findings, which were summarized in part of his Table 12-2, indicated that, in general, sleep deprivation and fatigue led to decreased autonomic responsiveness as measured by heart rate, blood pressure, skin conductance, GSR lability, skin temperature, and vascular volume.

In considering these effects of sleep deprivation, one should distinguish the arousal level of a sleep-deprived subject who must perform a difficult task (e.g., in a combat situation) and that of one who does not have any pressing tasks. It is the latter group for which the lowered autonomic responsiveness is more likely to hold. When tasks of moderate difficulty are administered to subjects and/or when motivating conditions for performance are introduced following sleep deprivation, it is very difficult to make inferences about arousal level on the basis of available data. In fact, the use of sleep deprivation as an experimental method of specifying different levels of arousal is inadequate since "the effects of a fall in stimulation may be either a fall or an over-compensating rise in arousal, depending upon the subjects, their motivation, and so on [Broadbent, 1963, p. 187]."

Knowledge of the emotions associated with different physiological states can have great significance in planning environments. For example, a work setting can be modified (with the introduction of music, noise, or some visual form of stimulation) to allow the workers to maintain an optimal level of arousal and a high level of pleasure, despite their increasing fatigue during the course of the day (e.g., Smith, 1947). In the case of monotonous environmental conditions associated with increasing levels of fatigue (e.g., those experienced by truck drivers on long journeys) one can seek stimuli that are not distracting but help maintain a higher and more preferred level of arousal.

In addition to these naturally occurring transitory drive states, another source of internal stimuli is artificial and direct physiological intervention. Drugs such as stimulants, depressants, hallucinogens, hormones, and brain toxins, as well as direct electrical stimulation of the brain, shortcut environmental stimulation and directly affect the three emotional dimensions.

The uses of drugs (e.g., alcohol) have been of particular interest, and their reinforcing effects have been thoroughly documented (e.g., Bandura, 1969). Whereas there is little documentation of their effects on dominance or pleasure, those on arousal are generally well known.

Very low blood-alcohol levels usually produce mild sedation, relaxation, or tranquility. Slightly higher levels, at least in some people, may produce behavioral changes which seem to suggest stimulation of the brain: garrulousness, aggressiveness, and excessive activity, but which may result from depression of neural function which normally inhibits or restrains such behavior. At still higher levels, greater depression may occur, producing incoordination, confusion, disorientation, stupor, anesthesia, coma, or death [Mendelson, 1970, p. 510].

Thus, it is seen that alcohol functions primarily to lower arousal, and its prevalence in Western cultures can be explained at least in part by the highly arousing quality of modern urban environments. In a similar way, other drugs can also be used as part of an attempt to reduce arousal to an intermediate and preferred level. The following comments of Jarvik (1969) describe this particular function of drugs.

Humans like to regulate their state of alertness with drugs. Caffeine is, by all odds, the favorite stimulant drug, and it is used by almost everyone in the form of coffee, tea, or coke in order to perk them up. Amphetamine is used by fewer people (but still a sizeable number), and cocaine by fewer still. The depressant drugs, alcohol and the barbiturates, are used sometimes in order to induce sleep, but, at other times, for the purpose of lowering arousal levels sufficiently to change the context of the environment, external and internal. How sedatives relieve anxiety is not known, but it must be more than a coincidence that anxiety prevents, and sedatives facilitate, sleep. Opiates also relieve anxiety or cause sleep, but apparently by a mechanism different from that of the sedatives. The drugs whose incentive value poses a real mystery are the psychotogenic drugs—for example, marihuana, LSD, mescaline, and the more commonly used, though not necessarily more benign drug, nicotine. People begin to take these drugs because of peer pressure in the teens, but there is something intrinsically pleasurable about them, just as there is with sugar. They are all stimulants and they cause varying degrees of sensory change depending on dose, susceptibility, and setting. . . . An alcoholic is happier drunk than sober, but the consequences of inebriation to himself and to those around him may be bad. Similarly, the frustrations and unhappiness produced by the poverty of the slums cause aggression and aroused states which can be quelled very effectively with drugs such as heroin. . . .

In summary, drugs are widely used, legally and illegally, for the purpose of regulating states of arousal, controlling anxiety, and assuaging the effects of stress [Jarvik, 1969, p. 47].

Summary

A person's feelings at any time can be characterized by the three dimensions in our framework. These feelings are a function of his personality, temporary conditions such as hunger or intoxication, and, of course, environmental stimuli. The resulting emotional state then regulates the individual's behavior (e.g., preference, approach, ability to work or affiliate) in a situation.

This chapter examined the emotional correlates of various personality traits and provided a series of regression equations expressing their relations. On the whole, our results were in accord with the definitions of the measures and with general expectations.

Of particular interest was the personality trait of arousal-seeking tendency, since variations in arousal-seeking behaviors (e.g., seeking out, exploring, remaining in, or preferring a place) are accounted for by the interaction of stimulus properties and by individual differences in preferred arousal level. The development of, as well as validating evidence for, our questionnaire measure of arousal-seeking tendency was reported. The scale was found to have satisfactory internal and test-retest reliabilities. Correlations with other scales provided preliminary evidence of validity.

A final section provided some preliminary discussion of drugs and alcohol within the proposed framework, that is, in terms of their effects on pleasure, arousal, and dominance. Further study of these effects may help to identify those environmental factors that contribute to increased use of alcohol or drugs.

Note

1. This section includes rewritten segments from Mehrabian and Russell's "A measure of arousal seeking tendency," reprinted from *Environment and Behavior 5,* no. 3 (Sept. 1973): 315–333, by permission of the publisher, Sage Publications, Inc.

4 The Emotional Correlates of Single Stimulus Dimensions

This chapter reviews evidence that related the proposed emotional dimensions to the more traditional stimulus categories based on sense modalities. We shall focus on the relation of pleasure and arousal to the physical aspects of the environment. Evidence that would relate dominance to single sensory dimensions is lacking and is therefore absent from our discussion. A fuller discussion would include human reactions to chemical pollutants, extremes in temperature, or vibrating stimulations. The effects of chemical pollutants are considered more appropriately in Chapter 6.

Color and Pleasure

There have been numerous studies of emotional reactions to color, such as studies of color-mood associations (e.g., Crane and Levy, 1962; Lawler and Lawler, 1965; Schaie, 1961a; 1961b; Wexner, 1954), color-warmth associations (e.g., Kimura, 1950; Wright, 1962), and color preferences (e.g., Choungourian, 1967; Eysenck, 1941; Kearney, 1966; Tinker, 1938). However, because of the lack of control for brightness and saturation, there are many inconsistencies in these studies (Norman and Scott, 1952). Guilford and Smith (1959) have shown that any hue can be made more pleasurable than another by varying brightness and saturation. Therefore, our discussion will rely primarily on the studies by Guilford (1934; 1939) and Guilford and Smith (1959), whose sample of 316 colors was systematically drawn from the entire color chart, varying saturation and brightness as well as hue. Their studies are especially relevant here because they employed pleasantness-unpleasantness as the dependent measure. Their major findings were as follows.

Brightness

In general there was a positive relationship between brightness and pleasure. At zero saturation (no color) this was the case except for a sharp reversal at low brightness (black). Thus white and black were both pleasant, while grays were unpleasant. At higher values of saturation, both hue and saturation interacted with brightness. For "cool" colors, pleasure increased with brightness, but the increase was a negatively accelerated function, such that in some instances there was a slight reversal in pleasure at high values of brightness. For "warm" colors, the increase in pleasure was a positively accelerated function.

Saturation

Similar interactions existed for saturation, but, for most values of hue and brightness, saturation was a direct correlate of pleasure. However, the minimum pleasure rating was often given to low rather than zero saturations.

Hue

As already noted, the pleasure associated with a hue varied with the value of saturation and brightness. However, for most values of brightness and saturation, maximal pleasure was reported in the region of green to blue, and minimal pleasure was reported on the green side of yellow. Thus, a typical ranking of pleasantness of hues (at constant saturation and brightness) was: blue, green, purple, red, and yellow, in descending order.

The preceding description is of necessity oversimplified, especially where there are interactive effects between hue, saturation, and brightness. Therefore the degree of pleasure for a specific color can be more easily ascertained from the extensive charts given by Guilford and Smith (1959).

Additional Evidence

Granger (1955a) measured the preference for Munsell chips varying in hue, saturation, and brightness. In his view, his results were essentially similar to those obtained by Guilford. Preference increased with saturation and brightness, although he found a significant reversal for very high saturation. Blues and greens were preferred most.

Wright and Rainwater (1962) used a small sample of colors, but varied all three dimensions. They obtained semantic differential judgments from 3660 subjects and found a "happiness" factor (happy, young, fresh, clear, social, and graceful). A regression equation expressed happiness as a function of the three stimulus dimensions and had a multiple correlation coefficient of 0.67:

Happiness = 0.194 brightness + 0.102 saturation + 0.014 hue.

As in Guilford and Smith (1959), pleasure significantly increased with brightness and saturation, but was not a significant linear function of hue.

Hogg (1969a) used a sample of thirty color cards varying in hue, saturation, and brightness. He presented pairs of colors simultaneously to his subjects, who judged the color pairs on semantic differential scales. A pleasantness factor emerged (pleasant-unpleasant, sharp-dull). Pleasure was high in the blue-purple region, low in the yellow-green region, with red occupying an intermediate position. Hogg (1969a) noted: "No systematic relation between brightness and the individual color weightings is seen in the present results, but

there is a tendency for colors in the mid-saturation region to be most preferred [p. 133] ." Sobol and Day (1967) used looking time at colored polygons as their measure of preference. The blue polygons were preferred most,
then red, yellow, and finally green.

Thus, despite differences in the dependent measures of evaluation (pleasantness in Guilford's experiment; preference ranking in Granger's, 1955a, study;
a semantic differential factor of pleasantness in Hogg's, 1969a, experiment;
a happiness factor in Wright and Rainwater's, 1962, study; and looking time
in Sobol and Day's, 1967, study), there is a general correspondence of results.
Slight discrepancies in the results are likely to be a function of less adequate
control and/or sampling of saturation and brightness of the various color
stimuli in some of these studies.

Color Combinations

The results from studies that employed color pairs (e.g., Allen and Guilford,
1936; Granger, 1955b; Kansaku, 1963) are valuable for understanding the
impact of stimuli that involve a variety of colors. The most thorough of these
studies in terms of the sampling of colors is that of Allen and Guilford (1936).
Their results led to the following conclusions: (1) The pleasantness of a combination of colors is highly dependent upon the pleasantness of the components. (2) There is some evidence that either very small or very large differences in hue (Munsell numbers) give more pleasing results than do medium
differences. (3) The pleasantness of a combination is positively correlated
with the amount of contrast in brightness. (4) There is a slight preference for
combinations with small differences in saturation rather than large differences.

Studies by Granger (1955d), Hogg (1969b), and Washburn, Haight, and
Regensburg (1921) confirmed the finding that preference for a pair of colors
presented simultaneously correlated with preferences for the individual
colors. Granger (1955c; 1955d) found preference to increase with greater
contrasts in hue. Seventy percent of the variance in preference for a pair in
his (1955d) study was accounted for by the preferences for the component
stimuli plus the contrast in their hue.

Granger (1955c) confirmed Allen and Guilford's (1936) finding that pleasure decreased with contrasts in saturation. However, in apparent contradiction to the latters' results, he also observed a decrease in pleasure with
increasing contrast in brightness.

In sum, the pleasure in reaction to a pair of colors is a weighted sum of the
pleasure in response to the individual colors. Contrast in hue adds an incre-

ment to pleasure, whereas contrast in saturation decreases pleasure. The effects of contrast in brightness are unclear.

Color and Arousal

Unfortunately there has not been any systematic work relating arousal to a thorough sampling of color brightness, hue, and saturation. In the available studies, three different types of measures of arousal were used: physiological reactions, behavioral indexes, and semantic differential ratings.

Using GSR as a measure of arousal, Wilson (1966) found that saturated red slides (with brightness unspecified) were more arousing than saturated green slides. Erwin, Lerner, Wilson, and Wilson (1961) used colored slides, two of which (red and green) were of approximately equal intensity. For these two slides, the EEG desynchronization (arousal) was significantly greater for red than for green. The effects of their white, yellow, and blue slides were difficult to assess, since these three differed in intensity from one another and from the red and green slides. In a discussion to follow, light intensity is hypothesized as a correlate of arousal, and therefore in studies that attempt to assess the arousing qualities of different colors, the intensity of color stimuli must be controlled.

In the next group of studies, arousal was assessed less directly, in terms of speed of movement, reaction time, or activity. In Nakshian's (1964) study, subjects were requested to trace a half-circle with a stylus as slowly as possible; they were also asked to hold a metal rod steadily between two guides – contact with the guides was automatically recorded, thus measuring hand tremor. In both tasks, subjects were surrounded by panels of uniform color. It was found that red panels increased both hand tremor and speed of movement more than gray panels. Gray panels, in turn, increased speed of movement more than green ones of maximum saturation. James and Domingos (1953) corroborated these results in a study where hand tremor was found to be greater under "deep red" than under white light. However, Hammes and Wiggins (1962) found no significant effect of red versus blue illumination conditions on a perceptual-motor steadiness task. Finally, in his review, Birren (1946) reported that muscular reactions were 12% faster than normal under red light, whereas green light had a retarding effect.

Although these studies used only a very small sampling of colors, the findings are generally consistent in showing red to be more arousing than green. The relation of arousal to other hues at varying levels of saturation and brightness is suggested by some indirect evidence. For example, Seaton (1968, p. 18) reported a study in which people were found to walk faster in hallways painted in "warm" colors than in those painted in "cool" colors. This observation, together with the previous evidence that red (a warm color) was arousing, suggested that color "warmth" is correlated with arousal.

Judgments of color warmth are highly reliable (Berry, 1961; Hogg, 1969a; Newhall, 1941; and Osgood, Suci, and Tannenbaum, 1957, p. 300). In general, a hot-cold color continuum ranges from red, orange, yellow, violet, blue, to green, with green being the coolest (Kimura, 1950).

Color warmth is also a direct correlate of saturation (Wright and Rainwater, 1962). This suggests that more saturated colors should be more arousing. More direct evidence was given by Hogg (1969a), who found that more saturated colors were rated as more active.

Although Hogg (1969a) did not find a relationship between color brightness and his activity factor (which consisted of semantic differential judgments of arousing and forceful quality), Wright and Rainwater (1962) did find consistent inverse correlations between brightness and warmth. In sum, it is hypothesized that color warmth and the associated level of arousal are roughly U-shaped functions of hue, red being judged warmer than orange, yellow, violet, blue, and green, in that order. Further, more saturated colors, or less bright colors, are warmer and more arousing.

Support for these conclusions was provided outside the experimental laboratory by Srivastava and Peel (1968). They found that in a museum people took more footsteps and covered more area per unit time when the walls were dark brown than when they were light brown. That is, activity or arousal increased in the warmer (high saturation, low brightness) color situation.

Further exploration of hue, saturation, and brightness in relation to the basic response dimensions could proceed in a way quite similar to Guilford and Smith's (1959) study, but with the inclusion of the dimensions of dominance and arousal. These dimensions could be defined for subjects by a single adjective pair as in the Guilford and Smith (1959) study or in terms of the semantic differential scales of Appendix B. Alternatively, other dependent measures that have been discussed could be used.

Incidentally, one study by Williams and Foley (1968) is of some use in interpreting studies that were based on subjective responses to color names only. The two sets of stimuli employed were ten dark and saturated hues and ten color names. Semantic differential ratings yielded the three factors of Osgood, Suci, and Tannenbaum (1957). Furthermore, the ratings of color names and actual colors were highly correlated. This implies that if color names are used to describe colors, subjects are likely to imagine dark and highly saturated hues.

Thermal Stimulation and Pleasure

Bedford (1961) provided a thorough review of thermal stimulation in relation to comfort, which we assume to be a correlate of pleasantness. Various aspects of thermal stimulation include temperature, humidity or vapor pressure, mean radiation temperature, speed of wind or convection, and temperature gradient from floor to head level.

For air temperatures between 50° and 76° Fahrenheit, Bedford (1961) reported that the range of 60° to 68° Fahrenheit was optimal for comfort. The distribution of heat in a room affected comfort in that a temperature gradient from floor to head level of greater than 5° Fahrenheit decreased comfort. For radiant heat, Bedford (1961) noted that although small degrees (i.e., a mean radiant temperature less than 4° Fahrenheit) had a refreshing effect, "with more intense radiation, whether due to the heating panels [walls, pipes, or heat from the sun] being hotter or of greater area, considerable discomfort may be experienced. One may find the radiation unpleasant even though the head does not feel to be over warm [p. 306]."

Bedford's (1961) approach to the characterization of thermal variables and comfort was based on the specification of optimal ranges. This makes it difficult to infer functional relationships from the findings that he summarized. Also, most of the preceding results were restricted to very narrow stimulus ranges and cannot be considered representative of the broader thermal fluctuations encountered outdoors.

Thermal Stimulation and Arousal

Bedford (1961) discussed the feeling of "freshness," which he also referred to as arousal. He reported a correlation of −0.24 between arousal and relative humidity, indicating that "a humid atmosphere was less stimulating than a dry one [p. 304]." Arousal was also related to mean radiation temperature and was greatest when the walls surrounding the area were 3° Fahrenheit warmer than the air (for both the 65° and 70° Fahrenheit conditions). Also, air speeds alternating between 12 and 30 feet per minute increased arousal at 66° Fahrenheit.

In another review article, Provins (1966) showed that small increases in temperature relative to adaptation level lowered arousal, whereas larger increases were arousing. Supporting evidence for the hypothesis was provided by the studies of Hoagland (1936), Okuma, Fujimori, and Hayashi (1965), ten Cate, Horsten, and Koopman (1949), Teschan and Gellhorn (1949), and von Euler and Söderberg (1956; 1957). For instance, in the study by Okuma, Fujimori, and Hayashi (1965) the arousal level of cats, as measured by EEG, was lower at air temperatures near the body temperature. Very high and very low temperatures increased arousal. Also, Barmack's (1939) subjects reported feeling more "alert" in a room of 15.6° Centigrade than at a normal room temperature of 24.7° Centigrade, although their heart rate was decreased.

Behavioral measures of arousal were used by Bell (1965) and Lovingood, Blyth, Peacock, and Lindsay (1967). Bell (1965) instructed his subjects to count or tap at a specified rate (e.g., once per second) and found that subjects counted or tapped faster at higher temperatures. Lovingood, Blyth, Peacock, and Lindsay's subjects showed increased hand strength, reaction time, and heart rate at a room temperature of 125.6° Fahrenheit, relative to the control room temperature of 74° Fahrenheit.

Additional studies of arousal used task performance as the dependent measure. Unfortunately, in such studies task characteristics (e.g., the routine versus variable quality of the task, its novelty or complexity) also contributed to arousal. As a consequence, there was a confounding of the experimental results with the specific tasks used. Reviews of this literature by Bell and Provins (1962) and Provins (1958; 1966) therefore did not provide any consistent relationships between thermal stimulation and performance levels. As the evidence reviewed in Chapter 6 will show, performance can be conceptualized as a function of both the arousing quality of the task and the arousing quality of the environment in which the task is performed. Specifically, performance is an inverted-U function of total arousal level due to these two sources.

In sum, arousal level increases with large changes in temperature (away from body temperature), small mean radiation temperature, alterations in air speed, and decreasing humidity.

Light Intensity and Pleasure

There is very little literature on the pleasure elicited by varying degrees of light intensity. The studies of color preference, already reviewed, showed that brighter colors were judged as more pleasant. It is thus possible that the intensity of white light is also a correlate of pleasure. This idea is supported by the finding that people walk nearest to the lighted areas in hallways, whether these are in the center or side of the hallway (Seaton, 1968, pp. 42–43). Alexander, Hirshen, Ishikawa, Coffin, and Angel (1969, p. 125) informally observed that people moved toward lighted areas. Also, Alexander, Ishikawa, and Silverstein (1968, p. 279) informally observed that in a room with adequate lighting everywhere and with only 28% of the seats next to lamps, thirteen of twenty-one subjects chose seats that were next to the lamps.

On the other hand, contrast of a bright area with darker surroundings (known as glare) was found to be unpleasant (Hopkinson and Collins, 1963; Hopkinson and Longmore, 1959). These investigators provided the relevant variables and formulas for calculating the glare of a given light source.

Light Intensity and Arousal

Alexander and Isaac (1965) found that the activity level of monkeys increased with the increasing intensity of white light. Their experiment confirmed an earlier result obtained by Isaac and DeVito (1958). However, a contradictory result was presented by Isaac and Kendall (1967), who found that the activity of rats decreased with the intensity of white light, and by Isaac and Reed (1961), who found a similar decrease in the activity of Siamese cats with light intensity. The discrepancy between the findings for monkeys and those for rats and Siamese cats can be explained in terms of their habits: the former are diurnal, whereas the latter are nocturnal. Since light intensity and temperature are correlated in natural settings, this explanation is also supported by Pereboom's (1968) finding that the activity of rats on a wheel decreased as temperatures increased from $50°-65°$ to $77°-92°$ Fahrenheit.

Thus, the findings for the monkeys, which have a greater bearing on human functioning, suggest that increasing light intensity, like thermal stimulation, should contribute to increasing levels of activity for humans. This conclusion conforms to the more general fluctuations in activity associated with waking and sleeping in response to the light intensity as well as temperature fluctuations of day and night.

Sound Stimulation and Pleasure

The effects of auditory stimulation are especially difficult to characterize because of the variety of stimulus categories. Despite similarities in loudness or frequency range, noise, music, and language can differ considerably in information rate, with consequent differences in response. For instance, noise is unpleasant, whereas music is pleasant (e.g., Newman, Hunt, and Rhodes, 1966; Smith, 1947; Middleton, Fay, Kerr, and Amft, 1944). The present discussion will be confined mostly to the effects of noise. However, some of the conclusions can be generalized to music and language when these more complex forms of sound stimulation are characterized in terms of information rate.

Kryter (1950) concluded that annoyance or lack of preference (an inverse correlate of pleasure) increased with the loudness, unexpected quality, inappropriateness, irregularity, variability, and reverberation (lack of localization) of a sound. Kryter's (1966a; 1966b) subsequent work provided more evidence bearing on the effects of noise and tones. Annoyance increased with loudness, with the pitch of a tone, with the complexity of the spectrum of sounds (i.e., the number of different tone frequencies present), and with duration (within the range of two to twelve seconds studied). These conclusions were also supported by other studies not included in his review. Alexander (1968) presented evidence of damage due to prolonged exposure to levels even as low as 85 db. Perret, Grandjean, and Lauber (1964), using airplane noise, found that reported discomfort (assumed to be a correlate of displeasure) increased with the loudness and duration of noise. Walsh (1966) found that comfort decreased when conversation noise exceeded 90 db. Also, Laird and Coye (1929) found a U-shaped function between annoyance and the frequencies of noise ranging from 64 to 8192 cps. The optimal frequency range for minimizing annoyance was approximately 100 to 1000 cps. Thus, either very high or very low frequencies were more annoying. Reports of the interactions between frequency and intensity of tones in determining pleasure are lacking.

In sum, the results in the preceding two paragraphs indicate that pleasantness increases with decreasing loudness and/or duration, intermediate frequencies, simplicity of the sound spectrum, less variability, and more expected quality of noises and pure tones. The latter two are related in that a less varied source of noise is also more expected. As will be seen in Chapter 5, many of these terms can be subsumed under the concept of information rate. The findings, then, are simply summarized: pleasure decreases with the rise in the information rate of a noise source. A more general implication of this conclusion is that increased arousal intensifies the prominent qualities of a stimulus (e.g., the unpleasantness of noise in this case).

Sound Stimulation and Arousal
Numerous studies have consistently indicated that arousal level increases with noise level. Nunnally, Knott, Duchnowski, and Parker (1967) used a 2000-cps tone and found that pupil dilation increased with the decibel level for the range of 64.2 to 94.2 db. Davies (1948) found that two- or four-second bursts of a 500-cps tone at 90 to 100 db increased muscle tension. Gaviria (1967) used heart rate, digital blood flow, and skin conductance and found that arousal was greater for white noise (two-second bursts), less for a voice recording, and least in a quiet condition. Costello and Hall (1967) found that heart rate increased during the performance of a mental task in a noisy versus a noiseless condition.

Freeman (1939) also found increases in total energy expenditure (oxygen consumption) and muscle tension in 50-db noise relative to a quiet condition. This increase occurred only in the first few days of exposure to noise. Gradually, within twelve days, both oxygen consumption and muscle tension became normal again. A similar habituation to noise was obtained by James and Hughes (1969), who used two-second bursts of white noise over eight trials at a mean interval of one minute. Their subjects' GSR responses decreased over the eight trials when the *same* noise was repeatedly presented, that is, as the information rate of the stimulus decreased.

Other studies explored the relation of noise to activity level as a measure of arousal. Isaac and Reed (1961) found that cats increased their activity with increasing decibels of white noise. Azrin (1958) found that the onset and offset of loud white noise produced increasing activity of persons who were engaged in a vigilance task. White noise at 100 db, when compared to ambient noise, increased the performance rate of turning over as many blocks as possible (Weinstein and Mackenzie, 1966). Miller (1953) found that a

90-db tone at 8000 cps produced an increase in hand trembling. Finally, Smith and Curnow (1966) reported that with loud music, shoppers in a supermarket bought the same quantities in a shorter period of time. Thus, in a variety of contexts and using a diversity of measures, increases in loudness of noise or music were found to increase arousal.

Arousal, as measured by EEG desynchronization, was found to be a U-shaped function of tone frequency and had a minimum value at 800 cps (Berlyne, McDonnell, Nicki, and Parham, 1967). In other words, the more unusual tones in the high- or low-frequency range (i.e., those of higher information content) were found to be more arousing. These investigators also found greater arousal with white noise than with pure tones.

In the case of music, studies indicated that the exciting versus calming quality of music was reliably judged. In one study, Zimny and Weidenfeller (1962) selected three pieces of music that had been reliably rated as exciting, neutral, and calming by fifty undergraduates. For children in the age range of five to twelve, arousal as measured by GSR was very high for the exciting and very low for the calming music. This relation also held for college students, but to a lesser extent (Zimny and Weidenfeller, 1963). Ellis and Brighouse (1952) used respiration rate and heart rate as measures of arousal level in response to music that was rated calming or exciting. Their findings did not show any significant difference in heart rate in response to the calming or exciting music. However, they did find a significant increase in respiration rate for the exciting music. Thus, these findings indicate that music can be reliably judged on a scale of its exciting or arousing quality and that, in turn, this quality is correlated with GSR response and respiration rate. It is also possible, considering the relationships that exist among these physiological indexes of arousal and activity level, that exciting music can produce a higher level of activity and movement. This is partially supported by the report of Smith and Curnow (1966) that louder music increased the speed of shopping. The exciting quality of music is in part determined by its speed. In this context, it is relevant to note that Rieber (1965) found children's activity rate to be greatest for fast music, less for slow music, and least in the absence of music.

Taste, Odor, Pleasure, and Arousal
Although a consideration of pleasant tastes and odors in terms of theories

about responses to chemical stimulation is beyond our scope, one important finding reported by Hess (1965) is relevant here. Using pupil diameter as a measure of arousal, he found arousal was greater for either pleasant- or unpleasant-tasting liquids than for water. A similar relation was found for arousal (GSR) and the pleasantness of odors (Shock and Coombs, 1937), although the unpleasant odors consistently elicited higher arousal. Thus, the more unusual stimuli were found to be more arousing.

Both odors and tastes are quite reliably judged as pleasant-unpleasant, and the pleasure of a pair of odors is simply a weighted sum of the pleasure of each one taken separately (Spence and Guilford, 1933).

Tactile Stimulation, Pleasure, and Arousal
The studies by Stevens and Harris (1962) and Stone (1967) both showed that subjective judgments of roughness versus smoothness were power functions of the grit number of emery cloths, although the exponent of this power function varied from experiment to experiment. Thus, there was a correspondence of this particular function with the general form of other psychophysical functions, such as those for pitch or intensity of sound. Incidentally, ratings of smoothness were inversely related to ratings for roughness (Stone, 1967). Ekman, Hosman, and Lindström (1965) confirmed the findings of Stevens and Harris (1962) by showing that judgments of roughness were a power function of the coefficient of friction, that smoothness was the inverse of roughness, and most importantly, that preference was directly proportional to smoothness.

These findings therefore show that the smooth-rough dimension can be fruitfully explored in subsequent studies of the emotional effects of textures. For instance, the relation of smoothness to arousal level can be explored readily, and then preference for a texture can be expressed as a function of its pleasurable and arousing qualities.

The Emotional Correlates of Verbally Described Stimuli
We encounter various environments not only through actual experience but also through others' verbal descriptions. An examination of these verbal descriptions can help clarify the ways in which humans know environments and how such cognitions relate to the emotions that are aroused. Also, in studies where subjects are asked to provide spontaneous verbal descriptions

of different situations (e.g., Lynch and Rivkin, 1959), it would be helpful to know what kinds of physical and emotional dimensions are primarily implied by different descriptions.

The exploratory study described below drew on the pioneering work of Kasmar (1970), who obtained an extensive list of adjectives that were specifically used to describe architectural spaces.

There was no readily available source of such items. Therefore, questionnaires were used to elicit descriptive adjectives; additional descriptive terms came from architectural and interior design magazines, as well as from previous research on the affective aspects of music, color and lines, art, and the theatre. . . .

Fifty-four undergraduate students (twenty-two males and thirty-two females) were asked to describe two rooms they liked and two rooms they disliked, listing the adjectives they believed to be descriptive of the four rooms. Upon completing this questionnaire, each S supplied the bipolar complement of each adjective he had listed. Additionally, eleven fourth- and fifth-year architecture students, after completing the first questionnaire, completed a second questionnaire which listed thirteen categories suggested by architects and designers as important in describing architectural space (size, volume, scale, mood, color, texture, function, illumination, esthetic quality, climate, odor, acoustical quality, and miscellaneous). The architecture students listed descriptive adjectives appropriate to each of the thirteen categories and then supplied the bipolar complement of each adjective listed [Kasmar, 1970, pp. 155-156].

Using these procedures, Kasmar obtained 500 bipolar pairs of adjectives that could be used to describe various environments. In proceeding to a more refined set of descriptors from this initial set, she employed a series of questionnaire studies in which only those pairs that were found to be relevant, meaningful, and usable by laymen were retained. The latter sixty-six descriptors were used in our own study.

In our questionnaire experiment, we employed 206 University of California undergraduates. These subjects each read four randomly selected situations from among the first forty listed in Appendix A and described each situation using the sixty-six descriptors developed by Kasmar (1970). In describing a given situation with each of the adjective pairs, the subjects checked off the appropriate spot on a nine-point continuum ranging from one adjective of the pair to the other. The instructions given to them were as follows:

Read situation number ___ [the situation identification number was entered here] very carefully, and then try to imagine yourself in it. Take about two minutes to really get into the mood of the situation; then rate your impressions in this situation below. Each pair of words below describes some aspect of the environment. Place a checkmark somewhere along each dimension to show your judgment of the situation.

The sixty-six pairs of verbal descriptors taken from Kasmar (1970) were listed following these instructions. After describing the situation, the subjects proceeded to record their emotional responses (i.e., their "state" emotions) to the situation using the scales of Appendix B. Thus, for each of the four situations given to him, the subject read the verbal description, described it using the sixty-six scales, and recorded his emotional reactions.

Factor Analysis of the Environmental Descriptors

Since each of 206 subjects described four situations, a total of 824 descriptions were available, each of which included a set of sixty-six judgments on the various adjective pairs. The 66 X 66 intercorrelation matrix was factor analyzed, and a principal component solution was obtained. Oblique rotation of these factors yielded the grouping of physical descriptors summarized in Table 4.1. The items within each factor are listed in decreasing magnitude of factor loadings, and the plus (+) and minus (−) signs following each item indicate the direction of loading. Factor names were selected that seemed most representative of the types of concepts subsumed in each factor. A casual examination of the various factors reveals that evaluative attitudes were given excessive representation in the sixty-six adjective pairs. Further, adjective pairs that described physical environments in visual terms were disproportionately represented at the expense of terms that might have referred to stimulation in other sense modalities.

Table 4.2 presents the intercorrelations among the nine factors of Table 4.1. To obtain these intercorrelations, factor scores were computed by algebraically summing each subject's item scores on each factor. In this way, the original matrix of 824 X 66 scores was reduced to an 824 X 9 matrix of factor scores. The factor correlations were then obtained from this matrix.

In order to show the extent to which evaluative attitudes permeated the particular list of sixty-six physical descriptors, a second-order factor analysis of the matrix of correlations given in Table 4.2 was performed. The results, summarized in Table 4.3, show that the primary factor underlying the various descriptive dimensions was pleasure, and it accounted for 45% of the total variance. Indeed, this set of factor loadings is quite analogous to the

Table 4.1   Results of the Factor Analysis of Sixty-Six Environmental Descriptors

Item	Loading Direction on Factor
Factor 1: Pleasant	
1. Unpleasant–pleasant	(+)
2. Attractive–unattractive	(–)
3. Repelling–inviting	(+)
4. Unappealing–appealing	(+)
5. Ugly–beautiful	(+)
6. Uncomfortable–comfortable	(+)
7. Bad colors–good colors	(+)
8. Pleasant odor–unpleasant odor	(–)
9. Dreary–gay	(+)
10. Good temperature–bad temperature	(–)
11. Bad lines–good lines	(+)
12. Cheerful–gloomy	(–)
13. Comfortable temperature–uncomfortable temperature	(–)
14. Inconvenient–convenient	(+)
15. Tasteful–tasteless	(–)
16. Good acoustics–poor acoustics	(–)
Factor 2: Bright and colorful	
1. Muted colors–bright colors	(+)
2. Colorful–drab	(–)
3. Bright–dull	(–)
4. Dark–light	(+)
5. Subdued colors–flashy colors	(+)
6. Good lighting–poor lighting	(–)
7. Dingy–sparkling	(+)
8. Diffuse lighting–direct lighting	(+)
9. Soft lighting–harsh lighting	(+)
Factor 3: Organized	
1. Neat–messy	(–)
2. Tidy–untidy	(–)
3. Well organized–poorly organized	(–)
4. Poorly planned–well planned	(+)
5. Orderly–chaotic	(–)
6. Disorganized–organized	(+)
7. Run down–well kept	(+)
8. Cluttered–uncluttered	(+)

Table 4.1. (Continued)

Item	Loading Direction on Factor
Factor 3: Organized	
9. Poorly balanced–well balanced	(+)
10. Dirty–clean	(+)
11. Well scaled–poorly scaled	(–)
12. Inefficient–efficient	(+)
13. Uncrowded–crowded	(–)
14. Noisy–quiet	(+)
Factor 4: Ventilated	
1. Stale odor–fresh odor	(+)
2. Poor ventilation–good ventilation	(+)
3. Drafty–stuffy	(–)
4. Warm–cool	(+)
Factor 5: Elegant	
1. Ornate–plain	(–)
2. Elegant–unadorned	(–)
3. Expensive–cheap	(–)
4. Unfashionable–fashionable	(+)
5. Full–empty	(–)
6. Simple–complex	(+)
7. Unstylish–stylish	(+)
Factor 6: Impressive	
1. Impressive–unimpressive	(–)
2. Ordinary–distinctive	(+)
3. Usual–unusual	(+)
4. Private–public	(–)
Factor 7: Large	
1. Free space–restricted space	(–)
2. Narrow–wide	(+)
3. Cramped–roomy	(+)
4. Huge–tiny	(–)
5. Large–small	(–)
6. Adequate size–inadequate size	(–)

Table 4.1. (Continued)

Item	Loading Direction on Factor
Factor 8: Modern	
1. Modern–old-fashioned	(–)
2. Contemporary–traditional	(–)
3. Old–new	(+)
Factor 9: Functional	
1. Functional–nonfunctional	(–)
2. Useful–useless	(–)
3. Single purpose–multiple purpose	(+)

Table 4.2   Intercorrelations among the Nine Factors Which Describe Environments[*]

Factor	2	3	4	5	6	7	8	9
1. Pleasant	0.56	0.74	0.68	0.32	0.56	0.63	0.08	0.56
2. Bright and colorful		0.29	0.33	0.40	0.19	0.35	0.23	0.33
3. Organized			0.53	0.18	0.46	0.52	0.00	0.50
4. Ventilated				0.07	0.50	0.59	0.00	0.41
5. Elegant					0.19	0.14	0.23	0.19
6. Impressive						0.51	– 0.08	0.22
7. Large							– 0.06	0.37
8. Modern								0.15
9. Functional								

[*]Correlations in excess of 0.18 are significant at the 0.01 level.

set of coefficients for the pleasure terms in the equations of Table 4.4. The second factor of Table 4.3 represents old-fashioned, unadorned, drab, and nonfunctional settings, with reasonably clear evaluative implications. Thus, it is not surprising that Factors 1 and 2 of Table 4.3 correlated –0.21.

To summarize, even though Kasmar (1970) attempted to provide a comprehensive list of descriptors, the end result fell short of this objective. Our analyses showed that care must be taken in developing such a series of physical descriptors to avoid disproportionate reliance on evaluative scales. Also,

Table 4.3   Rotated Factor Matrix of the Correlations in Table 4.2*

First-Order Factor	Second-Order Factor 1	Second-Order Factor 2
1. Pleasant	0.84	−0.24
2. Bright and colorful	0.33	−0.62
3. Organized	0.79	0.00
4. Ventilated	0.82	0.05
5. Elegant	0.12	−0.71
6. Impressive	0.74	0.14
7. Large	0.81	0.07
8. Modern	−0.25	−0.77
9. Functional	0.53	−0.31
Percent variance	45	16

*The second-order Factors 1 and 2 correlate −0.21 ($p < 0.01$).

it is important to give a more proportionate representation to descriptors that refer to stimulation in senses other than the visual one.

Environmental Descriptors Expressed in Terms of Emotions

The analyses in this section were carried out primarily for illustrative purposes. Our object was to show that any set of environmental descriptors can be described as possessing certain well-defined, emotion-eliciting qualities.

For each subject and each situation, factor scores of the environmental descriptors were available, and the three emotional response scores were computed that represented state measures of the subject's pleasure, arousal, and dominance in the situation.

Regression analyses were used in which each of the nine judgment factors was expressed as a function of the 0.05 level significant effects of pleasure, arousal, and dominance. The results of these regression analyses are given in Table 4.4.

These regression equations showed that the initial set of sixty-six physical descriptors and the nine factors that were based on the latter were heavily biased by evaluative judgments. In every equation but one, pleasure had the highest coefficient. It is instructive to consider differences in the magnitudes of the coefficients for pleasure in some of the nine equations. Under-

Table 4.4 Factors of Environmental Descriptors Expressed as Functions of the Three Basic Emotions*

Factor	Regression Equation	Multiple Correlation
1. Pleasant	$= + 0.83\,P - 0.06\,A$	(0.85)
2. Bright and colorful	$= + 0.44\,P + 0.17\,A$	(0.46)
3. Organized	$= + 0.60\,P - 0.27\,A$	(0.66)
4. Ventilated	$= + 0.61\,P$	(0.61)
5. Elegant	$= + 0.23\,P + 0.21\,A$	(0.30)
6. Impressive	$= + 0.56\,P + 0.07\,A - 0.13\,D$	(0.53)
7. Large	$= + 0.61\,P \quad\quad - 0.07\,D$	(0.59)
8. Modern	$= \quad\quad + 0.16\,A + 0.18\,D$	(0.23)
9. Functional	$= + 0.45\,P \quad\quad + 0.08\,D$	(0.48)

*P = state pleasure, A = state arousal, D = state dominance in these equations. All variables are normalized to facilitate the comparison of magnitudes of the various effects. The 0.05 level was used to assess the significance of all effects. Although state measures of emotion were used to compute these equations, quite similar results would have been obtained if the average pleasure (P), arousal (A), and dominance (D) eliciting qualities of the various situations were used.

standably, Factor 1, which was named "pleasant," exhibited the highest correlation with the emotional ratings of pleasure. At the other extreme, "modern" spaces were considered neither pleasant nor unpleasant, thus showing a lack of definite evaluative attitudes toward modern versus traditional environments. The "elegant" factor also had a low pleasure coefficient, indicating that elegant spaces were not considered pleasing by these college students.

The coefficients for arousal in the nine equations provided support for our conceptualization of this emotion and the way in which it was hypothesized to relate to the physical qualities of stimuli. For instance, discussions of brightness in this chapter led to the conclusion that it is a direct correlate of arousal. This indeed was the case in the second equation of Table 4.4.

"Organized," in contrast to disorganized and cluttered, spaces were rated as less arousing in the third equation, as would have been expected. Organization tends to provide an overall impression, thus minimizing the heterogeneity that is present in the stimulus components. That "elegant" situations were more arousing is understood in terms of their more ornate quality.

Finally, impressive situations that were unusual were also understandably more arousing.

All of these findings for arousal in relation to the physical qualities of environments are very much consistent with our more general discussion of theoretical information concepts in Chapter 5, where we shall hypothesize that information rate is a direct correlate of arousal. To avoid redundancy, we shall refrain from additional detailed discussion of these findings, since the following chapter provides the general rules for predicting the arousing qualities of different types of situations.

There were only four significant effects involving dominance in the nine equations of Table 4.4. Two of these can be discussed readily in terms of the basic inverse relationship between the dominant quality of a setting and the feeling of dominance that is experienced there. Since "impressive" or "large" places (the sixth and seventh equations) have a more dominant quality, persons in such places feel themselves to be more submissive. The last equation in Table 4.4 confirmed the idea that places that provide tools or increase flexibility of action (i.e., "functional" spaces) give people a more dominant feeling. Finally, the eighth equation in Table 4.4 showed that modern spaces elicited a more dominant feeling than old-fashioned ones. It is interesting here to speculate about the connotations of old-fashioned environments. These may include a certain degree of inflexibility, which can be almost intimidating when it is well-preserved, and so elicit a submissive feeling.

Summary

The object of this chapter was to review the available evidence relating important aspects of physical stimuli to feelings. The large number of studies that related colors to emotions led to the conclusions that brightness and saturation are directly correlated with pleasure. For hues, the following colors are ranked in descending order of pleasantness: blue, green, purple, red, and yellow.

Color "warmth" is correlated with arousal and ranges from red, orange, yellow, violet, blue, to green, with green being the coolest. Color warmth is also directly correlated with saturation and inversely correlated with brightness.

The results for thermal stimulation are complicated because several variables influence thermal comfort. The temperature range of 60° to 68° Fahrenheit is optimal for comfort (pleasure), and temperature gradients from floor to head level reduce comfort. Arousal increases with large deviations in temperature (away from body temperatures), small mean radiation temperature, alterations in air speed, and decreasing humidity.

For light intensity, the findings show that increased intensity of lighting is pleasant, but that discontinuities in lighting (glare) are unpleasant. Light intensity is a correlate of arousal.

For sound stimulation, most of the findings are based on noise or pure tones and show that pleasantness increases with decreasing loudness and/or duration, intermediate frequencies, simplicity of the sound spectrum, less variability, and more expected qualities of noise and pure tones. In other words, in the case of noise, pleasantness increases with lower information rates. On the other hand, arousal increases directly with the loudness of noise or music.

The remainder of this chapter consisted of the detailed analysis of one comprehensive set of adjective pairs for describing environments. The factor analysis of these physical descriptors yielded nine intercorrelated factors. These were the pleasant, bright and colorful, organized, ventilated, elegant, impressive, large, modern, and functional qualities of environments. The expressions of each of these factors in terms of basic emotional reactions showed that all but one of them were highly correlated with pleasure. These concepts, taken from the vocabulary of architects and environmental designers, not only primarily reflected evaluative attitudes but were also restricted mostly to the visual sense. Specific equations did, however, show some interesting differences in the other two emotions, arousal and dominance, elicited by each of the nine qualities of physical stimulation.

5 The Information Rate of Environments: Interrelations among Stimulus Components

In Chapter 4, we reviewed the available literature on the effects of stimulation along single-stimulus dimensions such as hue, pitch of sound, loudness, or temperature. However, most environments that are encountered are much more complex and simultaneously include stimulation in all the sense modalities, as well as along several stimulus dimensions within each modality (e.g., the many colors in a typical setting, together with various combinations of sounds, odors, temperatures, or textures). Many of these stimulus components also vary in time. The combination of all these variations results in different overall patterns, contrasts, and levels of information, which then determine responses. Furthermore, the responses are also affected by the relationship of the setting to previously encountered ones. Concepts, such as the following, have been proposed to account for the overall effect of the various components of stimulation in a given setting: complexity, diversity, unity, congruity, artificiality, crowding, symmetry, meaningfulness, harmony, and novelty. As will be seen, these terms, as well as others, can be related systematically along a single dimension by the use of information theory. The concept of average information rate can be used to characterize complex spatial and temporal arrangements of stimuli within and across settings. It also serves as the basis for a simple, yet powerful, hypothesis: Information rate is a direct correlate of arousal. Evidence for this hypothesis is reviewed after some definition of terms.

Information Rate

Although general discussions of information theory and the measurement of information rate are available (e.g., Attneave, 1959a; Cherry, 1966, Chapter 5; Garner, 1962), it is helpful to consider briefly the basic concepts of this approach at this point.

The uncertainty in the outcome of a coin toss is given by $\log_2 2 = 1$ bit. Alternatively, given that a certain outcome of a coin toss is observed, the information (i.e., the reduction in uncertainty) of that outcome is one bit. More generally, the uncertainty of an outcome that is one of k equally likely alternatives is $\log_2 k$. Thus, a specific outcome (the occurrence of one of these k alternatives) is said to have $\log_2 k$ bits of information. The amount of information for a series of independent events is simply specified. For instance, if n independent events occur and each of these events is one of k equally likely alternatives, then the amount of information (H) is given by $H = n \log_2 k$.

These considerations apply to the characterization of the information of a spatial configuration. For instance, of two paintings, one of which contains two, and the other eight, equally distributed colors, the latter has three times ($\log_2 8 = 3$) the information of the former ($\log_2 2 = 1$). The same reasoning is applied for characterizing any series of events, whether distributed over space or time or both. No distinction is made in information theory between spatial and temporal distributions of events. Both are treated as sequences.

When the various alternatives of an event are not equally likely, or when the various elements in a spatial configuration are not equally distributed, the amount of information is given simply by

$$H = \sum p_i \log_2 1/p_i = -\sum p_i \log_2 p_i$$

where p_i is the probability of alternative i. In the case of k equally probable outcomes, $p_i = p = 1/k$, and the formula reduces to the expected form:

$$H = \sum_{i=1}^{k} p_i \log_2 1/p_i = k\,(p \log_2 1/p) = \log_2 k.$$

One important implication of this measure of information is that when the alternatives of an outcome are not equally probable, the amount of information is less than when the alternatives are equally probable. Thus, in the case of a spatial configuration, the information is less when the various parts are not equally distributed. For example, a painting that has eight equally distributed colors has a higher amount of information than another one with the same eight colors, but where one color covers 90% of the surface area. A second important implication of the information measure is that rare or novel events contain more information, since the information of an event is $\log_2 1/p$, where p is the probability of that event.

Within a spatial or temporal distribution of events, the total amount of information is simply the sum of information from each event or component, provided that the component events are independent (i.e., provided that successive outcomes are independent of preceding ones in a temporal sequence or that the components are randomly distributed in a spatial configuration). In particular, given that the information of a stimulus configuration is specified for some particular time, each change in that configuration can be characterized as contributing additional information. The unchanging (redundant) quality of a stimulus configuration is thus reflected in a lower total amount of information within a time period. In contrast, a configuration in which the components are varying rapidly and randomly is characterized by a high amount of information.

If there is any patterning (regularity, redundancy, dependencies, or lawfulness) within the sequence of events, this means that the probability of a particular event occurring after a given sequence is higher. In other words, such patterning reduces the uncertainty of the next event in the sequence and therefore lowers the amount of information.

In general, any set of events is coded into a linear sequence of symbols (thus resembling a message, the type of subject matter for which information theory was developed). The number of alternative events, their frequencies, and any patterning within the total sequence determine the probability for each event. The set of probabilities, in turn, is used to calculate the amount of information by the formulas just given.

Attneave's (1959b) statement briefly summarizes the central idea so far:

Perhaps the most fundamental concept of information theory is that of a continuum extending from extreme lawfulness, or redundancy, or regularity on one hand, to extreme disorder, or unpredictability, or uncertainty on the other. One end of this continuum is homogeneity, the other chaos [p. 503].

Total sensory deprivation (single values for each modality with no spatial or temporal variation) constitutes an example of one extreme end of this continuum. At the opposite end is an environment with numerous components distributed in random fashion, all varying at a high speed in unpredictable directions.

For psychological problems, it is important to define the rate at which a person is receiving information (Cherry, 1966, p. 177). Average information rate is defined simply as the total amount of information per unit time.

Information Rate Used to Describe Stimuli

Various kinds of stimuli have been developed for which the amount of information is exactly specified: simple geometric figures (Attneave and Arnoult, 1956; Attneave, 1957; 1959b; Day, 1968c; Dorfman and McKenna,

1966; Terwilliger, 1963; Vitz, 1966a), combinations of tones (Vitz, 1964; 1966b), and sequences of letters or various approximations to English (Munsinger and Kessen, 1964).

Several problems should be considered that have been encountered in using such stimuli. First, when specific stimuli are devised so that they can be described exactly in informational terms, there is sometimes a failure to define information rate. When the subject is to observe some static configuration that is novel to him, information rate is the inverse of the number of repetitions (or length of time) of exposure to the stimulus. For instance, Vitz (1966a) presented the same series of stimuli to his subjects in two successive sessions and found quite different results in the two sessions. This difference in findings can be explained in terms of the decreased information rate of the second series due to its greater familiarity.

Familiarity can also be due to past exposures to similar stimuli. Thus, a set of randomly generated shapes may be meaningful to a subject who has encountered certain objects with similar shapes and therefore is able to assign a meaning to the random shapes. The possible contribution of meaningfulness must be considered for a psychologically adequate measure of information rate. For example, in Terwilliger's (1963) study, information was measured for a collection of rectangles drawn within a square border. All the figures were randomly generated; however, some of them looked like familiar plaids or windowpanes. A more accurate information score for such figures is possible only if their familiarity is taken into account.

There have been no attempts to measure the information of the complex stimuli in everyday environments, such as visual displays of houses or people. One approach to the computation of the information of such displays is their treatment as a two-dimensional mosaic consisting of light-dark blocks. As in the case of a picture on a cathode-ray tube, the display is reconstructed as a sequence of binary decisions. The size of each block (the grain) in the mosaic is determined by the needs of the experiment or by the complexity of the pictorial display. The information of the entire figure, coded into a sequence of binary digits, is then computed. Furthermore, color can be added to the display by expanding from binary to higher orders. For a complex visual display that changes over time, the amount of information in the display is measured in successive short intervals of time, thus allowing the computation of an overall index, information rate, for that display.

When there is patterning of stimuli (i.e., regularity, redundancy, dependencies, or lawfulness), the amount of information can be calculated from estimates of conditional probabilities for the various components. For instance, the frequency distribution with which subjects assign (predict) the next item in a sequence, given the preceding series of items, can be used to estimate the conditional probabilities. When such probability estimates are used in computing information rate, individual differences in past encounters with environments and differences in the discrimination of patterning are automatically taken into account.

It is also possible to extend this method of computing information to other modalities besides the visual one. In considering the simultaneous effects of two or more modalities, if stimulation in any one modality (e.g., visual) is completely independent of stimulation in any other modality (e.g., auditory or thermal), then total information is simply the sum of the information within each of these modalities measured separately. However, the studies of synesthesia and related evidence already reviewed show that, despite material differences, stimulation in different sense modalities can be partially redundant in terms of its emotional impact. In this case, the complication in the measurement of total information from different sense modalities can again be resolved by obtaining estimates of conditional probabilities. Such estimates can be obtained from the expected associations of stimulus categories across modalities. For instance, the frequencies with which each of a set of hues are judged by subjects as being congruent with different temperatures would identify the patterning within these two modalities.

Although patterning can be detected in certain sequences (and thus lead to accurate estimates of probabilities), no general method yet exists that detects all types of patterning in all sequences. Furthermore, for psychological studies, the important question is what patterning is noticed by the person encountering a situation. Besides the method already noted for computing conditional probabilities for each specific case, no a priori and general answer to this question is available today (Simon, 1972).

To summarize, approximate measures of information rate may be calculated for certain complex settings but are quite difficult to obtain. Thus, the general unavailability of exact measures of information rate, in all but the simplest cases, presents a pragmatic problem in research based on this concept. For this reason, it is important to find an adequate and simpler alternative to the measurement of information rate that would include possible contributions due to patterning, meaningfulness, and familiarity of stimuli. In this context, the objective of the following section is twofold: first, to illustrate specifically the heuristic value of the concept of information rate in studies of environmental psychology, and second, to provide a basis for the development of a verbal measure of information rate in the final section of this chapter.

Familiar Concepts Expressed in Terms of Information Rate
A number of familiar distinctions that are made in characterizing environments or specific stimuli can be translated and integrated within the concept of information rate. In characterizing everyday environments, the second term in each of the following pairs refers to an environment of higher information rate: *simple-complex, patterned-random, harmonious-jarring, homogeneous-heterogeneous, redundant-varied, similar-contrasting, consonant-dissonant, continuous-intermittent* (Berlyne, 1967). For example, electronic music compared to the traditional classical music, a highly, rather than simply, decorated room, a strobe-light compared to a stationary light, and cubism or surrealism relative to representational art, all represent increases in information rate.

The terms *novel, rare, unexpected,* and *surprising* all refer to the improbability of an event. As already noted, the information rate of more improbable events is greater.

A *meaningful* object or situation is recognizable, therefore patterned. Further, it is familiar and therefore probable. On both counts, meaningfulness contributes to a lowering of information rate.

Changing or *moving* situations have more information per unit time, relative to *static* ones. Furthermore, *fast, accelerated* movements contain more information per unit time than *slow* ones.

The Gestalt principles of *symmetry, closure,* and, generally, *good form* (e.g., Koffka, 1935) can be defined in terms of information rate. For instance, *symmetry* implies redundancy and therefore reduced information rate. Perceptual configurations that are characterized as having good form consist of redundant parts are more familiar and less novel, and therefore contain less information than those that are of poorer form (e.g., Attneave, 1957; Hochberg and McAlister, 1953; Terwilliger, 1963).

The concept of *distance* is increasingly used in the study of environments (e.g., Hall, 1966; McBride, King, and James, 1965; Mehrabian, 1971a, Chapter 5; Sommer, 1969; also see Chapter 7 of this book). As the distance to some stimulus object decreases, the details of the object become more apparent, and the information rate increases. Thus, information is minimized in open or *expansive* spaces where average distances to entities in the spaces are large.

The approach of another human, a varied source of stimulation, also increases information. More generally, *immediate* stimuli (e.g., closer stimuli that are also available in more sensory channels) are higher on information rate than nonimmediate ones. Thus, a house is more immediate than its photograph, and another person who is close, leaning forward, touching, or having eye contact is more immediate than when he is distant, leaning back, or looking away (Mehrabian, 1972a; 1972b).

The concepts of *crowding* and *density* have been used to characterize environments, and Calhoun's (1962a; 1962b; 1966; 1968; also see Chapter 7) experiments dramatically illustrated the adverse effects of crowding on rats. In general, high densities are associated with smaller distances between the subject and the sources of stimulation and thus with more varied stimuli. Since people are a varied source of information, a high density of persons is expected to involve a much greater information rate than a high density of inanimate objects. The striking behavioral effects observed in a crowded environment are explained in part by an excessive information rate that cannot be avoided.

The concept of *scale* is also related to information rate. Given a fixed distance to an object, with increasing scale, its features and details become more recognizable, and the information rate increases. Pictures of the Eiffel Tower or the Washington Monument, or even exact but small physical replicas, fail to have quite the emotional impact of the actual monuments. Also, an increase in the scale of a familiar object (e.g., a Campbell soup can) can be unexpected, thereby increasing its information. Both of these effects of large scale (more detail and unexpected quality) are obtained when pop artists reproduce simple and familiar objects on an enormous scale, with a surprising change in their emotional impact. The difference in response to the enormous scale is attributable in part to the novelty of such objects. As expected, then, part of the emotional effect dissipates for those who become familiar with such objects of art.

Outdoor, rural, or *natural* settings, as distinct from *indoor, urban,* or *man-made* ones, are characterized by larger distances, smaller density, and a slower pace of changes, thus having a lower information rate.

The Information Rate–Arousal Hypothesis

Within the present framework, the information rate from an environment is linked to the response variables by the following hypothesis: The arousal level elicited by an environment is a direct correlate of its information rate.

There are two lines of evidence bearing on this hypothesis: one for arousal in response to more or less complex static configurations and a second for arousal in response to changing stimulus configurations. The latter also subsumes response to novel situations.

Berlyne (1960), de Charms (1968), and Fiske and Maddi (1961) discussed the relation of arousal to information input. In addition to the theoretical notions and evidence brought forward by these authors, data are provided by Baker and Franken (1967), whose subjects had longer EEG desynchronization (indicating greater arousal) in response to more complex geometrical figures. In a similar study, Berlyne and McDonnell (1965) found that EEG desynchronization was longer in response to more complex patterns when the patterns were exposed to subjects for three seconds. Berlyne and Borsa (1968) used more or less blurred pictures as stimuli. Since blurred pictures are less patterned and have less obvious meanings, it follows from the discussion in the preceding section that such pictures have a higher information rate than clear ones. Subjects had longer EEG desynchronization in response to the more blurred pictures. Using GSR as a measure of arousal, Berlyne, Craw, Salapatek, and Lewis (1963) found increased arousal response for more complex, more irregular, or more incongruous figures. On the other hand, Berlyne and Lawrence (1964) failed to find any significant effects on GSR due to complexity of their figures. Also, Berlyne and Peckham (1966) had subjects rate the preceding figures on semantic differential scales. Contrary to our hypothesized positive linear relation, judged activity of the figures was an inverted-U-shaped function of complexity, such that intermediate degrees of complexity were judged highest in activity. Activity was represented by only a single item (fast-slow), however, so that this result may be unreliable.

There are more studies bearing on the relation of arousal to temporally varying stimuli. One special case is the novel stimulus, with greater novelty being a correlate of information rate. In the Baker and Franken (1967) study, as subjects continued to view the same figure, arousal (as measured by EEG desynchronization) decreased. The more arousing quality of novel stimuli was also explored by Berlyne, Craw, Salapatek, and Lewis (1963). They found the highest level of GSR at the first showing of any slide and decreased GSR at subsequent presentations of the same slide. Similarly, James and Hughes (1969) obtained a decrease in GSR with successive presentations of the same two-second bursts of white noise.

In another study, Berlyne and Lawrence (1964) observed a decrease in GSR of the subjects with successive exposures of the same figure, that is, with a decrease in novelty. Using a different measure of arousal, Nunnally, Knott, Duchnowski, and Parker (1967) found greater pupil dilation in their subjects in response to more novel pictures. Milerian's (1955) study involved a comparison of a changing, relative to a static, configuration. The subjects listened to a melody or single tones, and, as expected, EEG desynchronization was greater in response to the melody than to the single tones.

Work with the orienting reflex also provided support for the preceding hypothesis.

According to Sokolov (1960; 1963), a leading authority on the orienting reflex, an initial condition for elicitation of an OR is stimulus change. Any increase, decrease, qualitative or quantitative change in stimulation may evoke an OR. Consequent response changes defining an OR include cephalic vasodilation and peripheral constriction, the GSR, alpha desynchronization, and pupillary dilation. While any change in stereotyped stimulation may be followed by these physiological responses, repeated occurrence of stimuli in a uniform manner results in habituation of the OR. In addition to the above vegetative components of the OR there may be overt responses, such as turning of the head and eye movements, which also have the effect of facilitating stimulus reception [Maltzman, 1967, p. 96].

The preceding summary of findings for the orienting reflex provides further support for the concept of arousal and the particular grouping of physiological cues within it. It also provides support for the hypothesis that more variable and novel stimuli are more arousing.

In sum, the preponderance of relevant studies has indicated that information rate is a direct correlate of arousal. Despite its simplicity, this is a hypothesis of considerable scope because of the numerous relations it implies. It is easy to list derivative hypotheses that have not been adequately tested but that have an important bearing on the descriptions of the effects of everyday environments. For instance, there should be greater arousal in response to variability in colors or lighting, to unusual or ambiguous situations, and to more, or closer, people. More generally, arousal should be greater when a person confronts a densely decorated area relative to a sparsely decorated one (such as when there is more crowding or, more generally, in urban versus rural areas).

Several observations by Mason (1959b) with monkeys provided support for some of these conclusions. For instance, monkeys that were placed in cages from which other animals in the room were more visible were found to have more secretion from the adrenal cortex, which is considered an index of arousal (e.g., note our discussion in Chapter 6 of Selye's, 1950; 1952; 1956; 1959 General Adaptation Syndrome). This result supported the hypothesized increase in physiological arousal with the increases in information rate from others in the environment. Mason (1959b) also found that the corticoid secretion of the monkeys decreased by 30% over the weekends, when there were fewer people in the laboratory.

A related study by McBride, King, and James (1965) illustrates the results that can be obtained in some of these more familiar and less explored settings. They found that the GSR of their human subjects increased with decreasing distance from another person. Even more specifically, Nichols and Champness (1971) found that both frequency and amplitude of the GSR was greater when two subjects had eye contact than when they did not.

The studies of Mason (1959b), McBride, King, and James (1965), and Nichols and Champness (1971) thus showed that greater "immediacy" (i.e., proximity and directness of orientation leading to intensity of interpersonal cues) between persons or animals was more arousing. Their findings point to some unexplored areas of research that could help to clarify further the proposed hypothesis.

The Synchrony of External and Behavioral Rhythms

At this point, it is of interest to consider some rhythmic phenomena that provide a possible mechanism for the information rate–arousal correlation. Condon and Ogston (1966) and Kendon (1967) discussed the movements that a person produces in reaction to movements and speech produced by another. This relationship can be stated more generally as a person's synchronization of his movements to any rhythmic patterns in the environment. For example, some studies reviewed in Chapter 4 showed exciting, loud, or fast music to have the effect of increasing the physical activity rate of the persons who were listening to it (e.g., Rieber, 1965). When the stimulus was another person, Condon and Ogston's (1966) microanalysis of movement sequences produced evidence for "movement mirroring" and "punctuation."

There is a small amount of research which suggests that when subjects are exposed to an input that has a rhythmic organization, for instance music, they tend to move in time to it . . . and that if they are already performing some activity, such as tapping, or typing, they may bring the rhythm of this activity into relation with the rhythm of the input. . . . We have seen here, both from the data we have reported on, and also very strikingly from the data reported by Condon and Ogston, that the synchrony of the listener's behavior to that of the speaker may be very precise indeed. The precision of the synchrony suggests that the listeners are responding to a rhythm with which they are thoroughly familiar. This rhythm is, of course, largely the rhythm of speech, the rhythmical character of the syllabic pulse, and for those who have a given language in common this rhythm must be familiar. . . . It seems plausible, thus, that the minute synchrony observable between inter- actants is a product of their attention to an input where rhythmical struc- turing is highly familiar to them [Kendon, 1967, pp. 36–37].

These synchronous movements have been ascertained only from a very care- ful microanalysis of film records and, for the most part, are not evident from direct observations in real time. That is to say, the movements have to be slowed down considerably in order to be noted. The exceptions, of course, are when a person coordinates the rhythm of his bodily movements with a piece of music or with some other salient source of rhythmic stimulation in the background. Further exploration of this synchronous quality of move- ments of humans to the events around them could provide much needed data for explaining the link between arousal and information rate.

This phenomenon bears on environmental designs that deliberately or inadvertently control specific rhythmic behaviors or emotional states. For instance, suppose a highway is constructed in successive and equal sections of two distinct shades of gray, such that a driver encounters a repeated and rhythmic change in the visual input from the road as he drives. The section lengths, having been set to correspond to an optimal range of arousal for someone who is driving at the specified speed limit, are intended to serve as an indirect speed control device. In this case, individual differences in desired levels of arousal would probably lead to characteristic differences in driving speed, with concomitant undesirable consequences (e.g., higher accident rates). Also, the optimal range of arousal for an individual may be too broad to provide a useful solution to the speed control problem. This application illustrates some of the problems that are associated with environmental controls on behavioral rhythms. Such problems are more likely when the controls are inadvertent. For instance, workers engaged in repetitious work at a factory may find it extremely disturbing to hear a loud noise that rhythmically fluctuates in decibel level at a different frequency from that involved in their own movements.

In a deliberately designed and more pleasant application, the beat of a musical piece could be made to correspond initially to an average heart beat or breathing rhythm, thus casually producing a synchrony between musical and physiological rhythms. Once this "hookup" is made, the musical rhythm could be slowly changed in various directions to achieve the desired mood changes—a technique undoubtedly found today in films.

A Verbal Measure of Information Rate

For the complex and multimodality stimulation in everyday environments, the problems already reviewed indicate that the exact specification of information rate is quite cumbersome. The meaningfulness or familiarity of (various components of) a setting necessitate subjective estimates of conditional probabilities of each component event in a stimulus configuration; that is, the component events need to be assigned probability estimates that are based on the perceiver's own detection of patterning in the spatial and/or temporal arrangement of components.

Verbal report measures of information rate provide an alternative approach. Initial research with single verbal scales has been promising. Attneave (1957) found that judged complexity of polygons was a logarithmic function of the amount of information as specified by the number of independent turns in his figures. In Day's (1968c) study, judgments of the complexity of polygons were directly correlated with the number of sides of polygons. Vitz (1966b) constructed sequences of tones in which higher information rates were obtained with sequences that contained greater variance in the dimensions of loudness, duration, and pitch. His subjects' mean verbal rating of the "variation or unexpected quality" of each set of tones was highly correlated with the rank order of the information rate of that set.

Thus, for stimuli where the measurement of information rate is cumbersome, good estimates can be based on subjective judgments along verbal dimensions. An advantage of the use of subjects' own judgments over other measures of information is that the former automatically discounts the effects of familiarity and meaningfulness. In other words, subjects' own judgments provide estimates of information rate that are based on conditional probabilities of the various component events.

For these reasons, we attempted to develop a verbal measure of information rate. A number of concepts, assumed to relate to information rate, were available from our introductory discussions in this chapter and provided the initial set of adjective pairs. These adjective pairs, given in Table 5.1, were used in a study with two objectives: first, to provide preliminary validation for the conceptualization of information rate presented here, and second, to develop a more adequate verbal scale of information rate by eliminating items included in the initial set that were excessively confounded by an evaluative bias.

In the study, 214 University of California undergraduates each read a set of six situations taken from Appendix A (different sets being selected and randomly assigned to different subjects). Following the reading of each situation, a subject first characterized his emotional reactions to that situation, using the state measures given in Appendix B. He then rated the same situation on the adjective pairs of Table 5.1, using the instructions and format given there.

The nine-point response scales of Table 5.1 range from −4 (extreme left) to +4 (extreme right). Response bias was controlled by arranging the adjective pairs so that approximately half the time the adjective on the extreme right corresponded to judgments of higher information rate and the reverse was true in the other half of the instances. The plus (+) and minus (−) signs preceding each item in Table 5.1 indicate direction of scoring. These, of course, were omitted from the instructions given to the subjects.

Since each of 214 subjects rated six situations, there were a total of 1284 sets of ratings based on the response format given in Table 5.1. The 21 × 21 matrix of intercorrelations among the items of Table 5.1 was factor analyzed,

Table 5.1.   Initial Set of Adjective Pairs Relating to Information Rate*

Instructions to Subjects
Please use the adjective pairs below to describe situation [the situation identification
number was entered here]. Each of the following adjective pairs describes the situation
or the relation among the various parts of the situation. Put a check somewhere along
the line (Example: - - - -:- -✓- -:- - - -) to indicate what you think is an appropriate
description.

(+) simple	- - - -:- - - -:- - - -:- - - -:- - - -:- - - -:- - - -:- - - -	complex
(+) patterned	- - - -:- - - -:- - - -:- - - -:- - - -:- - - -:- - - -:- - - -	random
(−) novel	- - - -:- - - -:- - - -:- - - -:- - - -:- - - -:- - - -:- - - -	familiar
(+) meaningful	- - - -:- - - -:- - - -:- - - -:- - - -:- - - -:- - - -:- - - -	meaningless
(+) small scale	- - - -:- - - -:- - - -:- - - -:- - - -:- - - -:- - - -:- - - -	large scale
(−) immediate	- - - -:- - - -:- - - -:- - - -:- - - -:- - - -:- - - -:- - - -	distant
(+) good form	- - - -:- - - -:- - - -:- - - -:- - - -:- - - -:- - - -:- - - -	bad form
(−) varied	- - - -:- - - -:- - - -:- - - -:- - - -:- - - -:- - - -:- - - -	redundant
(−) dense	- - - -:- - - -:- - - -:- - - -:- - - -:- - - -:- - - -:- - - -	sparse
(+) common	- - - -:- - - -:- - - -:- - - -:- - - -:- - - -:- - - -:- - - -	rare
(−) heterogeneous	- - - -:- - - -:- - - -:- - - -:- - - -:- - - -:- - - -:- - - -	homogeneous
(−) intermittent	- - - -:- - - -:- - - -:- - - -:- - - -:- - - -:- - - -:- - - -	continuous
(−) crowded	- - - -:- - - -:- - - -:- - - -:- - - -:- - - -:- - - -:- - - -	uncrowded
(+) usual	- - - -:- - - -:- - - -:- - - -:- - - -:- - - -:- - - -:- - - -	surprising
(−) man-made	- - - -:- - - -:- - - -:- - - -:- - - -:- - - -:- - - -:- - - -	natural
(+) harmonious	- - - -:- - - -:- - - -:- - - -:- - - -:- - - -:- - - -:- - - -	jarring
(−) asymmetrical	- - - -:- - - -:- - - -:- - - -:- - - -:- - - -:- - - -:- - - -	symmetrical
(+) similar	- - - -:- - - -:- - - -:- - - -:- - - -:- - - -:- - - -:- - - -	contrasting
(+) rural	- - - -:- - - -:- - - -:- - - -:- - - -:- - - -:- - - -:- - - -	urban
(+) consonant	- - - -:- - - -:- - - -:- - - -:- - - -:- - - -:- - - -:- - - -	dissonant
(−) indoor	- - - -:- - - -:- - - -:- - - -:- - - -:- - - -:- - - -:- - - -	outdoor

*The signs preceding each adjective pair indicate the scoring direction.

and a principal component solution was obtained. There were five factors
with eigenvalues exceeding unity, which accounted for 60% of the total
variance. The composition of these factors is given in Table 5.2 in which the
items within each factor are listed in order of their factor loadings. The
scoring direction for each item is indicated to its left, and the factor loading
is given to the right. It is seen from Table 5.2 that the scoring-direction and
factor-loading signs corresponded in each case, thus providing support for the
a priori judgments about the significance of these adjective pairs.

Table 5.2.   The Factorial Composition of the Information Rate
Scales

Scoring Direction and Item	Factor Loading
Factor 1	
(+) good form–bad form	+0.84
(+) harmonious–jarring	+0.74
(+) meaningful–meaningless	+0.69
(+) consonant–dissonant	+0.64
Factor 2	
(+) common–rare	+0.80
(–) novel–familiar	−0.77
(+) usual–surprising	+0.71
Factor 3	
(+) small scale–large scale	+0.74
(+) simple–complex	+0.69
(–) dense–sparse	−0.63
(–) crowded–uncrowded	−0.48
(–) immediate–distant	−0.34
Factor 4	
(–) intermittent–continuous	−0.67
(–) heterogeneous–homogeneous	−0.64
(–) asymmetrical–symmetrical	−0.61
(+) similar–contrasting	+0.56
(+) patterned–random	+0.50
(–) varied–redundant	−0.41
Factor 5	
(–) indoor–outdoor	−0.83
(+) rural–urban	+0.78
(–) man-made–natural	−0.74

Factors 1 and 5 in Table 5.2 appeared to be heavily biased by evaluative
judgments. To assess the extent of this bias, the subject's emotional reactions
of pleasure, arousal, and dominance to each situation were computed from
his responses to the adjective pairs of Appendix B. Regression equations
were then written to express each adjective pair in terms of these emotional
reactions. These equations are listed in Table 5.3. Also, a composite score
for each factor of Table 5.2 was computed by summing a subject's ratings

for a particular situation on the adjective pairs listed in that factor. These composite scores were also expressed in terms of pleasure, arousal, and dominance in the regression equations of Table 5.3.

Based on the a priori judgments as to which adjective of each pair was cor-related with a higher information rate (i.e., the direction of scoring as indi-cated in Table 5.1), a total information rate score was computed for each situation as rated by each subject. The item-total correlations presented in Table 5.3 provide the correlation of scores on each adjective pair with this total score and are based on 1284 observations. With degrees of freedom $(df) = 212$, correlations in excess of 0.14 are significant at the 0.05 level, thus showing that in all but one instance the item-total correlations were significant. Furthermore, all correlations were in the anticipated direction, therefore providing preliminary validity for the hypothesized commonality among these items.

Construct validity for the assertion that the scales of Table 5.1 constituted measures of information rate was assessed through the information rate-arousal hypothesis. Examination of the coefficients in the twenty-one regression equations in Table 5.3 showed that in all but two cases, arousal was a significant component. With the use of the cumulative binomial distribution, the null hypothesis was rejected, since the probability of such an effect was less than 0.01.

More important, though, the regression equations and item-total correla-tions in Table 5.3 provided useful information for selecting a subset of the items for use as a verbal measure of information rate. Such a measure can be used for verbally described situations, photographic or pictorial presenta-tions, and video recordings, as well as direct viewing by a subject. The availability of this measure should facilitate the development of stimuli for experiments in which information rate needs to be specified. Further, such a measure can be useful in considering everyday design problems (e.g., how much information rate is there in a classroom filled with students, and is it excessive or tolerable for highly anxious students? How much information rate is there in a shopping center or discotheque, and, on the basis of this, how can we predict the kinds of people who will be attracted to it?).

In selecting the final set of items for the measure of Appendix D, items from Factors 1 and 5 were eliminated because these two factors charac-terized aspects of environments that primarily affected pleasure, even though

Table 5.3.   Items and Factors of the Information Rate Scale Expressed as Functions of Emotional States*

Item-Total Correlation	Item	Regression Equation	Multiple Correlation
0.51	good form–bad form	$= -0.78\,P$	0.78
0.68	harmonious–jarring	$= -0.62\,P + 0.32\,A$	0.72
0.29	meaningful–meaningless	$= -0.61\,P - 0.15\,A$	0.62
0.56	consonant–dissonant	$= -0.42\,P + 0.20\,A$	0.49
	Factor 1	$= -0.77\,P + 0.13\,A$	0.80
0.21	common–rare	$= +0.14\,P + 0.18\,A$	0.22
0.33	familiar–novel	$= +0.09\,P + 0.28\,A - 0.09\,D$	0.29
0.32	usual–surprising	$= +0.13\,P + 0.31\,A$	0.33
	Factor 2	$= +0.14\,P + 0.32\,A - 0.10\,D$	0.33
0.16	small scale–large scale	$= +0.20\,P + 0.32\,A - 0.12\,D$	0.36
0.59	simple–complex	$= -0.16\,P + 0.49\,A$	0.53
0.42	sparse–dense	$= + 0.27\,A$	0.27
0.63	uncrowded–crowded	$= -0.36\,P + 0.37\,A$	0.55
0.11	distant–immediate	$= +0.11\,P + 0.20\,A$	0.22
	Factor 3	$= -0.11\,P + 0.53\,A$	0.55
0.34	continuous–intermittent	$= + 0.11\,A$	0.11
0.50	homogeneous–heterogeneous	$= -0.09\,P + 0.24\,A$	0.26
0.57	symmetrical–asymmetrical	$= -0.23\,P + 0.22\,A$	0.34
0.51	similar–contrasting	$= + 0.34\,A$	0.34
0.26	patterned–random	$= + 0.13\,A + 0.08\,D$	0.17
0.14	redundant–varied	$= +0.44\,P + 0.29\,A$	0.50
	Factor 4	$= + 0.37\,A$	0.37
0.35	outdoor–indoor	$= -0.34\,P - 0.13\,A + 0.14\,D$	0.36
0.47	rural–urban	$= -0.32\,P + 0.10\,A$	0.35
0.50	natural–man-made	$= -0.42\,P + 0.10\,D$	0.43
	Factor 5	$= -0.44\,P + 0.12\,D$	0.44

*In these equations, P = state pleasure, A = state arousal, and D = state dominance. All variables were normalized before computing the equations. Significance of the various terms entered in each of these equations was assessed at the 0.05 level.

they also had smaller effects on arousal. Thus, the final scale in Appendix D includes the remaining fourteen items and provides a convenient and rapid means of assessing information rate of a situation. To compute total scores for this measure, the signs of subjects' responses to the negatively signed items of that scale are first changed, and then an algebraic sum is obtained over all items. Over the sixty-five situations of Appendix A, this scale has a mean of –2.2 and a standard deviation of 15.7, when each item is scored +4 to –4.

The measure of Appendix D was used to compute a total information rate score for each situation for each subject. The reactions of pleasure, arousal, and dominance by each subject had already been computed for each situation in carrying out the analyses of Table 5.3. A regression equation analogous to those given in Table 5.3 was computed to express total information rate in terms of pleasure, arousal, and dominance and yielded the following equation:

Information rate (Appendix D) = 0.57 arousal state

In other words, the information rate measure of Appendix D is not significantly related to either pleasure or dominance.

Summary

The concept of information rate is a very powerful tool for the analysis of environmental problems, since it unites within a coherent framework a large number of ideas that investigators have used in their studies of environmental psychology. These are concepts such as complex, random, intense, jarring, heterogeneous, dissonant, intermittent, rare, novel, surprising, meaningless, asymmetrical, close, crowded, or dense. All such concepts somehow relate to the idea of information because temporal or spatial patterning serves to increase disproportionately the conditional probabilities of certain compo-nents at various parts in an arrangement, thereby reducing uncertainty (i.e., the amount of information) in the total arrangement. In this context, it is useful to distinguish information rate from amount of information because this distinction allows one to understand the change in a person's emotional reactions to a static stimulus configuration (e.g., a painting) over time.

The concept of information rate is useful in that it not only subsumes a larger number of relevant concepts but also forms the basis of a central hy-pothesis: The information rate from a stimulus is a correlate of the arousal elicited by it. Available literature bearing on this hypothesis was reviewed, and some mechanisms were suggested to relate various stimuli to arousal level. Examples were the synchronous movements of a person in reaction to the movements of others (Condon and Ogston, 1966) and physical occurrences (Kendon, 1967).

Owing to the absence of a convenient measure for assessing the information rate in complex situations, a study was conducted to develop a verbal measure of information rate. The objectives in the study were (1) to confirm the idea that the adjective pairs identified (e.g., simple-complex) were indeed correlates of information rate, (2) to explore the factorial composition of these adjective pairs, (3) to assess construct validity by using the hypothesis that persons are more aroused in situations where information rate is higher, and (4) to use these analyses as a basis for developing a verbal measure of information rate that was not confounded by an evaluative bias. The measure that was obtained should be helpful in assessing the information rate of situations, whether the situations are described verbally, presented pictorially or with video recordings, or viewed directly by subjects.

6 The Determinants of Approach-Avoidance Behavior

Having characterized the emotions that are elicited by various environmental qualities, we can proceed to describe how these emotional responses affect behaviors in different settings. In the proposed approach, the emotional responses of pleasure, arousal, and dominance serve as intervening variables between physical or social stimuli in an environment and the various behaviors that occur in the environment. As in the case of describing emotional reactions, a parsimonious description of the latter behaviors is needed. We have used the generic concept of approach-avoidance, which is defined in a broad sense to include physical movement toward, or away from, an environment or stimulus, degree of attention, exploration, favorable attitudes such as verbally or nonverbally expressed preference or liking, approach to a task (the level of performance), and approach to another person (affiliation).

The concept of approach-avoidance, together with the three emotional-response dimensions, is used to integrate the diverse findings of environmental psychology. In the hypotheses that are based on a review of the available literature, it is important to distinguish pleasure, a feeling state, from approach behavior. This chapter is a review of those aspects of the literature that relate emotional reactions to physical stimuli in the environment to approach-avoidance. In Chapter 7, the same hypotheses are discussed by considering social stimuli, such as proxemic and immediacy cues and the ways in which the physical environment mediates interpersonal approach behaviors. In the absence of relevant data, we shall postpone the discussion of the effects of dominance on approach-avoidance until Chapter 8, where our own experimental findings are presented.

A final section on the urban environment was included in this chapter to provide an example of the application of our framework to relevant life problems. Thus, evidence concerning noise, odor, and chemical pollution is also reviewed in terms of the approach-avoidance concept.

Pleasure and Approach-Avoidance Behavior

It is hypothesized that approach behaviors of all types increase as a person experiences increased pleasure. An important implication of this hypothesis is that pleasure may be produced by any number of sources, including the object or person approached. For instance, approach toward one aspect of a situation (e.g., a task or another person) is enhanced by the pleasantness of other aspects of that situation. Also, approach or preference is increased by pleasant stimulations that are not contingent on the approach behavior. Rather, simply because of their association with a pleasant environment, tasks or persons within it have been shown to be judged as more pleasing, and therefore to elicit more approach.

This pleasure-approach hypothesis has far-reaching significance, and its implications for interpersonal approach behavior have been explored to some extent. Studies by Griffitt (1970), Griffitt and Veitch (1971), Janis, Kaye, and Kirschner (1965), Maslow and Mintz (1956), Mintz (1956), Razran (1938; 1940), and Rohles (1967) are reviewed in detail in Chapter 7 and consistently showed that interpersonal approach-avoidance behaviors (e.g., increased affiliation, attraction, positive evaluation) among strangers are correlated with the pleasant-unpleasant feelings of the persons within a situation. These feelings, in turn, were determined by the physical qualities of the situations and were not a function of the persons present.

Approach to the pleasant stimulus itself is considered here to be a special case of our more general hypothesis, and support for this derivative hypothesis is supplied by the learning literature. However, we need to review the relationships among definitions and findings in quite distinct areas of learning research to clarify this relationship between pleasure and approach.

The relation between pleasure and approach-avoidance may be established by considering the concept of reinforcement. A positively reinforcing stimulus is defined independently of its pleasure-eliciting quality—by the increased probability of the behavior it follows (Skinner, 1961). Available evidence, however, shows that pleasure-eliciting stimuli are also positively reinforcing. For example, work with cranial self-stimulation identified subcortical structures in which electrical or chemical stimulation produced verbal reports of pleasure (Delgado and Hamlin, 1960; Heath, 1954; 1963; 1964a; Heath and Mickle, 1960; Sem-Jacobsen and Torkildsen, 1960) and relief from pain (Heath and Mickle, 1960). These pleasure areas were found to be also associated with positive reinforcement. Heath (1963) and Bishop, Elder, and Heath (1964) planted electrodes in human subjects and allowed them to self-stimulate various areas of their brains by pressing a button. As expected, stimulation of the pleasure-eliciting areas reinforced the button pressing, and subjects took precautions to avoid stimulation in pain-eliciting areas. Pleasure, then, is a sufficient condition for positive reinforcement.

Heath (1963) found other areas, however, where stimulation was positively reinforcing but not pleasant. Stimulation of these areas produced, for example, partial memory recall or the beginning, but never the reaching, of orgasm. These findings imply that pleasure, while a sufficient condition, is not a necessary condition for positive reinforcement.

In turn, the learning literature links approach-avoidance to positive reinforcement. That positively reinforcing stimuli elicit approach and negatively reinforcing stimuli elicit avoidance behavior is thus a familiar hypothesis with both animal and human subjects. Further refinements of this hypothesis are provided in Miller's approach-avoidance model (e.g., Dollard and Miller, 1950; Miller, 1944; 1964). Approach-avoidance has also been used independently to define reinforcers (Premack, 1965, in the case of animal studies; Mehrabian, 1968, Chapter 4, in the case of human subjects). In this case increases in frequency of a given behavior following positive reinforcement constitute the well-established empirical generalization.

The network of definitions and empirical generalizations that relates pleasure, positive reinforcement, approach, preference, and so on, is summarized in Figure 6.1.

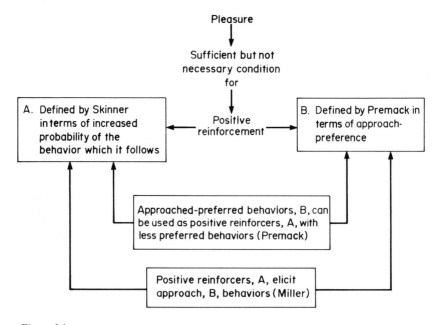

Figure 6.1.

To summarize, pleasure is a sufficient, but not a necessary, condition for positive reinforcement and the elicitation of approach (Figure 6.1). Also, studies have shown that approach is not limited to the pleasant stimulus itself but also applies to other temporally and spatially associated aspects of the pleasant stimulus. Thus, task performance or affiliation, for instance, can be increased (or decreased) by simply making the surrounding environment more pleasant (or unpleasant).

Arousal and Approach-Avoidance Behavior

Like pleasure, arousal level mediates approach-avoidance behavior. Calder (1970) observed:

The elaborate games and sports that humans organize for themselves are often far from pleasurable in any simple meaning of that word, if one judges by the subdued anger of the bridge table, the football field or the cockpit of a yacht. Quite sensible people will risk their lives on a mountainside or on a motorcycle rather than be bored, and war is unfortunately one of the most interesting games that man has invented. The arousal system of the brain probably holds more illuminating explanations of human conduct than does the recent emphasis on sexual and aggressive drives [pp. 34-35].

Evidence from very different sources is summarized in the hypothesis that approach-avoidance is an inverted-U-shaped function of arousal (e.g., Dember and Earl, 1957; Fiske and Maddi, 1961; Glanzer, 1958; Hunt, 1960). In other words, physical approach, preference, liking or positive attitudes, exploration, performance, and affiliation are all maximized at a moderate level of arousal. Extremely high or low levels of arousal are avoided. Arousal level, of course, is determined both by the environment (e.g., its information rate, or that from the task being performed) and by internal sources (e.g., level of anxiety or physiological changes caused by the intake of alcohol or drugs).

The evidence is reviewed in several sections. The first two sections discuss extremes in arousal and review the physiological basis for the observed avoidance behavior. Subsequent sections review areas of research that have systematically varied arousal level: animal studies of spontaneous learning and exploration as a function of environmental complexity, human preferences for stimuli differing in novelty and complexity, and performance of tasks as a function of arousal level. A final section deals with the effects of internally generated arousal.

Extremely Low Arousal: Sensory Deprivation Studies

Narrow prison quarters, long sea voyages, and exploration of the polar regions (Gunderson, 1963; 1968) are examples of situations of extremely low information rate. Studies of these environments, largely anecdotal or autobiographical (note the review by Solomon, Leiderman, Mendelson, and Wexler, 1957), have been consistent in showing severely deteriorated thinking, feeling, and perception.

Laboratory studies on sensory deprivation provided more detailed information but strongly confirmed these earlier reports (e.g., Zubek, 1964). Sensory deprivation (also called perceptual deprivation or isolation) has included a variety of procedures such as (1) water immersion with static, reduced input to the senses and instructions to avoid any motor activity, (2) placement in dark, soundproof rooms with no limitation to self-stimulation or motor activity, (3) restricted motor activity in a monotonous situation with normal, though unchanging, intensity of stimulation, (4) restricted movement in a normal environment, and (5) partially limited social contact but with unrestricted movement in a normal environment (Kubzansky, 1961).

Despite the heterogeneity of situations studied, strikingly similar results have been obtained. In reviewing both the anecdotal and the laboratory studies, Cohen (1967) stated:

Such conditions were seen, from the beginning, as an experimental means of inducing psychological stress leading to a number of psychopathologic-like phenomena. . . . Some of the rather profound psychological experiences reported by individuals exposed to life experiences in which they were isolated (cf. Burney, 1961; Byrd, 1938; Gibson, 1953; Hunter, 1953; Ritter, 1954; Slocum, 1962) and by subjects who were isolated in altered sensory environments for long periods (cf. Bexton, Heron, & Scott, 1954; Heron, Bexton, & Hebb, 1953; Vernon & Hoffman, 1956) were reported to be similar phenomena. Reports from both settings contained descriptions of illusions and hallucinations, disorganizations of goal-directed thinking, impaired time perception, distortion of body image, increased preoccupation with body sensations and inner thought processes [pp. 77–78].

Another common instance of sensory deprivation is the general absence of people, who are important sources of stimulation, in an infant's environment (Yarrow, 1961). The experiments of Harlow and his colleagues showed strong detrimental effects due to the absence of a mothering one or peers from the infant monkey's environment (e.g., Harlow and Harlow, 1962). The amount of social contact rather than the specific kind of social contact (e.g., presence of a mother) was the more important variable in these situations.

Besides the psychological deterioration, experimenters have also found physical avoidance by subjects of the sensory deprivation situations and of physical or mental tasks in these settings. Bexton, Heron, and Scott (1954), for instance, offered subjects twenty dollars a day, which exceeded what they normally earned, but the subjects typically left the sensory deprivation experiment after two or three days. Further, the less the information rate, the more avoidance has been observed. Davis, McCourt, and Solomon (1958) compared the length of stay of two groups of subjects placed into polio tank respirators with reduced visual, auditory, and motor input. The control group was allowed occasional brief conversations, while the experimental group was instructed to remain silent. All other conditions were the same for both groups. It was found that the control group stayed in the experiment significantly longer. In other words, the experimental group, which received the lower information rate, more quickly avoided the experimental condition.

The avoidance response elicited by sensory deprivation can be explained in terms of subjective feelings of low arousal in these situations. Several studies have shown progressively lower arousal during sensory deprivation. Heron (1961) found continually decreasing EEG activity in subjects isolated for four days. Zubek, Welch, and Saunders (1963) obtained the same result during fourteen days of perceptual deprivation. Myers (personal communication) used the Primary Affect Scale (Johnson and Myers, 1967), which includes a verbal report of arousal. He found that the sensory deprivation group was lower in reported arousal than a confined, but not sensory deprived, control group, which, in turn, was lower than an ambulatory control group.

In concluding, it is important to note that persons initially did volunteer for sensory deprivation, expected to like it, and, in the early stages of the experiment, gave subjective reports of relaxation and enjoyment (Kubzansky, 1961). Thus, in leaving the overly arousing urban climate (Toffler, 1970) in which most subjects were recruited, subjects found the initial arousal drop to their liking. However, with continued decline, their arousal levels became intolerably low, and avoidance responses were elicited.

Extremely High Arousal: General Adaptation Syndrome

The biologically adaptive basis for the avoidance of high-arousal environments was provided by Selye (1950; 1952; 1956; 1959), who explored physiological reactions to prolonged stressful stimulation. Selye initially studied toxins, diseases, and injuries and discovered a common stress reaction, which he termed the General Adaptation Syndrome (GAS). Subsequent work has shown that the GAS, sometimes in a milder form, occurs in response to a large variety of other stimulus conditions that are arousing, thus showing the broad relevance of Selye's findings to the study of environmental psychology.

The GAS consists of three stages. The initial "alarm reaction" stage includes the production of adrenaline and corticoid, with concomitant feelings of tension, nervousness, anxiety, or in our terms, high arousal and low pleasure. Specific physiological reactions at this stage include autonomic excitability, heart-rate changes, muscular tension, and blood content and gastrointestinal changes.

When the stressful stimulation persists, the alarm reaction gives way to a stage of resistance, characterized by a feeling of depression. The glands have depleted their stores, and various derangements in hormonal secretions lead to "diseases of adaptation." In other words, the body's own attempts at adaptation are unbalanced and therefore harmful. These "diseases" can include headaches, insomnia, gastric and duodenal ulcers, high blood pressure and other cardiovascular complaints, kidney diseases, and rheumatic and allergic reactions.

Diseases of Adaptation are those in which imperfections of the GAS play the major role. Many diseases are actually not the direct result of some external agent but rather the consequences of the body's inability to meet these agents by adequate adaptive reactions. Maladaptation plays a major role in diseases of the heart and blood vessels, diseases of the kidney, eclampsia, rheumatism and rheumatoid arthritis; inflammatory diseases of the skin and eyes, infections, allergy and hypersensitivity, nervous and mental diseases, sexual derangements, digestive and metabolic diseases, and cancer [Institut de Médecine et de Chirurgie Expérimentales, 1964, p. 23].

When the stressful stimulation has outlasted the body's ability to resist, a third and final stage is reached in which the adaptive mechanisms cease to function, and a feeling of exhaustion overwhelms the person.

Oken (1967) concluded from his review that the following anxiety-eliciting (i.e., both arousing and unpleasant) situations led to the GAS stress reaction.

Stimuli which have been found to be effective include competitive sports (Hill *et al.*, 1956; Frost *et al.*, 1951); paratrooper training (Basowitz *et al.*, 1955); admission to a research ward (Fishman *et al.*, 1962), to a mental hospital (Board *et al.*, 1956), or a surgical ward and the anticipation of surgery (Price *et al.*, 1957); college examinations (Bliss *et al.*, 1956); emotion-arousing interviews (Hetzel *et al.*, 1955; Persky *et al.*, 1958); perceptual distortion (Korchin *et al.*, 1958); and initial exposure to the psychosomatic laboratory (Sabshin *et al.*, 1957). In addition, similar changes have been produced in monkeys as a result of changes in housing or shifts in surrounding environmental activity as well as by conditioning techniques associated with avoidance, punishment (e.g., electric shock), and "anxiety" (Mason, 1958, 1959a, 1959b). This list is by no means exhaustive. Stress stimuli are a ubiquitous feature of real life [Oken, 1967, p. 45].

However, high arousal alone, without concomitant displeasure, may be sufficient to elicit the GAS stress reaction. Oken (1967) stated: " 'novelty' [is] one of the most consistently effective of stressors. A wide variety of environmental changes have been shown to be effective stress stimuli in many species (Mason, 1959a, 1959b; Fishman et al., 1962) [p. 47]."

In general, then, the human organism is unable to cope satisfactorily with persistently high-arousal situations. The bodily reactions are only temporary devices, which, when used excessively, become potential threats themselves. It is therefore understandable that highly arousing situations tend to elicit avoidance reactions. A second important fact to emerge from Selye's work is that the initial emotional state of arousal associated with persistent and highly arousing stimuli is only temporary. Internal stimuli, in subsequent stages, combine with the externally induced arousal to elicit feelings of fatigue, depression, and exhaustion.

Studies of the Exploratory Drive

The hypothesized inverted-U-shaped relation of preference to arousal level (and therefore, to information rate) was supported in experiments, mostly with animals, where the subjects sought increased or more varied stimulation. A review of studies by Dennis (1935; 1939), Dennis and Sollenberger (1934), and Wingfield and Dennis (1934) showed that "a rat that is permitted to make two successive choices of a T-maze usually displays a marked tendency to choose a different arm on its second trial than on the first [Glanzer, 1958, p. 302]." Montgomery (1954) and Montgomery and Segall (1955) found that rats learned to choose one arm of a Y-maze or learned to make a black-white discrimination in order to gain access to a Dashiell maze.

A common element in all of these experimental situations was that the animals were provided with an opportunity to decrease the monotony of a repetitive (i.e., unarousing) learning task. They were found to show a greater preference for more varied and arousing tasks, which provides support for the proposed hypothesis.

The tendency to seek higher levels of arousal was further evidenced by the following findings. Rats turned to the dissimilar and less familiar arm of a maze even though they had been rewarded more often in the alternative arm (Denny, 1957). Kish (1955) found that rats pressed a bar in order to change the lighting condition in their box. Similar findings were obtained by McCall (1965) and by Moon and Lodahl (1956). In two related animal studies (Chapman and Levy, 1957; May, 1968) rats were found to run faster to novel goal boxes. Chapman and Levy (1957) used two goal boxes, one brown and gray and one black and white. Goal box changes (novelty) induced faster running in the rats, irrespective of which one of the two boxes was used first. In May's (1968) study, speed of running also increased with changes in goal boxes. He used four different boxes in the experiment, all of which were patterned. Fantz (1958a; 1958b) found that young infants' and young chimps' looking time at a chessboard pattern was greater than that for solid colors. Finally, studies by Davis, Settlage, and Harlow (1950), Harlow (1950; 1953), Harlow, Harlow, and Meyer (1950), and Harlow and McClearn (1954) showed that animals learned to manipulate and solve mechanical puzzles without any reinforcers from the experimenter. Our assumption is that preoccupation with the puzzles served to increase arousal to more preferred levels compared to the arousal levels associated with the usual monotonous settings in which the animals were held captive.

Another source of evidence for the preference of moderately complex stimuli over less complex and familiar ones came from the exploratory behavior of animals in different mazes. Montgomery (1953) allowed rats to explore successively mazes that had been rated in degree of similarity. He found that as the dissimilarity of two successive mazes increased, the amount of exploration of the second maze increased. On the other hand, Calhoun (1962b) found that during their initial encounter with a very novel stimulus, rats exhibited avoidance and fear behavior. With increased familiarity, they began to explore it actively, and finally, with prolonged exposure, they decreased their exploration. Fear and avoidance reactions toward innocuous novel stimuli were also observed in dogs (Melzack, 1952).

This apparent inconsistency can be resolved by considering our hypothesis, according to which there should be increased preference for, or exploration of, a maze only when it is moderately novel (i.e., of moderate information rate) and not when it is excessively novel. Montgomery's (1955) study bears on this interpretation. He used two mazes, one of which was elevated and fear-evoking, while the other was enclosed. Two groups of rats were exposed to the mazes for two minutes on each of three days. On the first day, exploratory behavior in the enclosed maze was an inverted-U-shaped function of time. On the second and third days, no such function was found, but only a steady decline in exploration. On the other hand, there was very little exploratory behavior in the elevated maze. On all three days, there was only a slight increase in exploration over time. These findings of Montgomery (1955) are interpreted as follows. Information rate from an unchanging configuration decreases over time (see Chapter 5). Rats that encountered the enclosed maze showed the expected curvilinear relationship of level of exploration as a function of time (i.e., they initially avoided exploration, increased their level of exploration to a maximum with the increasing familiarity and optimal information rate, and subsequently decreased their exploration when the information rate was too low). However, rats who were exposed to the elevated maze that was excessively high in novelty and information rate only showed a slight increase in exploration over time. It is conceivable that with prolonged exposure to the elevated maze, the rats would have shown the same curvilinear function as that obtained for those in the enclosed maze.

To summarize, animal subjects have been found to show a greater preference for the moderate degrees of arousal associated with more novel and varied stimuli than for the uniform and monotonous tasks that are characteristic of the experimental situations in which they usually are placed. Most of the findings compared preferences for moderate, relative to low, levels of arousal. However, in a few studies employing excessively novel or unusual stimuli, initial fear or avoidance reactions were elicited, thus showing that highly arousing stimuli were less preferred than moderately arousing ones.

The Discrepancy Hypothesis

Research relating to the discrepancy (butterfly-curve) hypothesis of McClelland, Atkinson, Clark, and Lowell (1953) provides corroborative evidence for the proposed approach-arousal hypothesis. According to the discrepancy hypothesis, there is only moderate preference for stimuli to which the subject has adapted, maximum preference for stimuli that deviate slightly from the adaptation level, and least preference for stimuli that differ excessively from the adaptation level. For instance, in some experiments, stimuli are characterized in terms of intensity, and a certain level of intensity is the adaptation value. In these instances, preference for various degrees of intensity as a function of stimulus intensity is a butterfly curve (i.e., two juxtaposed inverted-U shapes, placed symmetrically about the adaptation level).

Evidence bearing on McClelland, Atkinson, Clark, and Lowell's (1953) hypothesis was reviewed by de Charms (1968, pp. 109–134). The following three studies, which employed human subjects, illustrate the methodology and results that were obtained. Haber (1958) used buckets of water at 33° Centigrade, and his subjects put their hands in the buckets to adapt to this temperature. Subjects next placed their hands into two other buckets and were instructed to remove the one hand that felt unpleasant. Haber (1958) found a peak preference for 1° Centigrade deviation from the adaptation level and very low levels of preference at ±15° Centigrade from the adaptation level. Pitts (1963) used musical pieces of varying degrees of complexity as his stimuli and once again found a butterfly-curve function when preference was plotted as a function of the complexity of the music. The same result was obtained by Terwilliger (1963), whose stimuli were various arrangements of rectangles within a rectangular frame.

The discrepancy (butterfly-curve) hypothesis is reinterpreted within the present framework as follows. When the subject has adapted to a stimulus (or a certain level of stimulus intensity), the stimulus has minimum novelty. For stimuli that are increasingly different from the adaptation level, novelty (and therefore arousal) is proportionately greater. It follows that the preference level is an inverted-U-shaped function of stimulus intensity for values both above and below the adaptation level, thus corresponding to the butterfly curve.

Preference for Complexity

Considerable work has been carried out on behavioral responses to stimuli varying in complexity. Berlyne (1960; 1963), Berlyne and Lawrence (1964), and Berlyne and Lewis (1963) proposed a number of hypotheses and distinctions. Their hypotheses, as well as results obtained by Day (1966; 1967a; 1967c; 1968b; 1968c), Day and Berlyne (1966), Day and Crawford (1969), and Sobol and Day (1967), are summarized best as follows: The preference for high- or low-complexity stimuli is low, and the preference for moderately complex stimuli is high. Complexity, of course, is an aspect of information and a correlate of arousal.

Other investigators used different methods from those of Berlyne, Day, and their colleagues and obtained similar results. Jones (1964) found that subjects in a sensory isolation study had a greater preference for the more complex stimuli that were presented to them. Jones (1966) corroborated these findings in an extended series of experiments. Cheek, Maxwell, and Weisman (1971) found that hospitalized patients had a greater preference for carpeted wards. Alternative interpretations of the latter result are possible. Nevertheless, one possible reason for the greater preference of carpeted wards is that in the relatively simple hospital environment, carpeting introduces colors, textures, and varied kinesthetic sensations, thus providing much-needed complexity.

In experiments that involved the presentation of a series of stimuli varying in complexity, looking time was generally used to measure preference. In Minton's (1963) study, the subjects pressed a button to observe slides and obtained a 0.14-second viewing time with each press. Minton found a positive correlation between looking time and stimulus complexity. Cantor, Cantor, and Ditrichs (1963) found a direct correlation between looking time of preschool children and the complexity of the stimuli presented to them. Leckart and Bakan (1965) also found a positive correlation between looking time and judged complexity of slides of landscapes, objects, and arrays of objects. When slides of the geographic environment and modern art were used, the subjects' self-selected number of exposures to each slide was found to be a direct correlate of the judged complexity of the slide (Wohlwill, 1968). Finally, Fromkin (1969) described four different rooms to his subjects, one of which was said to be the "most unusual thing I have ever experienced." The subjects were given a choice of entering one of these four rooms, and this novel room was most frequently selected.

In only a few studies, an inverted-U-shaped relationship was found between looking time and complexity of stimuli. Day (1966) found such a curvilinear relation between looking time, or liking, and degree of complexity of polygons. In one of the most thorough studies of the problem where the meaningfulness of stimuli was controlled, Munsinger and Kessen (1964) employed several sets of stimuli including polygons, strings of letters, and various degrees of approximation to English. They consistently obtained the hypothesized curvilinear relationship.

Vitz (1966a) used angular figures with independent number of turns ranging from 8 up to 1024. The number of turns for this particular series was a direct correlate of information content. Preference for the various shapes was found to be an inverted-U-shaped function of information content or complexity. An interesting result was obtained when the same subjects were asked to show their preferences for the entire set of figures after a number of exposures to these shapes. The same inverted-U-shaped function was obtained, but with a shift of the curve toward a general preference for more complex figures. This can be understood in terms of the decreased information rate from the same figure with greater familiarity (see Chapter 5). Consistent with this interpretation, art students (who can be assumed to have had more experience with design and drawings) showed a greater preference for the more complex figures.

Vitz (1966a) replicated his first experiment, using another series of shapes that consisted of crossed lines within a square. He found the same inverted-U-shaped function between information content of the shapes and preference.

Task Performance

Several investigators have provided a theoretical basis and support for the hypothesis that task performance is an inverted-U-shaped function of arousal (e.g., Duffy, 1957; 1962; Hebb, 1955; Malmo, 1959; Schroder, Driver, and Streufert, 1967; Stennett, 1957).

Schroder, Driver, and Streufert's (1967) studies exemplify a broad-scoped approach to this problem involving the development of new methods. Their measure of performance was information-processing ability. Both in their own and in others' studies that they reviewed, information-processing ability was found to be an inverted-U-shaped function of arousal as measured, for instance, by various manipulations of stress or "information load" (the latter corresponding to information rate).

Stennett (1957) used an auditory tracking task and found strong support for the inverted-U-shaped relation between arousal and performance. The hypothesis was supported for each of five physiological measures relating to palmar conductance and the tension levels of four different muscle groups.

The bulk of available studies explored the contribution of noise and/or music to task performance. The results were contradictory in that with almost equal frequency the introduction of noise or music improved performance, impaired it, or had no effect (e.g., note Uhrbrock's, 1961, review of the effects of music).

These apparent inconsistencies can be resolved by noting that arousal level is influenced by the complexity of the environment and complexity of the task itself. According to the performance-arousal hypothesis, a person should prefer to remain in a situation and perform the task if his arousal level is moderate but not if his arousal level is high or low. A moderate level of arousal may be achieved through the combination of a boring-monotonous task with a moderately arousing setting (e.g., when there is some noise or music). Alternatively, an optimal level of arousal can be obtained through a combination of a moderately complex task with a nonarousing setting. In contrast, when both the task and the setting are of low complexity, or when the task is complex and the environment is also moderately complex, then a decrement in performance is expected. In all cases, however, the complexity of noise or music that is introduced into a work situation should not exceed a moderate level. If the auditory stimuli are very novel or very intense, they can cause excessive arousal and detract from performance.

Consistent with the preceding discussion, performance on monotonous or vigilance tasks has been found to improve with the introduction of sound (e.g., Berlyne, Borsa, Hamacher, and Koenig, 1966; Corcoran, 1963b; Houston, 1968; Houston and Jones, 1967; Humes, 1941; Kirk and Hecht, 1963; McBain, 1961; Oltman, 1964; Schwartz, 1967; Smith, 1947; Weinstein and Mackenzie, 1966).

A few methodological details were as follows: Weinstein and Mackenzie (1966) found that the introduction of white noise at 100 db significantly increased performance on a manual task that involved turning over as many blocks as possible. Kirk and Hecht (1963) used a vigilance task in which subjects were asked to watch a TV screen for beam deflections occurring every one-half to three and a half minutes. They found that the introduction of variable noise of an average value of 64.5 db improved performance more than continuous noise at 64.5 db or a quiet condition of 61 db. Corcoran (1963b) found that performance on a vigilance task improved with increasing rate of signals given to sleep-deprived subjects. On the Stroop Color-Word test (a task in which subjects are to give the color of ink in which the color name is printed) the introduction of familiar and loud, but not uncomfortable, noises facilitated performance (Houston and Jones, 1967). In the semiskilled labor of manufacturing radio tubes, slow, as well as fast, music resulted in fewer errors by the workers (Humes, 1941). Again, on highly repetitive assembly-line work, the introduction of music increased piecework production an average of 7% by day and 17% by night (Smith, 1947). The greater effectiveness of music at night attests to its greater value in increasing the arousal level of the low-aroused (sleepy) workers to an optimal level.

In a somewhat different context, Ayres (1911) found that lively music stimulated athletes to respond with greater effort even though they were functioning close to the point of exhaustion (i.e., low arousal) in a six-day bicycle race.

Finally, Schwartz (1967) used white noise paired with food reinforcement for bar-pressing of his animal subjects. Response rate (assumed to be performance) was a positive function of sound intensity. Extinction data showed, however, that response-contingent sound in conjunction with food reinforcement exerted its influence on performance and not on learning.

The detrimental effect of increased arousal on the performance of a moderately complex task was illustrated by Smith (1951). His subjects were required to perform the moderately complex task of discriminating between pairs of identical names and pairs of slightly dissimilar names. A second task required the subjects to identify the result of assembling a given group of isolated plane figures. A third task involved checking numbers. In the first two tasks, subjects who were exposed to 100-db intermittent bursts of ten- to fifty-second noise attempted significantly more items but were significantly less accurate. The third task, involving checking numbers, did not produce any significant result. Thus, the noise, together with task complexity, contributed to excessive arousal that was detrimental to performance for two of the tasks. In another study, Stikar and Hlavac (1963) found that the introduction of noise caused a decrement in typing performance.

The subjects of Teichner, Arees, and Reilly (1963) were shown ten alphabetic letters on successive trials and were to report when one of a set of previously memorized three-letter combinations was present. On this moderately complex task, learning was slower in the conditions where the change in noise level was greater (i.e., when the greater change in noise level contributed to more arousal).

Other studies also showed that the introduction of arousing stimuli to a complex task was detrimental to performance (e.g., Bindra, 1959; Boggs and Simon, 1968; Broadbent, 1954; Plutchik, 1959; Woodhead, 1966). In his review, Plutchik (1959) concluded that intermittent sounds were more likely to impair performance than continual ones, especially when the task was a difficult one. Since intermittent noise is more complex than continuous noise, it is understandable that the former has a greater detrimental effect on the performance of a more complex task.

In Broadbent's (1954) study, the subjects were keeping watch on a display of steam-pressure gauges, and performance was impaired in 100-db, relative to 70-db, noise. In Boggs and Simon's (1968) study, subjects engaged in two simultaneous tasks. While performing a primary task, subjects were also instructed to perform a secondary, or less important, task. The primary task varied in level of complexity. When 92-db bursts of noise were introduced, subjects made significantly more errors in the secondary task, especially when the primary task was more complex. Similarly, Woodhead (1966) found more errors in the performance of the second task when bursts of 105-db noise were introduced during the performance of a complex task.

Other studies of the effects of noise or music on the performance of complex tasks failed to support the proposed hypothesis and discussions. Brown, Galloway, and Gildersleeve (1965), Carlson and Hergenhahn (1967), Hoffman (1966), Konz (1964), McGehee and Gardner (1949), Park and Payne (1963), Slater (1968), and Smith (1961) introduced noise or music during the performance of complex tasks but found no significant differences relative to quiet conditions. For instance, McGehee and Gardner (1949) played eighty-minute selections of music on some days over a five-week period. Complex tasks that required six to fifteen months of training and two years of experience for adequate performance were not affected by the introduction of music. The employees, nevertheless, believed the music was beneficial to performance. Of course, the excess arousal here may have been compensated for by the increased pleasure from the music. Again, in Freeman and Neidt's (1959) study, the introduction of familiar, rather than unfamiliar, background music had no significant effect on the memory of the contents of a film subjects had watched while the music was playing.

The study of Fine, Cohen, and Crist (1960) was relevant to the arousing-nonarousing effects of various temperatures and humidity levels on the performance of tasks varying in complexity. They used four combinations of temperature and humidity on sixteen days. The subjects were asked to work on an anagram and an auditory discrimination task before and after the six and a half hour experimental conditions, but no significant effects on performance of either task were observed as a function of these conditions.

To clarify some of these contradictions in the results reported in the literature, future experimentation along these lines can test our hypothesis with more exact measures of information rate than are currently available:

(1)   Performance $= c_1$ (pleasure) $- c_2$ $(c_3\ H_T + c_4\ H_{TS})^2$

where c_1 through c_4 are positive constants, H_T is the information rate of the task (e.g., according to the measure provided in Appendix D) and H_{TS} is the information rate of the place where the task is performed. The first hypothesized effect follows from our general discussion of approach-avoidance behavior in relation to pleasure in the first section of this chapter and is supported by studies such as that of Podvin (1967). Stated otherwise, the remaining effects hypothesize that performance is an inverted-U-shaped function of a weighted sum of information rate from the task and from the setting. It should thus be possible to use a variety of tasks and settings to obtain an accurate answer to this important industrial and everyday problem (e.g., what kind of office design can be combined with a certain type of office work to maximize performance).

Internally Generated Arousal

As noted in Chapter 3, internally generated stimuli combine with external ones in determining arousal (or pleasure) and thus can be used to account for some interesting effects. Internal arousal can produce a main effect, or, in combination with the complexity of the task or setting, produce an interaction effect on performance. Martens and Landers (1970) illustrated the contribution of the main effect of trait arousal on performance. Their junior-high-school male subjects were required to move a ring along a tube without touching the sides. Performance was found to be an inverted-U-shaped function of scores on the children's form of the manifest anxiety scale (Castanada, McCandless, and Palermo, 1956). (It should be recalled that anxiety is a correlate of arousal.) They also showed that stress (which was induced by threat of shock and instructions that emphasized good performance) was significantly correlated with subjective arousal and, furthermore, that performance was also an inverted-U-shaped function of the stress manipulation.

An interactive effect between internal level of arousal and externally induced arousal was demonstrated by Cohen, Hummel, Turner, and Dukes-Dobos (1966). They found that anxious subjects, compared to nonanxious ones, did worse on a task during the high-noise (high-arousal) condition. Corcoran (1963b) introduced noise during the performance of a monotonous task, and his sleep-deprived subjects (who were in a low-arousal state) improved their performance more than a control group of subjects who were not sleep-deprived. In Chapter 3 we discussed the problems associated with the use of sleep deprivation as an experimental manipulation of arousal level. Those cautionary remarks are relevant in considering the preceding results of Corcoran (1963b), as well as in considering studies that employed more complex combinations of sleep deprivation with other experimental conditions (e.g., Corcoran, 1965).

According to our discussion in Chapter 3, extroverts are more responsive to arousing cues than introverts. So it is expected that the introduction of distractions (e.g., noise or music) should be more helpful to extroverts than introverts, when the tasks being performed are simple and repetitious. Consistent with this, Davies and Hockey (1966) found that in performing a "visual cancellation task" (i.e., crossing out certain items and modifying others), introduction of 95-db noise (relative to quiet, which was 70-db) was beneficial to the performance of the extroverts but not the introverts. Also, in an auditory vigilance situation, Bakan (1959) found that the introduction of a secondary task improved the extroverts' performance on the primary vigilance task more than that of introverts.

Since anxiety is a correlate of arousal, more anxious subjects should have less preference for more complex stimuli because the latter increase their total arousal to an intolerable level. Consistent with this, Day (1967c) found that less anxious subjects paid more attention to complex materials, whereas more anxious subjects paid less attention to complex materials. Again, Day (1967b, p. 15) used high- and low-arousal conditions (noise versus quiet) with high- and low-anxiety subjects, and the dependent measure was selective attention to one of two slides differing in level of complexity. He found that under the high-arousal (noisy) condition, low-anxiety subjects increased their selective attention to the more complex figure, whereas in the same noisy condition, high-anxiety subjects decreased their selective attention to the more complex figure.

In a study that employed a different paradigm from those just reported, Mehrabian (1970d) requested subjects who were high versus low on sensitivity to rejection to report their preference for persons holding different degrees of discrepant attitudes from their own. In Study 3 of Chapter 3, sensitivity to rejection correlated -0.30 ($p < 0.01$) with arousal-seeking tendency. Further, the average difference in the attitudes of another person from one's own is an estimate of his arousing quality for oneself (note the discussion of the discrepancy hypothesis of McClelland, Atkinson, Clark, and Lowell, 1953). The results showed that for sensitive subjects, preference of another was a monotonically decreasing function of the discrepancy of the other's attitudes. In contrast, for those who were insensitive to rejection, the expected inverted-U-shaped function was obtained, showing the highest level of preference for others holding slightly different attitudes.

It will be recalled that the more immediate, that is, closer and higher density, interpersonal cues were found to be more arousing (Chapter 5). This implies that more anxious persons should have less tolerance for high rates of information from interpersonal cues. In this connection, Luft (1966) found that more anxious subjects judged the distance to another to be less than the corresponding judgments made by less anxious subjects—a result that indicates that their tolerance for the proximity of another would be less. Such an effect can also be obtained because of temporary changes in anxiety state. For instance, in one informal study in Vietnam, Bourne (1970) identified a pronounced and interesting variant of territorial behavior in Marine camps, where the soldiers were generally anxious because of persistent stresses. He found that these soldiers staked out certain areas of the camp, where nobody else was allowed to enter. Such territoriality minimized interpersonal contact and the consequent high-arousal levels that could not be tolerated.

With regard to sex differences, equations 14A and 14C in Table 3.4 show that females have a generally higher arousal level than males. Since there is a decrease in arousal level over time in sensory-deprivation situations, the concomitant decrease in preference for these situations over time should be delayed more in the case of females than in males. Indeed, Zubek (1964) reported that females were better able to tolerate sensory-deprivation situations than males.

A related result was obtained from the subjects of Diespecker and Davenport (1967), who learned to match nine different tactile signals varying in duration and intensity with the numbers one through nine. It was found that the introduction of a 90-db continuous tone was detrimental to the female subjects' performance on this moderately complex task, whereas no significant difference was obtained for the males under the noise, versus noiseless, conditions. However, no results were obtained in a second experiment where a different noise condition was employed.

Finally, in apparent contrast to expectations, when Day and Thomas (1967) used d-amphetamine to induce arousal, they found the opposite effect—the subjects who were administered d-amphetamine attended to the more complex stimuli. Their result raises an important question about the function of d-amphetamine. Does this drug directly increase arousal level, or does it induce a condition that leads to arousal-seeking behavior with a consequent increase in arousal level? Day and Thomas's (1967) results are consistent with the latter interpretation.

The following equation resembles the one offered in the preceding section and is part of our attempt to reconcile and integrate the many findings bearing on performance, an important aspect of approach-avoidance behavior.

(2)   Performance $= k_1 \text{ (pleasure)} - k_2 (k_3 H_T + k_4 H_{TS} + k_5 \text{ trait arousal})^2$

Where k_1 through k_5 are positive constants, H_T is the information rate of the task (e.g., according to the measure provided in Appendix D), and H_{TS} is the information rate of the place where the task is performed. Trait arousal can be measured, for example, by the scales of Appendix B. This equation would apply in most instances but does not include those contributions of arousal state to approach-avoidance behavior that are due to drive levels and/ or drug-induced states.

Dominance and Approach-Avoidance Behavior
Owing to lack of evidence, dominance-submissiveness cannot be related to approach behavior. However, the phenomenon of territoriality shows that there is generally a greater preference on the part of males for an area in which the organism is more dominant. One of the reasons for such a preference is the greater psychological advantage of being in one's own territory. For instance, an animal who fights in his own territory almost

invariably wins. Even a physically more able and larger animal becomes
a less able fighter in another's territory (Braddock, 1949; Lorenz, 1966).

Approach-Avoidance in Urban Environments
The psychological problems that are associated with urban environments
can also be examined within the proposed approach-avoidance framework.
Thus, it should be possible to examine the emotional reactions of humans
to various aspects of the city and then predict approach-avoidance behaviors
to these aspects. Unfortunately, as noted in Chapter 4, there is insufficient
evidence on the emotional reactions of humans to various aspects of pollution. Moreover, since either displeasure or extremes in arousal may be
responsible for the observed avoidance reactions, we have no way to infer
the mediating emotions. There is, however, some work relating pollutants
directly to approach-avoidance behaviors, and this work is reviewed later.
The effects of crowding have been considered in some detail and will be
taken up again in Chapter 7, which deals specifically with interpersonal
approach-avoidance behaviors.

Noise Pollution
Previous sections have shown that noise, as its intensity and unexpected
quality increase, is both highly arousing and unpleasant and leads to an
avoidance reaction. Since anxiety is associated with displeasure and arousal
(see Table 3.4), a noise-anxiety correlation can be hypothesized, and evidence supports this view. Cohen (1968a) reported one study in which steel-
workers in the noisiest parts of a factory were observed to have greater frequencies of social conflict both at work and at home. Other studies reported
by Cohen (1968a; 1968b) showed that those workers who were daily exposed
to high levels of industrial noise (e.g., 110-db in one study) showed chronic
fatigue and had neurotic complaints. This fatigue can be understood in terms
of the General Adaptation Syndrome, that is, as a result of prolonged arousal
or anxiety.

As already noted, more anxious persons or neurotics have a generally higher
level of arousal and are thus more intolerant of highly arousing cues than are
less anxious persons. Consistent with this observation, one of the studies
reviewed by Broadbent (1957) showed that more neurotic persons found the
noises in their environments to be more annoying.

Since noise is arousing, then it obviously follows that it should discourage
sleep, a low-arousal state. Indeed, in communities where aircraft noise pre-

dominates, the interruption of relaxation and sleep due to noise was found to be a major complaint (Cohen, 1968a). Similar results were obtained from studies in Los Angeles, New York, and Boston (Bolt Beranek and Newman, 1967). We assume that even when noise does not fully awaken a person, it may deprive him of "deep sleep," the stage of sleep where dreaming primarily occurs. Such disruption results in irritability, fatigue, and difficulty in concentration (Dement, 1965).

Most of the evidence on the anxiety-producing effects of noise in the urban environment was obtained from questionnaire studies lacking carefully controlled designs. Nevertheless, there is corroborating evidence from laboratory studies, which shows that the important question is not whether noise is bothersome or anxiety-producing—this relationship is documented quite adequately. Rather, the question of importance is how information rate due to noise, the information rate (complexity) of situations or tasks, the trait arousal, and the arousal-seeking tendency of an individual contribute singly or interactively to determine his various approach-avoidance behaviors in a setting.

Chemical Pollution

Horvath, Raven, Drinkwater, O'Hanlon, and Dahms (1970) noted that our ignorance of the psychological effects of pollutants is approximately complete. The establishment of legal limits for concentrations of chemicals in the atmosphere has therefore relied on medical health data (e.g., Grut, Astrup, Challen, and Gerhardsson, 1970). Apart from severe physical damage caused by high concentrations of pollutants (e.g., brain damage due to carbon monoxide), there has been increasing evidence that small concentrations of pollutants, previously not considered to be "harmful," have serious psychological effects on the individual. In view of these recent findings and of the high magnitude of air pollution, research on these psychological effects of pollutants is of great importance. Some recent evidence shows avoidance reactions to various kinds of pollutants and also suggests the qualities of the mediating emotional responses.

Some general effects of air pollution. A commonly used measure of pollution is oxidant level. This concept refers to a "complex mixture of substances which . . . determines the net oxidizing activity of the atmosphere and includes ozone, nitrogen dioxide and peroxyacyl nitrates [Hitchcock, 1969, p. 1]."

Several studies have shown decreases in spontaneous activity (that is, an avoidance reaction) when chemical pollutants increase. Emik and Plata (1969) found that rats in a high-temperature and high-pollution condition (a high oxidant concentration obtained by mixing air with the exhaust from automobiles) decreased their voluntary running activity. In corroboration, Boche and Quilligan (1960) also found a decrease in spontaneous running of mice who had a mixture of gasoline vapors and ozone in their cages. Campbell, Emik, Clarke, and Plata (1970) reported a decrease in spontaneous activity of mice who inhaled peroxyacetyl nitrate (PAN) for a six-hour period at any of five concentrations ranging from 2.8 ppm (parts per million) to 8.5 ppm. Recovery of normal activity took about two days for subjects exposed to 2.8 ppm of PAN and about four days for those exposed to 8.5 ppm. On the basis of their own data and those available from previous studies (Boche and Quilligan, 1960; Murphy, 1964; Murphy, Ulrich, and Leng, 1963), these workers also compared the toxic potency of PAN to other pollutants and provided the following list of decreasing toxicity, with ozone being the most toxic: ozone, acrolein, nitro-olefins, ozonized gasoline vapor, PAN, nitrogen dioxide, carbon monoxide, and irradiated and non-irradiated auto exhaust. Toxicity was defined as that concentration producing a 50% reduction in the voluntary running activity of mice.

Such findings have been replicated with human subjects. Lewis, Baddeley, Bonham, and Lovett (1970) obtained air from a street that had an average traffic density of 830 vehicles per hour. Subjects who performed auditory vigilance, mental computation, or verbal comprehension tasks in this polluted air had lower performances than those performing in pure air.

Wayne, Wehrle, and Carroll (1967) did a longitudinal study over a five-year period on air pollution and athletic performance. Decline in team performance was defined as the percentage of team members who showed an increase in time taken to run the same cross-country track from one meet to the next. This decline in team performance correlated highly and significantly ($r = 0.88$) with the level of oxidant air pollution during the hour preceding the cross-country meet. These researchers commented that no physical cause for this finding was known and that they suspected it was due to decreased motivation.

The effects of metallic ions.   Additional studies explored the effects of specific chemical pollutants. Weir and Hine (1970) studied goldfish, using a conditioned avoidance technique. Significant performance decrements in the learned avoidance of shock were observed when fish were exposed to small concentrations (at fractions of lethal doses) of sodium arsenate, lead nitrate, mercuric chloride, or selenium dioxide. For example, mercury ions produced impaired ability to perform the avoidance reaction at 0.003 ppm. Weir and Hine (1970) noted that "these experimental results are reliable and demonstrate deleterious effects below levels of the four metals currently accepted as 'safe' [p. 50]."

Nitrous oxide. Human subjects in Steinberg's (1954) study performed ten tasks ranging in complexity from speed of finger tapping to difficult tests of reasoning by analogy. When the air contained 30% nitrous oxide (with the smell of this chemical having been camouflaged), performance on all of the tasks decreased.

Carbon monoxide. Carbon monoxide (CO) concentration is commonly measured in the atmosphere in parts per million or in the blood in percentage carboxyhemoglobin. A theoretical equation for predicting carboxyhemo-globin concentrations from atmospheric concentrations of carbon monoxide was given by Peterson and Stewart (1970).

Schulte (1963) found significant inverse correlations between carbon monoxide concentrations (ranging from 0% to 20% carboxyhemoglobin) and performance on arithmetic problems and other mental tasks. Correlations ranged from -0.54 to -0.91. Impaired performance in a vigilance task, where brightness of the signal was the cue, was observed in individuals subjected to air containing 111 ppm carbon monoxide, which resulted in 4% to 7% carboxyhemoglobin during the task (Horvath, Dahms, and O'Hanlon, 1971). The subjects in this experiment were young, healthy, nonsmoking males. MacFarland, Roughton, Halperin, and Niven (1944) also found that low concentrations of carbon monoxide (resulting in 4% carboxyhemoglobin) impaired visual discrimination of brightness. Again, Beard and Grandstaff (1970) found that carbon monoxide affected the ability to make relative brightness discriminations. The effect was significant in forty-nine minutes at 50 ppm of carbon monoxide and significant in only seventeen minutes at 150 ppm of carbon monoxide.

Such findings are disturbing in light of observed concentrations of this pollutant. Goldsmith and Rogers (1959) found that 9% of the vehicles in California had over 50 ppm of carbon monoxide in the driver's compartment. Haagen-Smit (1966) reported that on Los Angeles freeways the carbon mon-

oxide concentrations reach 120 ppm. In reviewing the effects of urban concentrations of carbon monoxide, Godin, Wright, and Shepard (1972) concluded: "The city-dweller is always close to the postulated point of impaired
psychomotor performance (and indeed in Los Angeles may have passed this
threshold). The drive to work can be sufficient to produce impairment, even
when the general atmospheric contamination (3 to 5 ppm) is well below the
accepted danger point. Groups who drive regularly in the city (bus, truck,
and police drivers) or stand on the sidewalk (foot police, vehicle inspectors,
and parking attendants) are at a much greater risk [p. 313]."

Carbon monoxide also affects the ability to make time judgments. Beard
and Wertheim (1967) put rats on a fixed-interval schedule while their cages
contained air with 250 ppm of carbon monoxide. The rats decreased their
rate of responding, but the rate returned to normal when the carbon monoxide was removed. Of course, this decrement in performance could simply
have been due to a lowering of activity (arousal) level. However, a series
of related experiments supported the conclusion that the rats had lost some
of their ability to make time discriminations. For instance, rats put on a
DRL schedule (i.e., one in which they had to wait a fixed period of time
before a response would yield a reinforcer) showed significantly more errors
when carbon monoxide was present. The effect was observable after only
eleven minutes of exposure to carbon monoxide at 100 ppm (Beard and
Wertheim, 1967). In Beard and Grandstaff's (1970) study, human subjects
attempted to estimate the passage of thirty seconds. A sixty-four-minute
exposure to 50 ppm carbon monoxide produced significant performance
decrements. In Beard and Wertheim's (1967) study, humans showed a significant loss of ability to judge short time intervals by comparing durations of
auditory signals. This effect was obtained with ninety-minutes exposure to
50 ppm carbon monoxide and the fifty-minutes exposure at 100 ppm.

A laboratory accident led to the discovery that methylene chloride, an
ingredient in paint remover, has a similar effect to carbon monoxide in that
it raises the blood concentration of carboxyhemoglobin. In an experimental
test, sustained rises in percentage carboxyhemoglobin were found in subjects
exposed to methylene chloride in concentrations of 500 to 1000 ppm, which
are below the legal thresholds (Stewart, Fisher, Hosko, Peterson, Baretta,
and Dodd, 1972). The report states: "Since 400 million pounds of methylene chloride are produced annually in the United States, with more than

one-sixth being consumed in the rapidly expanding retail market for paint removers, it was apparent that a large number of persons in the nonindustrial environment, including the elderly and those with significant cardiovascular disease, could be subjected unknowingly to the anoxic effects of carbon monoxide [p. 343] ."

Since the physiological result of carbon monoxide or methylene chloride is lowered oxygen concentration in the blood, increased concentrations of either chemical are especially harmful to "hypoxic" persons, who are normally low in blood oxygen concentration. Ramsey (1970) measured reaction time to a visual stimulus in normal and hypoxic subjects, all of whom were nonsmoking. For both groups, a decrease in blood oxygen level and an increase in reaction time were found after exposure to carbon monoxide by riding in an automobile for ninety minutes. The change in reaction time and blood oxygen level in the hypoxic subjects was significantly more than that for the normal subjects. No changes were found in a control group not exposed to carbon monoxide.

Finally, one experimental result from Schulte's (1963) study is of considerable importance. In this study, the levels of carbon monoxide employed were not found to affect any of the physiological measures (pulse rate, respiratory rate, systolic and diastolic blood pressure). However, such levels of carbon monoxide did affect performance on mental tasks and impaired visual discrimination and limb coordination. Similarly, Horvath, Dahms, and O'Hanlon (1971) concluded from their experiment that "impairment [on a behavioral task] can occur at much lower COHb [carboxyhemoglobin] levels than those commonly associated with relatively gross physiological signs of CO poisoning [p. 346] ." These results are important in showing how the emotional and behavioral effects of pollutants may be more readily apparent than the effects on commonly used physiological measures.

Odor.   Another aspect of chemical pollution is the concomitant odor. The evidence introduced in Chapter 4 showed that unpleasant odors are also arousing and thus anxiety-producing.

McCord and Witheridge (1949) reported a study by Winslow and Herrington (1936) in which eight subjects were employed, and on randomly picked test days over several months, the odor of "burnt dust" was gradually introduced into their workroom. The introduction was gradual enough that the subjects were never aware of its presence. It was, however, noticeable to anyone entering the room suddenly. Subjects ate less lunch on test days than on other days, with the types and variety of foods having been carefully controlled.

Mediating emotional reactions.   Several studies suggest that low pleasure may be the mediating emotion in the observed avoidance reactions to carbon monoxide. Stewart, Peterson, Baretta, Bachand, Hosko, and Herrmann (1970) found headaches in a group of healthy medical students and faculty members exposed to 200 ppm carbon monoxide for four hours. Headaches, vertigo, and exhaustion were found in a Japanese population with 20% to 30% carboxyhemoglobin (Goldsmith, 1970).

Schulte (1963) reviewed additional evidence that led him to make the following statement:

> . . . many authors have found that the symptoms which occur in subjects with levels of carboxyhemoglobin below 20% are vague and nondescript, and include such subjective complaints as mild frontal headache, vague generalized weakness, fatigue, lassitude, and drowsiness. These symptoms become progressively more severe when the concentration of carbon monoxide in the blood increases beyond 25%, and under these circumstances it is reasonably certain that the symptoms which develop are attributable to carbon monoxide [p. 524].

The preceding results of Goldsmith (1970) and Schulte (1963) suggest that a major effect of carbon monoxide is to lower arousal level. In summary, the effects of carbon monoxide on the emotions are lowered arousal and displeasure.

On the other hand, a study by Weybrew (1963) suggested that the effects of carbon dioxide were higher arousal and displeasure. The data were obtained daily during a three-month submarine voyage from a sample of forty men from the crew. An anxiety factor based on subjective ratings (with high loadings from adjectives such as "jittery," "anxious," "excited," "clutched up," and "uncomfortable") correlated with increased hydrogen, carbon dioxide, and oxygen levels and barometric pressure. Exact concentrations of the gases were not given, however.

This finding requires further study in light of the fact that the total atmospheric carbon dioxide concentration is slowly but steadily increasing (Keeling, 1970).

Summary
Quite diverse aspects of psychological research can be brought to bear on

the relation between approach-avoidance to a situation and the emotions
that are elicited there. The configuration of relations among pleasure,
preference, approach-avoidance, positive reinforcement, and increases in the
frequencies of reinforced behavior was discussed in terms of the available
literature in the learning and physiological areas and was summarized in
Figure 6.1. It was concluded that it is legitimate to distinguish pleasure
from approach-avoidance but to view them as being correlated.

The relation of approach-avoidance to arousal can be considered in the
context of (1) sensory deprivation studies, (2) the General Adaptation
Syndrome, (3) the effects of crowding that are reviewed in Chapter 7,
(4) studies of animal exploratory and curiosity drive, (5) the discrepancy
(butterfly-curve) hypothesis for humans, (6) experiments dealing with
human preferences for stimulus displays varying in level of complexity,
(7) work output in industrial settings as a function of extraneous stimuli
such as noise and music, (8) performance levels of persons differing in trait
anxiety or extroversion, and (9) pollution in the urban environment. Even
though the various sources of evidence support the hypothesized inverted-
U-shaped relationship between approach-avoidance and arousal, it is recognized that a more encompassing experimental approach to the study of
the problem is still required. More differentiated hypotheses relating
approach to the various emotional responses can only be tested if measures
of (1) approach-avoidance, (2) pleasure, arousal, and dominance, and
(3) information rate are developed and standardized across a variety of
settings. This is of paramount importance for comparisons of results
obtained from different experiments. Measures of a quite general scope
are given in Appendixes B, D, and E, and it is possible to use anchor stimuli
(e.g., in the form of slides) in conjunction with some of these scales to allow
comparisons of judgments across experiments.

Even though the evidence relating to urban pollution problems was
quite sketchy, some patterns of results were identified. Avoidance reactions, including lowered ability and motivation to perform, were found in
studies on the effects of noise, crowding, odors, and chemical pollutants.
Such reactions were more pronounced for certain (e.g., more hypoxic or
anxious) individuals. Lowered pleasure and increased arousal (i.e., anxiety)
were the mediating emotional reactions to noise, crowding, and odors. On
the other hand, the emotional reactions to most aspects of air pollution
(i.e., oxidant level and carbon monoxide) consisted of displeasure and

lowered arousal. In terms of our basic hypothesis relating pleasure to performance, the findings that showed decrements in performance can be explained as being due to a lowering of pleasure. The contribution of high arousal (from noise) and low arousal (from chemical pollution) to performance is more difficult to assess in that the exact levels of arousal in these studies were unknown. It is possible that the performance decrements in the various studies were partially determined by extremes (rather than moderate and optimal) levels of arousal. Further exploration of these important problems can be carried out by first determining the emotional reactions of subjects in settings that vary with respect of levels of pollution. This is a particularly important step in research, since verbal reports or behavioral impairments have sometimes been found to be even more sensitive to pollutants than commonly used physiological measures.

7 The Determinants of Interpersonal Approach-Avoidance Behavior[1]

Interpersonal stimuli are an important part of the environment. Interpersonal approach-avoidance behaviors are variously described as affiliation, conformity, cooperation, liking, aggression, and hostility and are examined in this chapter in terms of our framework. A consideration of the relation between affiliative behavior and pleasure in the first section also provides a definition of this important component of social interaction. Our second section bears on the relation between affiliative behavior and arousal, and a third section deals with the contribution of unpleasant and arousing settings to interpersonal hostility.

Pleasure and Affiliative Behavior

Evidence shows that the reinforcing quality of the other person (target) is the primary determinant of the degree of affiliative behavior elicited from a subject. For instance, Byrne (1969; 1971) reviewed the supporting evidence for his attraction-similarity hypothesis. Similar persons are found to be more attracted to each other, that is, they are more desirous of affiliating. Byrne explained that persons with less similar attitudes are more likely to have disagreements, and since disagreements are negatively reinforcing, their desire to affiliate is diminished.

In their review of this and other sources of evidence, Mehrabian and Ksionzky (1970; 1974) hypothesized that affiliative behavior consists of the exchange of positive reinforcers and is a direct correlate of a target's positively reinforcing quality and an inverse correlate of his negatively reinforcing quality. This hypothesis was substantiated by the results of Mehrabian (1971b) and Mehrabian and Ksionzky (1972). In each of these studies, some two dozen verbal and nonverbal cues were scored during a waiting situation involving pairs of strangers. It was found that the exchange of verbal and nonverbal messages of liking, together with the speech duration of the participants, defined the primary factor, affiliative behavior, in social interaction.

Affiliation, then, is an approach behavior and is perpetuated by mutual exchanges of positive social cues. Since affiliative behavior is a primary factor in social interaction, the most important effects of environments on social behavior may be considered in terms of how environments enhance positive feelings and the communication of these feelings among the persons within them. The two aspects of this problem are (1) how the physical aspects of the environment affect liking among the persons within it and (2) how the spatial arrangement of persons, as dictated by the environment, affects affiliation.

Pleasantness of the Social Setting

Our answer to the first question draws on the pleasure and approach-avoidance hypothesis developed in Chapter 6. Persons within a more pleasant environment are expected to elicit more approach, that is, affiliation, cooperation, and agreement. Supporting evidence was given by Griffitt (1970), Maslow and Mintz (1956), Mintz (1956), Razran (1938; 1940), and Rohles (1967).

Razran (1938) asked subjects to rate thirty photographs of college girls on a five-point scale for "beauty, intelligence, character, entertainingness, ambition, and composite general liking [p. 693]." The subjects rerated the pictures while enjoying a free lunch, that is, a noncontingent pleasant stimulation. Their ratings on all the scales increased, thus showing that a pleasurable experience increased their interpersonal approach behavior.

In the Maslow and Mintz (1956) study, photographs of persons were judged as more pleasant under more pleasant circumstances. Griffitt (1970) found a greater attraction among those subjects who interacted under a comfortable temperature condition than among those who met in an uncomfortable temperature condition.

The next two studies provided evidence for socially cooperative and conforming attitudes, which are also correlates of affiliative behavior (e.g., Mehrabian and Ksionzky, 1974, Chapter 3). Razran's (1940) subjects rated sociopolitical slogans (e.g., "America for Americans!", "Workers of the World Unite!") for personal approval, social effectiveness, and literary value. One half of the slogans was later presented again while the subjects were enjoying a free lunch. The other half was presented along with putrid odors. All of the slogans were then rated again by the subjects. Compared to the first rating, those slogans presented during lunch received higher scores; whereas those presented with the putrid odors received lower scores. Janis, Kaye, and Kirschner (1965) found that subjects significantly increased their acceptance, over pretest scores, of unpopular communications when the experimenter gave them food and drink. No significant changes in amount of acceptance were found in control groups that received neither food nor exposure to an unpleasant odor.

Immediacy: The Spatial Arrangement of Persons in a Social Setting

Our second concern was the way in which the spatial arrangement of persons, as dictated by the environment, affects affiliation. In other words, what is the significance of the design and architecture of microenvironments in determining social interaction patterns? Hall (1959; 1963; 1966), Osmond

(1957; 1959; 1969), and Sommer (1969) most clearly denoted the importance of the effect of spatial arrangements of persons on their affiliation. Osmond's concept of sociofugal and sociopetal spaces distinguished areas of buildings that tended to segregate people from those that brought people together, respectively. Explicit criteria for distinguishing these spaces were not offered, however, even though the concept was proposed and recognized as an important attribute of man-made environments.

Mehrabian (1971a, Chapter 5) provided one set of criteria to describe the effects of spaces on the people who interact within them. These criteria were based on the concept of proxemics (Hall, 1963; 1966) or immediacy (Mehrabian, 1970a; Wiener and Mehrabian, 1968). Immediacy refers to the extent of mutual sensory stimulation between two persons and is measured in terms of spatiotemporal proximity or by the number of available "communication channels." (Communication channels are the means by which one conveys his thoughts and feelings to another; they include words, facial and vocal expressions, postures, and movements.) For example, the closer two people are to each other, the more immediate their interaction. Sitting side by side is less immediate than an arrangement that permits them to face each other more directly. The greater immediacy associated with more channels for communication is illustrated as follows: Telegrams and letters are two of the least immediate ways of communicating, permitting the verbal channel alone. These are followed in order by telephone conversations (utilizing verbal and vocal channels), picturephone (which also includes the facial channel), and then face to face. In recorded video messages or face-to-face communications, more extensive visibility of each person to the other also increases the immediacy. It is thus seen that a person who increases immediacy with another is approaching that person.

The effect of spatial arrangement on liking and the consequent affiliative behaviors can be described best in terms of a two-sided relation between immediacy and liking: liking encourages greater immediacy, and immediacy produces more liking. Findings have consistently shown that when people like each other, or when they are basically more friendly or affiliative, they choose to be more immediate. When together, they sit closer, orient more directly, lean toward each other, touch, have more eye contact, and converse more (Mehrabian, 1972a; 1972b). Sommer's (1969) review also showed that when a variety of seating arrangements were made available to two persons, the actual arrangement selected by the pair was a function of the type of friendly, or unfriendly, activity in which they were engaged. For instance, Russo (1967) required subjects to give semantic differential ratings of diagrams representing two persons seated around a rectangular table surrounded by six chairs. The three rating scales used were intimate-unacquainted, friendly-hostile, and talkative-untalkative. These ratings were highly intercorrelated and defined an affiliative behavior dimension. Subjects rated all possible arrangements of two persons for this configuration of rectangular table and six chairs. Arrangements in which subjects were closest to one another were rated as most affiliative. Russo's (1967) findings also indicated that for two equally distant positions between two persons (e.g., eight feet), a more direct orientation (e.g., face to face) of the two persons was considered more friendly than a less direct one (e.g., if they were to sit at a 90° angle).

The reciprocal of this relation between immediacy and liking is also valid. Zajonc (1968) provided extensive evidence that familiarity through increased immediacy induced liking. Available reviews consistently supported the idea (Berscheid and Walster, 1969). For instance, it has been shown that college students who had more opportunities to be closer together, whether in their dormitories, apartments, or classes, were more likely to form friendships and like one another (Byrne, 1961; Byrne and Buehler, 1955; Festinger, 1953; Maisonneuve, Palmade, and Fourment, 1952; Willerman and Swanson, 1952). Similarly, persons in various occupations who were assigned working positions closer to one another were more likely to develop closer relationships and to like each other more (Gullahorn, 1952; Kipnis, 1957; Zander and Havelin, 1960). The following comments of Festinger (1951), which were quoted by Berscheid and Walster (1969), are based on a study of developing friendships in a new housing project, where few residents had previously known each other. It is evident that the architecturally determined and accidental arrangement of persons can have dramatic effects on their relationships (Festinger, 1951; Festinger, Schachter, and Back, 1963).

It is a fair summary to say that the two major factors affecting the friendships which developed were (1) sheer distance between houses and (2) the direction in which a house faced. Friendships developed more frequently between next-door neighbors, less frequently between people whose houses were separated by another house, and so on. As the distance between houses increased, the number of friendships fell off so rapidly that it was rare to find a friendship between persons who lived in houses that were separated by more than four or five other houses. . . .

There were instances in which the site plan of the project had more profound effects than merely to determine with whom one associated. Indeed, on occasion the arrangements of the houses severely limited the social life of their occupants. . . . In order to have the street appear "lived on," ten of the houses near the street had been turned so that they faced the street rather than the court area as did the other houses. This apparently small change in the direction in which a housed faced had a considerable effect on the lives of the people who, by accident, happened to occupy these end houses. They had less than half as many friends in the project as did those whose houses faced the court area. The consistency of this finding left no doubt that the turning of these houses toward the street had made involuntary social isolates out of the persons who lived in them [Festinger, 1951, pp. 156–157].

The results from a few studies of this type can be attributed to the fact that some of the persons were friends to begin with and elected to become close neighbors because of this friendship. In a number of studies, however, some strangers were accidentally assigned close positions to one another, and it was found that closeness led to greater liking (Festinger, Schachter, and Back, 1963; Newcomb, 1961). Thus, greater immediacy was indeed instrumental in enhancing the possibility of liking and friendships.

Using a very different approach, Mehrabian and Diamond (1971a; 1971b) replicated these findings on the consequences of immediacy on liking. Pairs of subjects who were strangers were brought together in a waiting room. The various experimental conditions involved different arrangements of the furniture. In one study, subjects were assigned particular seats in the room; in another, they were allowed to select their seats from among several possible positions. The findings showed more affiliative behavior among persons when a particular furniture arrangement required them to assume more immediate (i.e., closer and more face to face) positions relative to one another. Since affiliation involves the communication of positive affect (e.g., Mehrabian, 1971b), these findings showed that the very simple manipulation of the immediacy of participants in a situation was conducive to greater liking among them.

Some of the earlier research on prejudice reduction is also of considerable interest in this context. Studies by Deutsch and Collins (1951), Jahoda and West (1951), and Wilner, Walkley, and Cook (1955) showed that proximity of blacks and whites, which was a function of their living quarters, increased friendships and reduced prejudicial attitudes in the whites. Again, Works (1961) found that proximity due to residential arrangements was conducive to decreases in black prejudicial attitudes toward whites. Irish (1952) reported that Caucasian and Japanese persons whose residences were closer tended to have more mutually friendly attitudes and affiliative patterns. In short, environmentally determined physical proximity was conducive to decreasing negative (prejudicial) attitudes and increasing positive attitudes, as reflected in reports of affiliation, cooperative behavior, mutual assistance, and friendships. If negative feelings are reduced and even altered to positive ones through increased contact, such contact should be even more effective in eliciting positive feelings when initial attitudes are neutral, as would be the case with two strangers. There is one important exception, however, which should be noted. When hostile groups of persons are brought together, the increased contact does nothing to improve their relations (Sherif, Harvey, White, Hood, and Sherif, 1961).

In a somewhat different context, Mehrabian and Reed (1968) concluded from their review of the available literature that communication accuracy increases with the immediacy of the arrangement of the communicators (e.g., the increasing possibility of feedback or the increasing availability of communication channels). Thus, to the extent that accurate communications are more conducive to positive interpersonal exchanges than inaccurate ones, immediacy can contribute to positive exchanges because it enhances accurate communication.

Arousal and Affiliative Behavior: Crowding
The relationship between immediacy and liking-affiliation must be qualified, however, in two related ways that are based on the fact that excessive immediacy is overly arousing and, therefore, undesirable. First, there are limits to how much immediacy a person will spontaneously select even with someone he likes, so understandably even less immediacy will be preferred with strangers (i.e., with novel interpersonal stimuli, which are generally more arousing than familiar ones). Second, excessive immediacy that is forced upon a person because of environmental conditions is avoided. Many sources of evidence, which are reviewed later, show that the forced immediacy of contact in highly populated areas induces high arousal levels that are difficult to tolerate and, when prolonged, are physiologically damaging.

Hall (1966, Chapter 3) reviewed evidence showing that social disorganization, excessive aggression, and massive death rates were the effects of crowding in animal colonies. Carson's (1969) review also supported the hypothesis that crowding in animals and humans produced a stress reaction with the physiological effects characteristic of the General Adaptation Syndrome. For instance, Christian, Flyger, and Davis (1960) observed a herd of deer whose population rose and eventually exceeded the normal density. Despite an abundance of food and absence of disease, a massive death rate occurred. Examination of the dead revealed prolonged hyperactivity of the adrenals, and the investigators concluded that death was due to a stress reaction. Christian (1959) studied both tame and wild mice and found that increasing population density produced hypertrophy of the adrenals and atrophy of the gonads. Similar results were obtained with monkeys. Mason (1959b) found that monkeys who were placed in cages from which others were more visible showed higher corticoid secretion than those placed in more secluded cages. It will be recalled that higher corticoid secretion is part of the stress reaction.

The effects of crowding on the psychological well-being of human subjects are exemplified by Chombart de Lauwe's (1959) findings with French workers. He used the surface area allotted each person per dwelling unit as the density measure and found that when the available area per person per unit dropped below eight to ten square meters, physical and psychological disturbances doubled. Less direct evidence on the effect of crowding was provided by Hollingshead and Redlich (1958), whose "Index of Social Position" included area of residence as well as occupation and education. The lowest position, for example, was typically occupied by persons dwelling in tenements. A highly significant relation showed that the lower the social position, the more likely it was that the person was being treated for psychiatric complaints. Social class was, of course, confounded in this study with area of residence, but the evidence reviewed in this section provides a partial explanation of this finding. Similar detrimental effects of crowding on psychological well-being were noted by Loring (1956).

Other findings showed that crowded situations were avoided or that "abbreviated" avoidance behaviors occurred when individuals were confined to crowded situations (Sommer, 1969). For instance, in two studies summarized by Seaton (1968, p. 9) cafeterias that were 50% occupied were considered full, larger tables that sat eight persons were never used to full capacity, and groups preferred the large rectangular tables to smaller square ones. All of these findings indicated a lack of preference for crowded situations. Studies also showed that excessive proximity of two strangers induced avoidance reactions. For example, Felipe and Sommer (1966) explored the consequences of assuming a very close position to a stranger. When the intruder approached and took a seat at a distance of less than a foot from the subject, more than two-thirds of the subjects left within a thirty-minute period. Among those not approached by an intruder (the control subjects), less than one-third left within that same period.

Two other sources reported a phenomenon, analogous to crowding, that can be explained in terms of the lack of preference for high arousal levels that are due to high information rates from interpersonal cues. Ekman and Friesen (1969) noted that people were uncomfortable during conversations if they were totally exposed (i.e., when there was no desk or table to screen them partially from one another and reduce information rate). This can be especially true when the subjects are unfamiliar with one another, that is, when arousal is very high because of the unfamiliarity and the total visibility. Also, in therapy situations, clients resisted being seated out in the open and preferred to sit behind a desk or table. When they were fully visible, fidgeting increased, and females tugged on their skirts (Alexander, Ishikawa, and Silverstein, 1968, p. 245).

The excessive arousal and associated discomfort due to a high level of immediacy is readily observed in experimental or everyday situations. Argyle and Dean (1965) found that as people approached each other they tended to orient away and use less eye contact to compensate for the increasing closeness. Similar findings were reported in other studies reviewed by Mehrabian (1969). The discomfort that is due to excessive closeness to a stranger is altogether too familiar from everyday experiences in elevators. Persons in an elevator show a strong preference for large distances from others. They look at the elevator dial, the floor, or walls rather than the unfamiliar persons within it. This demonstrates the greater preference for the less arousing aspects of a congested situation (e.g., Seaton, 1968, p. 25). Similarly, in congested rooms, persons preferred locations close to windows (e.g., Alexander, Ishikawa, and Silverstein, 1968, p. 134, for work settings; Seaton, 1968, pp. 9–10 for cafeterias). In the latter situations, orientation toward the lower-density view apparently helped to diminish the level of arousal from the congested rooms.

Interpersonal Hostility in Unpleasant and Arousing Settings
Even though hostility must be distinguished from approach-avoidance reactions, with which we are primarily concerned, its study is of considerable

importance from a social standpoint. Studies have shown that the unpleasant and arousing effects of crowded environments lead not only to avoidance but also to hostile reactions. The earlier observations of Calhoun (1962a; 1962b) with rats in crowded situations showed dramatic increases in hostility. These findings were generalized to humans in a study by Griffitt and Veitch (1971). They showed that in hotter and more crowded rooms, people felt more negative in general, and more negative toward each other in particular.

One important question that remains unanswered, however, is the differential contribution of the unpleasant and arousing quality of environments to interpersonal hostility, that is, which one of these is a more potent factor. Relevant data were available from the subjects in the third study reported in Chapter 3. These subjects had rated their feelings of hostility in each of the various situations that were described to them. It was thus possible to express hostile feelings (a composite of ratings on three scales: aggressive–nonaggressive, hostile–not hostile, and angry–not angry) in the various situations as a function of the significant main and interactive effects of mean values for the pleasure, arousal, and dominance elicited in these situations.

To analyze these data, a multiple regression technique was used instead of the analysis of variance. Cohen (1968) described the procedures whereby multiple regression can be employed as a substitute for the analysis of variance, and our rationale for, and computation procedures in, using such regressions are detailed in Chapter 8. The following equation shows that only two main effects and one interaction effect attained the 0.05 level of significance. In the equations, all variables are standardized (mean = 0, standard deviation = 1) to facilitate comparisons of the relative magnitudes of the various effects. The symbol P is the mean pleasure, A is the mean arousal, and D is the mean dominance elicited in a situation. The multiple correlation coefficient is given to the right of the equation.

$$\text{Hostile feeling} = -0.53\,P + 0.29\,A - 0.07\,PD \qquad (0.66)$$

It should be noted that the possible contribution of A^2 to hostile feeling was also explored in this regression analysis, but this term was not found to be significant. These findings corroborated the evidence that was reviewed in both of the preceding sections. Unpleasantness of situations was most important in determining hostile feelings, and the arousing quality of situations was the second most important contributor. It was seen that average pleasure and average arousal levels elicited in a situation did not interact in determining hostile feelings, whereas average pleasure and average dominance did. Figure 7.1 shows the cell means for the **P** X **D** effect. It is seen that, irrespective of how dominant a person felt, more displeasure was always associated with a higher degree of hostile feeling. However, hostile feeling also increased with increasing dominance, but only in unpleasant situations.

With hostile feeling as the dependent measure, additional regression analyses of incidental interest were conducted. In these analyses, possible interactions of each item of the following list of personality measures with the **P, A,** and **D** factors were explored: sex, extroversion and neuroticism (Eysenck and Eysenck, 1968), trait anxiety (Spielberger, Gorsuch, and Lushene, 1970), arousal-seeking tendency (Appendix C), and affiliative tendency and sensitivity to rejection (Mehrabian, 1970c; Mehrabian and Ksionzky, 1974, Appendix B). Only the following interactions were found to be significant: **P** X trait anxiety; **P** X neuroticism; **P** X arousal-seeking tendency, and **A** X sex. Examination of the cell means for these effects showed that in unpleasant situations, highly anxious or neurotic subjects felt more hostile than less anxious or less neurotic subjects. Similarly, in unpleasant situations, high-arousal seekers felt more hostile than low-arousal seekers. Comparisons of the cell means for the **A** X sex interaction showed that females felt significantly less hostile than males only in extremely unarousing situations; otherwise, there were no differences in reported levels of hostile feelings of males and females.

These findings summarize how the feelings that are elicited by environments contribute to hostility and aggression. Together with our discussions of the emotional correlates of single-stimulus dimensions in Chapter 4 and the arousal-information rate hypothesis in Chapter 5, they provide a basis for understanding the increasing criminal activity and general deterioration of social conditions in the congested and economically depressed areas of various cities.

Summary
The discussions and data presented in this chapter bear on some pressing social problems in modern urban environments. The first of these is the loneliness and social alienation of the residents of large cities—a problem that is inadvertently perpetuated by the design (or lack of design) of cities, residential and office buildings, and even the interior of buildings (Mehrabian,

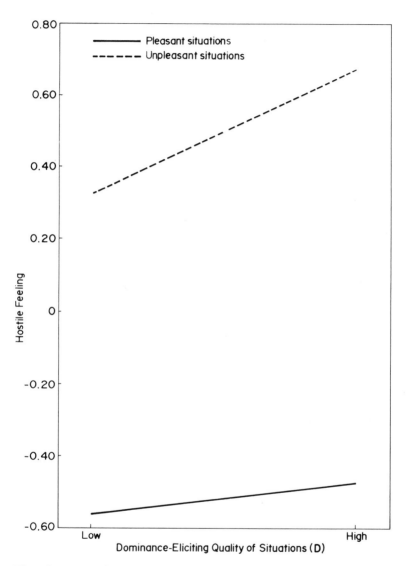

Figure 7.1. Hostile feeling as a function of the pleasure **(P)** and dominance **(D)** eliciting quality of situations*

*These are unadjusted cell means. Based on *t*-tests, the pair of cell means corresponding to unpleasant situations differ significantly at the 0.05 level. Of course, both simple effects of **P** were significant.

1971a, Chapter 5). The second problem relates to stresses of crowding and the necessity for privacy. These apparently contradictory problems present a challenge to the environmental psychologist and to the city planner, architect, and interior designer. A possible answer to this dilemma can be based on the generalizations emerging from our reviews of experimental findings. Architectural designs or even more specific concerns such as seating arrangements that allow greater immediacy (e.g., more frequent contacts because of crossing paths or common recreation areas) are more conducive to the development of positive attitudes—an essential component of sustained affiliation. This hypothesis, together with the provision that persons be allowed to have privacy when they need it (i.e., frequent contact remains a matter of choice for the residents), provides a powerful tool to the designer. It allows him to plan specifically an environment that can either enhance or discourage social interaction and positive feelings among the individuals within it. The typical modern office or apartment building that consists of segregated levels connected by elevators and long corridors leading up to individual offices or apartments is a case in point. Such designs illustrate an arrangement where, for the total number of persons within a given unit volume, interaction is close to a minimum. These arrangements, which are dictated mostly by economic and engineering considerations, are far from satisfactory from the standpoint of the residents' social needs.

Note

1. Acknowledgment is given to Wadsworth Publishing Company for permission to use in this chapter a small modified segment from Chapter 5 of Mehrabian's *Silent Messages.*

8 Investigations of Approach-Avoidance to Varied Environments

Review of the available literature in Chapters 6 and 7 led to a number of hypotheses that were tested directly in the studies reported later in this chapter. Among the three major hypotheses, the first was that preference, exploration, work performance, and affiliation are intercorrelated aspects of response to a situation and can all be subsumed under the generic concept of approach-avoidance. The second hypothesis was that approach to a situation is a direct correlate of that situation's pleasure-eliciting quality. The third hypothesis was that approach to a situation is an inverted-U-shaped function of the arousing quality of (or information rate from) the situation. In addition, there were a number of hypotheses regarding the interactive effects of certain personality variables (e.g., trait anxiety, extroversion, and arousal-seeking tendency) with the arousing quality of a setting in determining approach to it. Relative to persons with characteristically low arousal, those who are generally high in arousal (anxious or neurotic) are less likely to approach situations of highly arousing quality. Also, high-arousal seekers are more likely to approach environments of highly arousing quality. In addition, the following hypothesis was developed in Chapter 3: The state arousal of high-arousal seekers, compared to that of low-arousal seekers, is more sensitive to variations in the arousing quality of environments.

Three extensive questionnaire experiments were conducted to test these hypotheses and to provide additional data of interest for which no specific hypotheses had been proposed. The three experiments were basically of the same design, except that the measures of approach-avoidance to situations used in Experiment 1 were different from those used in the other two. Also, for each experiment, a different set of situations from those in Appendix A was employed. These slight variations in measures and stimuli provide results of greater generality than would be obtained with identical replications of the same experiment.

The methods in these experiments were as follows: In the first session, each subject was presented with a subset of situations taken from Appendix A. After reading each situation, the subject reported his emotional reactions to it, using the measures of Appendix B, and next characterized his approach-avoidance responses to that situation, using either the scales of Table 8.1 (in Experiment 1) or those of Appendix E (in Experiments 2 and 3). In Experiment 1, subjects also returned for a second session, one to two weeks later, during which they were administered a series of personality questionnaires. The subjects of Experiment 2 did not provide any personality data. The subjects of Experiment 3 provided the personality questionnaire data immediately following this first session.

The first section of this chapter attempts to characterize the relationships among the various approach-avoidance behaviors that can be elicited by situations. The second section analyzes these approach-avoidance responses as functions of the average degrees of pleasure, arousal, and dominance elicited in each situation. In both sections, data from all three experiments were used. Finally, the third section utilizes the personality data obtained in Experiments 1 and 3, as well as the results relating to sex differences obtained in Experiment 2, to test some of the hypothesized interactions involving the personality variables.

Characterizing Approach-Avoidance Responses to Environments
Experiment 1. In this experiment, 103 University of California under-graduates were each presented with a subset of eight of the situations from among the first forty described in Appendix A. After reading about each situation, the subjects were asked to respond to a random presentation of the questions listed in Table 8.1. Questions 1 through 9 were designed to measure different aspects of approach-avoidance response, and subjects provided their answers on a scale that ranged from 0 (not at all) to 7 (extremely so). Items 10 through 12 constituted our measure of state anxiety, and subjects responded to these by checking the appropriate spot along each continuum to indicate their feelings in the situation. Thus, the twelve dependent measures consisted of nine approach-avoidance items and three anxiety items.

Each of the 103 subjects provided eight sets of the dependent measures (i.e., one for each situation), so that there were a total of 824 sets of reactions to the various situations. These were factor analyzed, and a principal component solution was obtained. There were four factors with eigenvalues exceeding unity, and these four factors accounted for 79% of the total variance. Oblique rotation of the first four factors yielded the item group-ings shown in Table 8.1. The intercorrelations among the twelve items are given in Table 8.2.

Factor 1 characterized the variations in preference for a situation and consisted of liking, preference, tendencies to seek and explore the situation, and the converse of avoidance. The composition of this factor provided

Table 8.1.   Results of the Factor Analysis of Approach-Avoidance and State-Anxiety Reactions to Forty Situations*

Factor 1: Preference for the situation

1. How much do you LIKE this situation?

2. How much do you PREFER this situation?

3. How much would you SEEK OUT or TRY TO FIND this situation?

4. Once in the situation, how much would you EXPLORE it?

5. Once in the situation, how much would you try to LEAVE, or get out of it? (Negatively worded item.)

Factor 2: Desire to affiliate in the situation

6. To what extent is this a situation in which you would be friendly and talkative to a stranger who happens to be near you?

7. In this situation would you initiate a conversation just to be friendly?

Factor 3: Desire to solve problems in the situation

8. To what extent is this situation a good opportunity to think out some DIFFICULT problem you have been assigned in class?

9. If the problem is an EASY one, would you use this situation as an opportunity to solve the problem?

Factor 4: State anxiety

10. tense	- - - -:- - - -:- - - -:- - - -:- - - -:- - - -:- - - -:- - - -:- - - -	at ease
11. nervous	- - - -:- - - -:- - - -:- - - -:- - - -:- - - -:- - - -:- - - -:- - - -	not nervous
12. anxious	- - - -:- - - -:- - - -:- - - -:- - - -:- - - -:- - - -:- - - -:- - - -	nonanxious

*Subjects answered questions 1 through 9 on a scale ranging from zero (not at all) to 7 (extremely so).

support for our earlier assumption that these particular behavioral reactions to a situation were indeed related and that together they characterized a general preference reaction. Factors 2 and 3 characterized affiliative and problem-solving responses, respectively.

Items 10 through 12 in Table 8.1 were assumed to be measures of anxiety. The grouping of cues in Factor 4 clearly indicated that the adjective pairs, anxious–nonanxious, tense–at ease, and nervous–not nervous, together provided a reliable measure of state anxiety and constituted a factor distinct from the other three listed in Table 8.1. The separation of the state anxiety measures from the various approach-avoidance behaviors in Table 8.1 provided additional discriminant validation for the latter measures.

For further analyses, a composite score was computed on each factor

Table 8.2. Intercorrelations of the Measures of Table 8.1*

	2	3	4	5	6	7	8	9	10	11	12
1. Liking of	+0.92	+0.86	+0.56	-0.75	+0.22	+0.21	+0.35	+0.27	-0.53	-0.31	-0.45
2. Preference for		+0.90	+0.54	-0.73	+0.20	+0.21	+0.37	+0.29	-0.50	-0.31	-0.42
3. Tendency to seek			+0.57	-0.70	+0.18	+0.16	+0.37	+0.28	-0.50	-0.29	-0.43
4. Desire to explore				-0.49	+0.21	+0.15	+0.21	+0.14	-0.30	-0.15	-0.27
5. Desire to leave					-0.12	-0.12	-0.32	-0.27	+0.46	+0.26	+0.40
6. Desire to be friendly						+0.72	+0.12	+0.10	-0.13	-0.07	-0.13
7. Desire to initiate conversation							+0.18	+0.17	-0.18	-0.11	-0.15
8. Desire to solve difficult problems								+0.72	-0.43	-0.32	-0.37
9. Desire to solve easy problems									-0.32	-0.20	-0.24
10. Tense feeling										+0.58	+0.76
11. Nervous feeling											+0.56
12. Anxious feeling											

*Intercorrelations among scales from each factor are boxed separately.

from a subject's responses to each situation. Thus, for each subject's ratings of a particular situation, the responses to questions 1 through 5 were algebraically summed to assess his overall preference for that situation. His overall desire to affiliate, desire to solve problems, and state anxiety in the particular situation were similarly computed. The intercorrelations among these four composite scores are given in Table 8.3. It is seen that preference for a situation, desire to affiliate, and desire to engage in problem-solving activities in it were positively intercorrelated; however, the correlation between desire to affiliate and solve problems in a situation did not attain significance. State anxiety in a situation was inversely related to preference for it and the desire to solve problems in it.

Experiment 2. To provide a further check on the groupings of the approach-avoidance responses to everyday environments, a second experiment was carried out in which 163 subjects characterized their behavioral responses to an average of twenty (from the full list of sixty-five) situations given in Appendix A. In this case, subjects' approach-avoidance responses were assessed using a random presentation of the items listed in Appendix E. These items are rewritten versions of those in Table 8.1 and were designed to include equal numbers of positively and negatively worded items in each of the factors identified in the first experiment. The state-anxiety items were not included in this experiment.

There were a total of 3260 sets of responses to the questions of Appendix E, obtained from the 163 subjects. The intercorrelations among the eight approach-avoidance responses are given in Table 8.4. The 8 × 8 matrix of correlations among these dependent measures was factor analyzed, and a principal component solution was obtained. There were two factors with eigenvalues exceeding unity, and these two factors accounted for 61% of the total variance. The first of these factors, preference, consisted of the items

Table 8.3. Intercorrelations among the Three Approach-Avoidance Response Factors and the State-Anxiety Factor of Table 8.1*

	2	3	4
1. Preference for the situation	0.22	0.36	−0.49
2. Desire to affiliate in the situation		0.17	−0.16
3. Desire to solve problems in the situation			−0.39
4. State anxiety			

*Correlations in excess of 0.20 are significant at the 0.05 level.

relating to desire to stay, explore, and work in a situation; the two items for desire to affiliate in a situation constituted the second factor. The composite preference factor was significantly correlated with the affiliation factor ($r = 0.16, p < 0.05$). Thus, these results closely replicate those found in Experiment 1. The one difference found is simply that desire to work (an analogue of the problem-solving factor in Experiment 1) did not constitute a separate factor here.

Experiment 3. Since the approach-avoidance response scales developed in Experiment 2 were to be the basis for other studies, it was important to cross-validate the results obtained in Experiment 2. In this experiment, therefore, 214 subjects were each presented with six different situations from among the first fifty-four situations in Appendix A and were asked to describe their reactions to each situation by responding to a random presentation of the approach-avoidance questions of Appendix E.

There were a total number of 1284 sets of responses to the eight questions of Appendix E, obtained from the various subjects over the different situations. Intercorrelations among these eight dependent measures are presented in Table 8.5. The 8 × 8 matrix of correlations was factor-analyzed, and a principal component solution was obtained. Once again, only two factors had eigenvalues exceeding unity, and they accounted for 61% of the total variance. Oblique rotation of the first two factors yielded a pattern of factor loadings quite similar to that obtained in Experiment 2. For comparison, Table 8.6 presents the rotated factor matrices obtained in Experiments 2

Table 8.4. Intercorrelations among the Measures of Appendix E as Obtained in Experiment 2*

	2	3	4	5	6	7	8
1. Desire to stay	−0.66	0.49	−0.42	0.40	−0.48	0.13	0.00
2. Desire to leave		−0.45	0.46	−0.32	0.48	−0.10	0.03
3. Desire to explore			−0.62	0.27	−0.32	0.29	−0.16
4. Avoidance of exploration				−0.25	0.37	−0.24	0.26
5. Desire to think about difficult task					−0.38	0.11	0.03
6. Dislike to work						−0.11	0.07
7. Friendly feeling							−0.58
8. Avoidance of people							

*Intercorrelations among scales from each of the two factors are boxed separately. Correlations in excess of 0.21 are significant at the 0.01 level.

Table 8.5.   Intercorrelations among the Measures of Appendix E as obtained in Experiment 3*

	2	3	4	5	6	7	8
1. Desire to stay	−0.72	0.61	−0.48	0.43	−0.48	0.25	−0.07
2. Desire to leave		−0.51	0.48	−0.35	0.48	−0.22	0.08
3. Desire to explore			−0.62	0.28	−0.33	0.34	−0.16
4. Avoidance of exploration				−0.20	0.35	−0.31	0.25
5. Desire to think about difficult task					−0.36	0.17	−0.03
6. Desire to work						−0.16	0.12
7. Friendly feeling							−0.55
8. Avoidance of people							

*Intercorrelations among scales from each of the two factors are boxed separately. Correlations in excess of 0.18 are significant at the 0.01 level.

Table 8.6.   Rotated Factor Matrices from Experiments 2 and 3

	Factor 1	Factor 2
Experiment 2*		
1. Desire to stay	0.84	−0.08
2. Desire to leave	−0.82	0.07
3. Desire to explore	0.66	0.29
4. Avoidance of exploration	−0.63	−0.33
5. Desire to think about difficult task	0.61	−0.12
6. Desire to work	−0.71	0.04
7. Friendly feeling	0.05	0.84
8. Avoidance of people	0.10	−0.89
Percent variance	41%	20%
Experiment 3**		
1. Desire to stay	0.88	−0.03
2. Desire to leave	−0.84	0.04
3. Desire to explore	0.70	0.22
4. Avoidance of exploration	−0.60	−0.32
5. Desire to think about difficult task	0.61	−0.12
6. Desire to work	−0.69	0.05
7. Friendly feeling	0.11	0.82
8. Avoidance of people	0.11	−0.89
Percent variance	44%	17%

*Factors 1 and 2 correlated 0.16 ($p < 0.05$) in Experiment 2.
**Factors 1 and 2 correlated 0.23 ($p < 0.01$) in Experiment 3.

and 3. In this experiment also, the composite preference factor was significantly correlated with the affiliation factor (r = 0.23, p<0.01).

   An overview of the findings reported in this section shows that, as expected,
all the behaviors that were assumed to be part of a generic approach-avoidance
reaction to situations were indeed significantly intercorrelated. There were,
however, a number of noteworthy differences among this set of behaviors.
First, desire for affiliation was identified as a separate factor in all three
experiments. Second, problem-solving in Experiment 1 was similar to desire
to work in Experiments 2 and 3; it was identified as a separate factor and did
not relate significantly to affiliation. Thus, there were grounds for also
treating it and desire for work as separate dependent measures. In fact, it is
suggested that the four approach-avoidance indexes of Appendix E be analyzed separately when the object of a study is to obtain detailed answers for
the particular environmental influences on each of these—this, indeed, was
the approach taken in the following sections of this chapter. Some everyday
design problems, however, may not necessitate such fine distinctions. For
instance, in designing an office, a gallery, or a schoolroom, the distinctions
among exploration, staying, and work are less critical, and the entire setting
can be designed to maximize a composite of these three preferences. The
findings reported here indicated that such a composite index of preference is
quite legitimate, although it must be distinguished from the desire for affiliation.

Approach-Avoidance Behaviors as Functions of the Emotion-Eliciting Qualities of Situations

Experiment 1. As noted, each of 103 subjects was presented with a subset
of eight situations from among the first forty described in Appendix A. The
subjects read each situation presented to them, described their emotional
reactions to the situation using the measures of Appendix B, and next described their anticipated behavioral responses to that situation using the
measures of Table 8.1. The mean pleasure-, arousal-, and dominance-eliciting
qualities (**P, A, D**) of each situation were computed from reports of the
emotional reactions of all the subjects who responded to that particular
situation. The sets of **P, A,** and **D** scores for the different situations were
then used in the analyses of the data, since these were based on group norms
and were independent of individual personality biases.

In the following analyses, the various approach-avoidance behaviors were each explored as functions of the average pleasure-, arousal-, and dominance-eliciting qualities of the forty situations in this experiment. Regression analyses were used in preference to analyses of variance, since the former did not necessitate the elimination of cases to achieve cell proportionality. The particular multiple regression method used permitted the assessment of the significance of interactions as well as main effects (Cohen, 1968). Each regression analysis tested the contribution of the following four terms and all their possible interactions: P, A, A^2, and D. The term A^2 was included in the analysis since a curvilinear relationship of the arousing quality of environments to approach-avoidance responses to them had been hypothesized. The specific computation methods that were employed have been described by Efroymsen (1960). In each successive step of a stepwise regression analysis, the significance of the next most powerful effect (i.e., the effect that accounted for the largest amount of variance in the dependent measure) was tested, and the effect was entered into the equation if the 0.05 level of significance was attained.

Cohen (1968) discussed the possible value of such regression analyses not only as substitutes for analyses of variance but also as substitutes for analyses of covariance. The generality of the method was particularly suited to the analyses of the present data since, as will be seen, the interpretation of the data required some kind of covariance technique (i.e., a method that would make it possible to partial out the main effect of P in assessing the main and interaction effects of A).

The dependent measures in the analyses of the data of Experiment 1 were the three approach-avoidance factors of Table 8.1. Thus, for each subject's responses to each situation, composite scores for "desire to affiliate," "desire to solve problems," and "preference" were computed by normalizing and algebraically summing the responses to items within each factor and then normalizing the composite scores.

The 0.05 level significant results from the regression analyses[1] of these three sets of factor scores are given in equations 1, 4, and 7 of Table 8.7.

In considering the results in Table 8.7 and the remainder of this chapter, it is important to note another aspect of the data analyses. Even though t-tests were used occasionally to test for significant differences between pairs of cell means in some of the interactions, it should be noted that the trends

Table 8.7. Approach-Avoidance Behaviors Expressed as Functions of Average Pleasure-Eliciting (P), Arousal-Eliciting (A), and Dominance-Eliciting (D) Qualities of Situations*

1. Desire to affiliate (Experiment 1) $= + 0.19\ P$

2. Desire to affiliate (Experiment 2) $= + 0.14\ P - 0.15\ A \times D + 0.11\ P \times A - 0.06\ P \times A^2$

3. Desire to affiliate (Experiment 3) $= + 0.10\ P + 0.12\ P \times D - 0.09\ D$

4. Desire to solve problems (Experiment 1) $= + 0.16\ P - 0.53\ A + 0.09\ P \times A \times D$

5. Desire to work (Experiment 2) $= + 0.51\ P - 0.39\ A - 0.09\ P \times A^2 + 0.05\ P \times A \times D$

6. Desire to work (Experiment 3) $= + 0.46\ P - 0.37\ A - 0.13\ P \times A^2$

7. Preference (Experiment 1) $= + 0.69\ P - 0.24\ D - 0.08\ A^2 + 0.09\ D \times A^2$

8. Desire to explore (Experiment 2) $= + 0.39\ P - 0.09\ A^2 + 0.11\ P \times A - 0.08\ P \times D$

9. Desire to explore (Experiment 3) $= + 0.42\ P + 0.09\ A - 0.07\ A^2 - 0.11\ D$

10. Desire to stay (Experiment 2) $= + 0.58\ P$

11. Desire to stay (Experiment 3) $= + 0.59\ P$

*These equations were obtained using a stepwise regression procedure in which a uniform 0.05 level was used to assess the significance of all effects. Since all variables are normalized, the magnitudes of the coefficients in these equations reflect the relative strengths of the effects.

of the various dependent measures as functions of the arousing qualities of
environments were of particular concern in this context and the significance
of those trends was assessed directly from the regression equations. Thus,
for instance, a $(-A^2)$ term or a $(+ A - A^2)$ pair of terms in an equation supported the inverted-U-shaped relation between the dependent measure and
the arousing quality of settings. Another frequently encountered effect,
particularly when personality variables were included, was a positive two-
way interaction involving A, such as $+ A \times P$ or $+ A \times$ extroversion. Such
interactions indicated that the effects of the variables that interacted with
A (i.e., pleasantness of settings or extroversion in the examples here) were
generally greater in the more arousing situations and smaller in the less
arousing settings.

Experiment 2. The data of Experiment 2 were obtained from 163 subjects
who characterized their approach-avoidance responses as well as their emotional reactions to an average of about twenty situations from the full list
of sixty-five situations given in Appendix A. Once again, on the basis of
the emotional responses of all the subjects who read a situation, average
pleasure-, arousal-, and dominance-eliciting qualities (P, A, D) for that situation were computed and used in the regression analyses. The dependent
measures in this experiment were the four approach-avoidance measures of
Appendix E. The same kind of regression analyses as those employed in
Experiment 1 were used, and results, significant at the 0.05 level, are summarized in equations 2, 5, 8, and 10 of Table 8.7.

Experiment 3. There were 214 subjects in this experiment, and each of
them read and described his reactions to six different situations from the
first fifty-four situations in Appendix A. As in Experiment 2, regression
analyses were employed in which the dependent measures were the four
approach-avoidance categories of Appendix E. The results of the regression
analyses are summarized in equations 3, 6, 9, and 11 of Table 8.7. Significance of all the effects included in the equations was assessed at the 0.05
level.

  The description of results in the various figures given in the remainder of
this chapter must be prefaced with a discussion of the rationale for the use
of covariance methods and adjusted cell means (i.e., cell means in which the
effects of P were partialed out). Even though the correlations among state

pleasure, state arousal, and state dominance were generally low across the experiments reported in Chapter 2, a search for possible curvilinear relationships among P, A, and D showed that in all three experiments P was a U-shaped function of A. The implication of this relationship, shown in Table 8.8, was that, to assess an effect involving A, a covariance method was required to partial out the confounding effect of P. Our regression method was equally suited to covariance analyses, and the results reported in the equations of Table 8.7 can be rewritten readily in analysis of covariance form. This is done by simply moving the confounding terms that must be partialed out to the left-hand side of the equation. Thus, for instance, the analysis of covariance results[2] for equation 2 of Table 8.7 is summarized as

$$\text{Desire to affiliate} - 0.14\,P = -0.15\,A \times D + 0.11\,P \times A - 0.06\,P \times A^2.$$

From this form of the equation, adjusted cell means were computed. In other words, in computing the adjusted cell means, the effect of P for each of the four levels of A (as given in Table 8.8) was first subtracted from the obtained cell means. When a significant effect of Table 8.7 did not involve an A term, the interpretation of results was based on unadjusted cell means.

Desire to Affiliate

The results bearing on the desire to affiliate in the various situations of all three experiments are summarized in equations 1, 2, and 3 of Table 8.7. As expected, this particular aspect of approach-avoidance was indeed directly proportional to the pleasantness of the situations. There were no additional effects in equation 1; however, equation 2 showed an interaction between the arousing quality (A) and the dominance-eliciting quality (D) of the situations. Figure 8.1 provides the adjusted cell means for this interaction. The

Table 8.8. Relations among the Pleasure-Eliciting (P) and Arousal-Eliciting (A) Qualities of Situations in Each of the Three Experiments*

	Low A	Moderately Low A	Moderately High A	High A
Values of P in Experiment 1	0.60	0.00	−0.34	−0.19
Values of P in Experiment 2	0.03	−0.16	−0.07	0.36
Values of P in Experiment 3	0.48	0.18	−0.50	0.15

*In each experiment, values for P and A were computed for each situation by averaging reports of state pleasure and state arousal, respectively, of all subjects who read that situation. It will be noticed that the U-shaped relation between P and A was weakest in Experiment 2, where the full list of sixty-five situations in Appendix A was used.

next two effects in equation 2 showed that the pleasantness (**P**) and arousing quality (**A**) of situations interacted in determining the desire to affiliate, and the corresponding adjusted cell means are given in Figure 8.2.

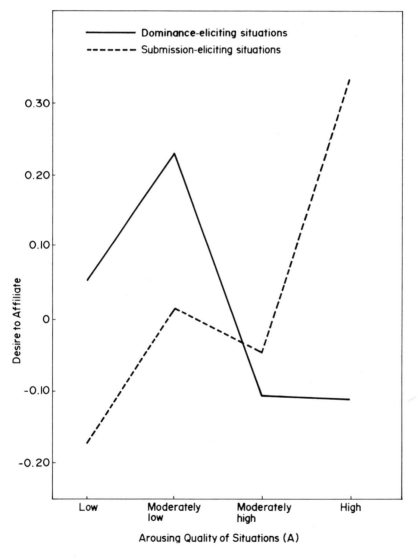

Figure 8.1. The effect of the A × D interaction of Experiment 2 on desire to affiliate*
*These are adjusted cell means, with the effect of **P** partialed out.

It should be noted that in computing cell means for these as well as all other figures in this chapter, average values were used to determine the high-low cutoff on the dichotomized **P** and **D** factors. For the four-way sub-division of the **A** factor, first a mean split on **A** was obtained, and then the mean splits of each of the high and low halves were used. As a consequence of these procedures, the number of observations in the various interaction cells were generally unequal. This did not present any problems, since significance levels of the various trends were directly noted from the regression equations. The cell means used for the figures were thus based on data samples from appropriate ranges of each variable and provided a pictorial representation of the trends given in the equations. Occasional comments about t-tests in the footnotes of the figures are designed to clarify the trends that are noted, and these tests were based on the actual number of observations from which each cell mean was computed.

Figure 8.1 shows that the hypothesized curvilinear relation between desire to affiliate and **A** was found only in dominance-eliciting situations. For situations that elicited a submissive feeling from the subjects, the desire to affiliate was maximized, quite unexpectedly, at a high **A** level. A similar unexpected increase in desire to affiliate was also observed in unpleasant and highly arousing situations (Figure 8.2). Together, these effects show that among highly arousing situations, those that were unpleasant and/or conducive to a submissive feeling elicited a very high desire for affiliation. These findings were contrary to our expectations but were in accord with Schachter's (1959) results, which showed that stressful situations tended to elicit affiliative reactions from some of his female subjects. In terms of our discussions of stress and anxiety, arousing situations that are unpleasant or that elicit submissive feelings may indeed be considered as stressful (note, for example, the equations of Table 3.4, which show that anxiety-related traits are associated with displeasure, arousal, and submissiveness).

The various effects of equation 3 are best described in terms of the un-adjusted cell means for the **P** X **D** interaction in Figure 8.3. The desire to affiliate was significantly less in unpleasant and dominance-eliciting situations than in the other three types of situations, and it did not differ significantly in the latter three situations. The results of Figure 8.3 were obtained in Experiment 3. An examination of the corresponding cell means in Experiment 2 showed an identical, but weaker, pattern of results that did not attain significance. Thus, the results given in Figure 8.3 do have some

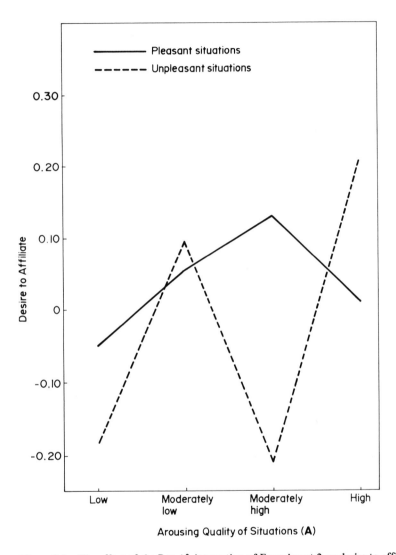

Figure 8.2.   The effect of the $P \times A^2$ interaction of Experiment 2 on desire to affiliate*
*These are adjusted cell means, with the effect of P partialed out.

generality. Furthermore, our data in Chapter 7 showed that the greatest amount of hostility was felt by persons in unpleasant and dominance-eliciting situations, relative to those in the other three types of situations (note Figure 7.1). Since hostile and negative feelings discourage affiliation

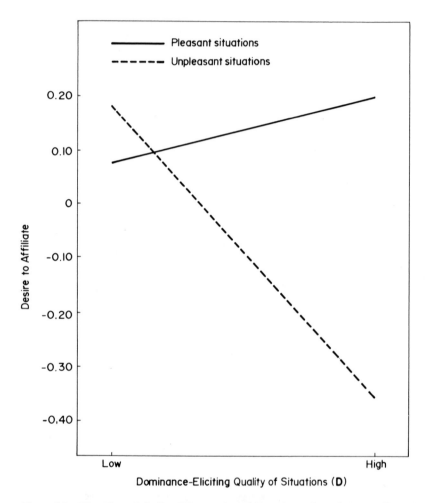

Figure 8.3.   The effect of the P × D interaction of Experiment 3 on desire to affiliate*
*These are unadjusted cell means.

(Mehrabian and Ksionzky, 1970), the results obtained for hostility and affiliation as functions of the emotions elicited in various situations are consistent.

An overview of the results for desire to affiliate shows that even though the
hypothesized effect of **P** was consistently supported, the effects of **A** differed
somewhat from expectations. Thus, the desire to affiliate in a situation cannot be conceptualized simply in terms of the proposed three-dimensional

scheme, and there are additional determiners, such as those identified by Schachter (1959) or by Mehrabian and Ksionzky (1970), that are peculiar to this factor of approach-avoidance behavior. Indeed, this explains the results in the first section of this chapter where desire to affiliate was found to have only a weak relationship to the other components of approach-avoidance.

Desire to Work

The results for desire to work in a situation as a function of the emotions typically elicited in that situation are summarized in equations 4, 5, and 6 of Table 8.7. Several consistent patterns were observed. First, as hypothesized, pleasantness (P) of situations was directly related to this particular variant of approach behavior in all three of the experiments. A second consistent result, which was contrary to our hypothesis, was that the desire to work generally decreased with the increasingly arousing quality (A) of the situation (note the strong and negative effects of A in all three equations).

The adjusted cell means (i.e., with the P effect partialed out) for the P × A^2 effect of equation 5 are given in Figure 8.4. For both pleasant and unpleasant situations, there was a decrease in the desire to work as a function of the arousing quality of situations.

Next, the corresponding cell means for the P × A^2 effect of equation 6 are given in Figure 8.5. In this case, the expected inverted-U shaped relation between desire to work and arousal-eliciting quality of work settings was obtained, but only for pleasant situations. For unpleasant situations, there was simply a drop in desire to work in the more arousing situations. This contrast implied that higher arousal levels were tolerated in the more pleasant situations.

Finally, the cell means were computed for the P × A × D interactions in equations 4 and 5, and the corresponding cell means for the two interactions were then averaged to obtain a more reliable estimate of the effects associated with this interaction. There were several reasons for averaging. First, the effects that influenced desire to work in all the experiments were comparable. Second, similar patterns of results were obtained when the P × A × D interactions in Experiments 1 and 2 were graphed separately. Third, higher-order interaction effects have lower reliability than main or second-order effects; as a consequence, the combination of data from different experiments bearing on the same interaction pattern can provide more reliable results.

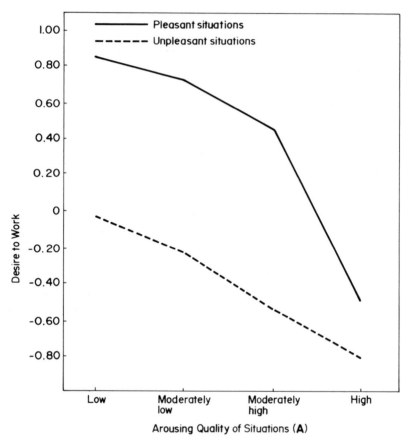

Figure 8.4.   The effect of the $\mathbf{P} \times \mathbf{A}^2$ interaction of Experiment 2 on desire to work*
*These are adjusted cell means, with the effect of $\mathbf{P}$ partialed out.

Figure 8.6, then, provides the summary of findings from Experiments 1 and 2 for the $\mathbf{P} \times \mathbf{A} \times \mathbf{D}$ effect on the desire to work. It shows that, for all four types of situations, the desire to work diminished with the increasingly arousing quality of the work setting. However, in pleasant environments that also elicited a submissive feeling, the desire to work remained unchanged, even with increases in the arousing quality of the settings up to a moderately high level. It was only for highly arousing situations that a sharp drop in desire to work was observed. These findings have some implications for

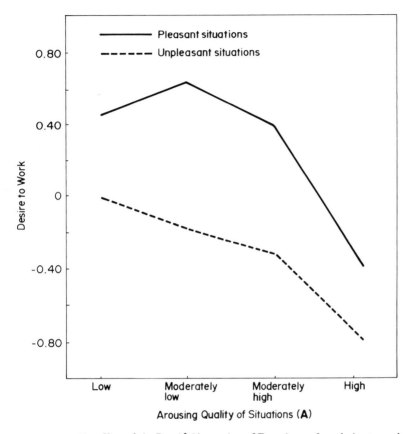

Figure 8.5. The effect of the **P** × **A²** interaction of Experiment 3 on desire to work

most work situations in which the employees are in a relatively submissive role. In such situations, employees would be better able to tolerate higher information rates from the work setting, provided the work situation is pleasant rather than unpleasant.

Excluding the single exception noted in Figure 8.6, the results from all three experiments showed that increased arousing quality of work settings was detrimental to the motivation to perform. This finding, which contradicts our hypothesis, can be considered in terms of our discussion of related phenomena in Chapter 6. In addition to the arousing quality of a work

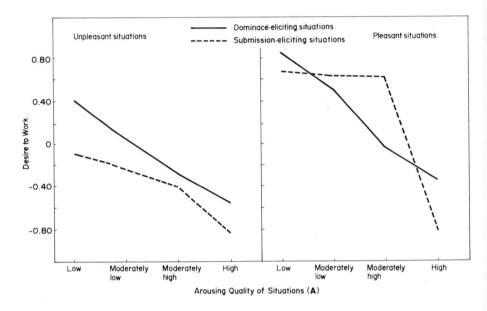

Figure 8.6. The summed **P** × **A** × **D** effects of Experiments 1 and 2 on desire to work

setting, the arousing quality of the task to be performed must be included in
considering the arousing quality of the total situation. The questions that
measured desire to work in our experiments were: "To what extent is this
situation a good opportunity to think out some difficult task you have been
working on?" and "How much would you dislike having to work in this
situation?" Thus, the first question elicited attitudes toward work of moderate or high complexity, and, in general, for these student subjects, work
meant homework or reading of abstract course materials that were usually of
high complexity. Quite understandably, then, our results departed from those
obtained from the results, reviewed in Chapter 6, for performance on simple
assembly-line work. Taking task complexity into consideration, the present
findings were consistent with the rationale that led to the inverted-U-shaped

hypothesis. These findings indicate that further exploration of the inverted-U relation must also include exact measurements of the arousing quality (i.e., the information rate) of tasks.

Preference and Desire to Explore

The preference factor obtained in Experiment 1 and described in Table 8.1 was a combined measure of liking, desires to seek out, explore, stay in, and not avoid a situation. The results for this composite measure are given in equation 7, and the corresponding results from Experiments 2 and 3 are given in equations 8, 9, 10, and 11 of Table 8.7. Once again, the most consistent result is that preference, desire to explore, and desire to stay in a situation are strongly affected by the pleasantness (**P**) of that situation. The adjusted cell means for the $D \times A^2$ interaction in equation 7, given in Figure 8.7, show that the effect of the arousing quality of a situation on preference was quite different, depending on the level of dominance-submissiveness that was elicited. Highly arousing situations were strongly preferred if they elicited a dominant feeling, but they were strongly avoided if they elicited a submissive feeling. This interaction in Figure 8.7 was obtained in only one out of three experiments and must be interpreted with some caution. Nevertheless, since a combination of high arousal and submissive feelings (with the effects of pleasantness having been partialed out) more closely resembles an anxiety state, it seems reasonable that it should be preferred less than a combination of high arousal and dominant feelings.

The cell means representing the combined effects of the $P \times A$ and A^2 terms on desire to explore in equation 8 are given in Figure 8.8. For both levels of pleasantness, the obtained results corresponded to the hypothesized inverted-U-shaped curve. Figure 8.8 also indicates that the optimal arousing quality of situations was moderately high for the pleasant, and moderately low for the unpleasant, situations. In other words, more arousing situations were explored when the situations were more pleasant. Together with the main effect of **P** in equation 8, these findings show that pleasantness of a situation per se elicits preference and exploration of the situation but can also facilitate the introduction of increased information rate in the situation without inhibiting approach behavior (note the analogous results for work in Figure 8.5).

The effects of **A** on exploration in Experiment 3 did not differ in pleasant, compared to unpleasant, situations. The adjusted cell means for the effects related to **A** in equation 9 show a relation that is consistent with the inverted-

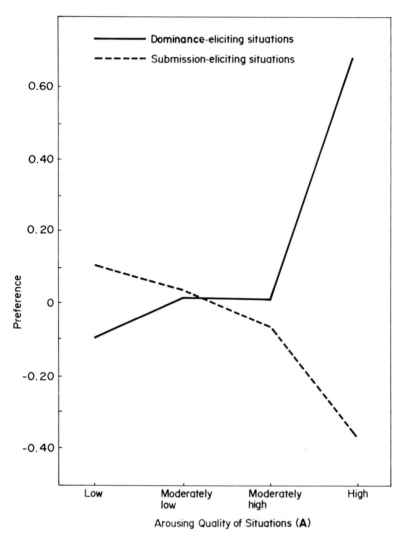

Figure 8.7.   The effect of the $D \times A^2$ interaction of Experiment 1 on preference*
*These are adjusted cell means, with the effect of P partialed out.

U hypothesis (Figure 8.9). The $+A$ and $-A^2$ terms in equation 9 indicate that the graphed curvilinear trend is indeed significant.

   The unadjusted cell means for the $P \times D$ effect of equation 8 are given in

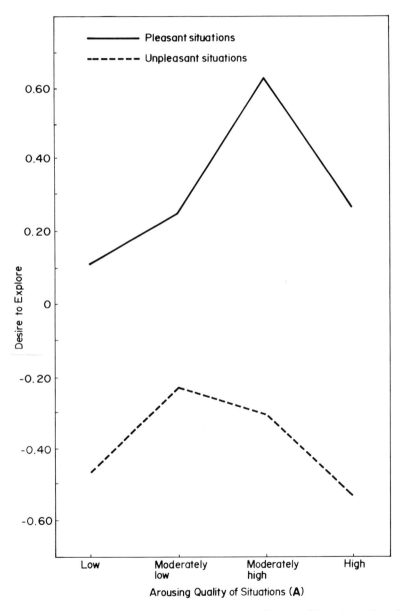

Figure 8.8. The combined effects of the P × A and A² terms of Experiment 2 on desire to explore

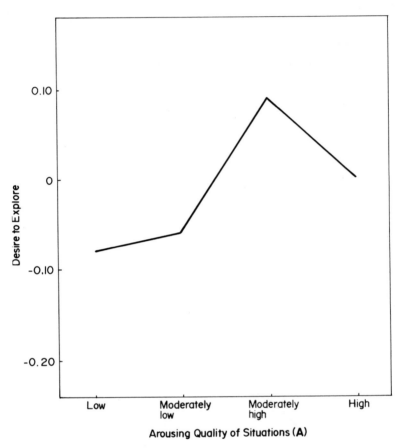

Figure 8.9.   The combined effects of the A and A^2 terms of Experiment 3 on desire to explore*
*These are adjusted cell means, with the effect of P partialed out.

Figure 8.10. In pleasant situations the desire to explore was not significantly different for the two degrees of dominance. In unpleasant situations, however, there was a significant drop in desire to explore the more dominance-eliciting situations. This finding is reminiscent of the P X D interaction that was reported for the desire to affiliate in Experiment 3 (Figure 8.3); however, the effect in Figure 8.10 is a weaker one. Both sets of effects show that approach-avoidance behaviors are discouraged when a situation is unpleasant and elicits dominant feelings from the persons within it.

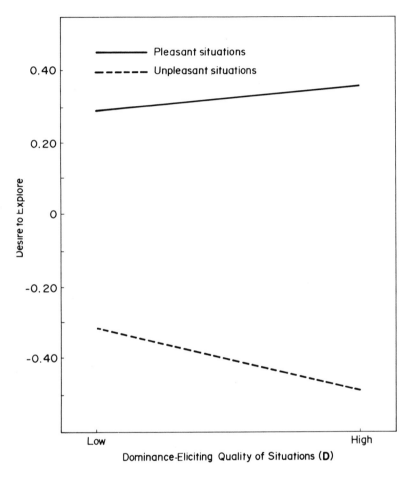

Figure 8.10. The effect of the **P** × **D** interaction of Experiment 2 on desire to explore*
*These are unadjusted cell means. Based on *t*-tests, the pair of cell means corresponding
to unpleasant situations differ significantly at the 0.05 level; of course, both simple
effects of **P** were significant.

To summarize, the results for preference in Experiment 1 and desire for
exploration in Experiments 2 and 3 provided some of the best confirmation
for the inverted-U hypothesis. Also, Figure 8.8 showed that the optimal
arousing quality of situations was higher for the pleasant than for the unpleasant ones among these. The exceptions were obtained in Experiment 1

where the preference of dominance-eliciting situations increased and the preference of submission-eliciting situations decreased with increases in the arousing quality of the situations.

Finally, equations 10 and 11 of Table 8.7 simply indicated that the desire to stay in a situation was determined only by the pleasure-eliciting quality of that situation and by no other factor.

The Contribution of Personality Variables to Approach-Avoidance Behaviors
The personality questionnaires that were administered to the subjects in Experiment 1 were measures of trait anxiety (Spielberger, Gorsuch, and Lushene, 1970), neuroticism and extroversion (Eysenck and Eysenck, 1968), and arousal-seeking tendency (Appendix C). The sex of each subject, an additional individual difference variable, was also known. There were no personality questionnaires in Experiment 2; therefore, only the sex of subjects was available for personality-related analyses. Experiment 3 included all the personality measures employed in Experiment 1, as well as measures of affiliative tendency and sensitivity to rejection (Mehrabian, 1970c; 1972b, Appendix B).

The method of multiple regression analysis was again used to analyze the data of this section. Each of the regression analyses for a dependent measure explored the possible main and interactive effects of P, A, A^2, D, and one personality measure. For instance, exploration of the possible contributions of sex in determining desire to affiliate in Experiment 1 yielded the following regression equation:

$$\text{Desire to affiliate} = 0.19\,P - 0.10\,A \times \text{sex,}$$

where male = 1 and female = −1. Repetition of the same procedure for each of the other personality variables in this experiment yielded the following regression equations:

$$\text{Desire to affiliate} = 0.19\,P - 0.12\,\text{trait anxiety} - 0.08\,P \times \text{trait anxiety;}$$

$$\text{Desire to affiliate} = 0.19\,P - 0.12\,P \times \text{neuroticism;}$$

$$\text{Desire to affiliate} = 0.19\,P + 0.11\,\text{extroversion.}$$

Since the fifth regression analysis, which explored possible contributions of arousal-seeking tendency, yielded no significant effects, no equation was written for this particular personality variable. Similar procedures were used to compute the contributions of the same five personality variables to each of the remaining two dependent measures of Experiment 1: desire to engage in problem-solving behavior in a situation and preference for the situation.

In Experiments 2 and 3, the dependent measures were the desires to affiliate, work, explore, and stay in a situation. As in Experiment 1, each regression analysis explored the possible main and interactive effects of P, A, A^2, D, and one personality measure on each dependent measure.

The significant effects for all three experiments are reported in Table 8.9. To avoid redundancy of presentation, all the significant effects for a given dependent measure are reported in the same equation; however, the effects of each personality measure in an equation are written on a different line to emphasize that they were obtained from separate regression analyses. Thus, the first set of eleven equations in Table 8.9 corresponds to that in Table 8.7 but also includes the contributions of the personality factors. (Since affiliative tendency and sensitivity to rejection are related personality attributes, their combined effects were tested in the same regression equations, e.g., note equation 3 of Table 8.9).

The last six equations in Table 8.9 report the results of regression analyses from the data of Experiments 2 and 3 in which state emotions were expressed as functions of the average emotion-eliciting qualities of situations (i.e., P, A, and D) and interactions of the latter with the personality measures. The computation method used for these equations was identical to that used for the initial set of equations of that table.

Desire to Affiliate

Equations 1, 2, and 3 of Table 8.9 summarize all the significant determinants of desire for affiliation in the three experiments. The adjusted cell means for the $A \times$ sex interaction in Figure 8.11 show that females' desire for affiliation increased with the arousing quality of the setting, whereas males' desire for affiliation was not significantly affected (note that no significant curvilinear trend was shown for this interaction in equation 1). This finding relates to the characteristically more submissive feelings of females relative to males (Table 3.4). It will be recalled that in Figure 8.1, desire for affiliation was high in submission-eliciting situations that were highly arousing. Thus, a

Table 8.9.   Approach-Avoidance Behaviors and State Emotions Expressed as Functions of Average Pleasure-Eliciting (P), Arousal-Eliciting (A), and Dominance-Eliciting (D) Qualities of Situations and Personality Variables*

1. Desire to affiliate (Experiment 1)
$$= + 0.19\ P$$
$$- 0.10\ A \times \text{sex}$$
$$- 0.12\ \text{trait anxiety} - 0.08\ P \times \text{trait anxiety}$$
$$- 0.12\ P \times \text{neuroticism}$$
$$+ 0.11\ \text{extroversion}$$

2. Desire to affiliate (Experiment 2)
$$= + 0.14\ P - 0.15\ A \times D + 0.11\ P \times A - 0.06\ P \times A^2$$
$$+ \text{no effect for sex}$$

3. Desire to affiliate (Experiment 3)
$$= + 0.10\ P + 0.12\ P \times D - 0.09\ D$$
$$+ 0.11\ \text{extroversion}$$
$$+ 0.10\ \text{arousal-seeking tendency}$$
$$+ 0.16\ \text{affiliative tendency} - 0.06\ \text{sensitivity to rejection}$$

4. Desire to solve problems (Experiment 1)
$$= - 0.53\ A + 0.16\ P + 0.09\ P \times A \times D$$
$$- 0.08\ P \times A^2 \times \text{trait anxiety}$$

5. Desire to work (Experiment 2)
$$= + 0.51\ P - 0.39\ A - 0.09\ P \times A^2 + 0.05\ P \times A \times D$$
$$+ \text{no effect for sex}$$

6. Desire to work (Experiment 3)
$$= + 0.46\ P - 0.37\ A - 0.13\ P \times A^2$$
$$+ 0.07\ P \times A \times \text{neuroticism}$$

7. Preference (Experiment 1)
$$= + 0.69\ P - 0.24\ D - 0.08\ A^2 + 0.09\ D \times A^2$$
$$- 0.13\ A \times D \times \text{trait anxiety}$$
$$+ 0.07\ P \times D \times \text{extroversion}$$

Table 8.9   (Continued)

8. Desire to explore (Experiment 2)
$$= + 0.39 \text{ P} - 0.09 \text{ A}^2 + 0.11 \text{ P} \times \text{A} - 0.08 \text{ P} \times \text{D}$$
$$- 0.06 \text{ D} \times \text{sex}$$

9. Desire to explore (Experiment 3)
$$= + 0.42 \text{ P} + 0.09 \text{ A} - 0.07 \text{ A}^2 - 0.11 \text{ D}$$
$$- 0.07 \text{ P} \times \text{sex}$$
$$+ 0.13 \text{ arousal-seeking tendency}$$
$$+ 0.08 \text{ affiliative tendency}$$

10. Desire to stay (Experiment 2)
$$= + 0.58 \text{ P}$$
$$- 0.06 \text{ D} \times \text{sex} + 0.02 \text{ A}^2 \times \text{sex} + 0.05 \text{ A} \times \text{D} \times \text{sex}$$

11. Desire to stay (Experiment 3)
$$= + 0.59 \text{ P}$$
$$+ 0.07 \text{ arousal-seeking tendency} + 0.08 \text{ A} \times \text{arousal-seeking tendency}$$

12. State pleasure (Experiment 2)
$$= + 0.68 \text{ P}$$
$$+ \text{no effect for sex}$$

13. State pleasure (Experiment 3)
$$= + 0.68 \text{ P}$$
$$- 0.09 \text{ trait anxiety} + 0.07 \text{ P} \times \text{trait anxiety}$$
$$- 0.06 \text{ neuroticism} + 0.07 \text{ P} \times \text{neuroticism}$$
$$+ 0.06 \text{ A} \times \text{arousal-seeking tendency}$$
$$- 0.08 \text{ sensitivity to rejection}$$

14. State arousal (Experiment 2)
$$= + 0.70 \text{ A}$$
$$- 0.04 \text{ sex} - 0.05 \text{ A} \times \text{sex}$$

Table 8.9 (Continued)

15. State arousal (Experiment 3)

$$= + 0.70 \text{ A}$$
$$- 0.07 \text{ A} \times \text{sex}$$
$$+ 0.05 \text{ A} \times \text{neuroticism}$$
$$+ 0.06 \text{ A} \times \text{extroversion}$$
$$+ 0.09 \text{ arousal-seeking tendency} + 0.06 \text{ A} \times \text{arousal-seeking tendency}$$
$$+ 0.07 \text{ affiliative tendency} + 0.08 \text{ A} \times \text{affiliative tendency}$$

16. State dominance (Experiment 2)

$$= + 0.49 \text{ D}$$
$$+ 0.08 \text{ P} \times \text{sex} - 0.07 \text{ D} \times \text{sex}$$

17. State dominance (Experiment 3)

$$= + 0.35 \text{ D}$$
$$+ 0.09 \text{ sex}$$
$$- 0.07 \text{ trait anxiety}$$
$$- 0.13 \text{ sensitivity to rejection}$$

*For each of the equations 1, 4, and 7 of Experiment 1, the results are based on five separate stepwise regression analyses. Each of these analyses tested the possible contribution of the main and interactive effects of only one personality measure and P, A, A², and D. The personality measures explored in Experiment 1 were sex, trait anxiety, neuroticism, extroversion, and arousal-seeking tendency. The results for Experiment 2 reported in equations 2, 5, 8, and 10 are based on a total of four stepwise regression analyses, which tested the interactive contributions of sex. For Experiment 3, seven regression analyses were conducted to test separately the contributions of sex, trait anxiety, neuroticism, extroversion, arousal-seeking tendency, affiliative tendency, and sensitivity to rejection, for each of the dependent measures in equations 3, 6, 9, and 11. Only effects that attained the 0.05 level of significance are reported in this table, and all the variables in the equations are normalized to facilitate comparisons of the relative strengths of the various effects. In all the equations involving sex, male = +1 and female = −1.

combination of high arousal and submissive feelings, whether because of the setting (as in Figure 8.1) or because of the setting and the subject's characteristic feelings (as in the case of the females in Figure 8.11), leads to a heightened desire for affiliation.

The two effects for trait anxiety in equation 1 are related, and the consideration of the cell means for the **P** X trait anxiety effect is sufficient for understanding both effects. The unadjusted cell means in Figure 8.12 show that less anxious persons were more desirous of affiliation, but only in the pleasant situations. A similar effect was obtained for the **P** X neuroticism interaction in equation 1: Less neurotic persons were more desirous of affiliation, but only in pleasant settings (note Figure 8.13 for the unadjusted cell means). The last effect in equation 1 shows that extroverts, who by definition are more outgoing, desired to affiliate more than introverts.

These results for trait anxiety, neuroticism, and extroversion are consistent with Mehrabian and Ksionzky's (1970) model for affiliative behavior. According to that model and its supporting evidence (e.g., Mehrabian, 1971b), affiliative behavior consists of the exchange of positive reinforcers, and persons who have generalized expectations of positive interpersonal exchanges are therefore more likely to engage in affiliative behavior. Since the more neurotic and anxious persons were less likely to have such positive expectations, they showed less desire to affiliate. In further support of the Mehrabian and Ksionzky (1970; 1974) model, no difference was obtained in unpleasant situations between high- and low-anxiety subjects' desire to affiliate. Similarly, in unpleasant situations, highly and slightly neurotic subjects both showed a similar low desire to affiliate. As noted in Chapter 7, the positiveness of interpersonal exchanges is directly correlated with the pleasantness of the setting in which the exchanges take place. Understandably, then, irrespective of their personality, subjects did not expect to have positive interpersonal exchanges in unpleasant settings.

Equation 3 shows that more extroverted subjects were generally more desirous of affiliation—a replication of the effect noted in equation 1. It also shows that high-arousal seekers were more desirous of affiliation than low-arousal seekers. Our review of the studies of McBride, King, and James (1965), Nichols and Champness (1971), and related studies with animal subjects by Mason (1959b) in Chapter 5 led to the hypothesis that the immediacy of interpersonal cues (i.e., increased mutual sensory stimulation due

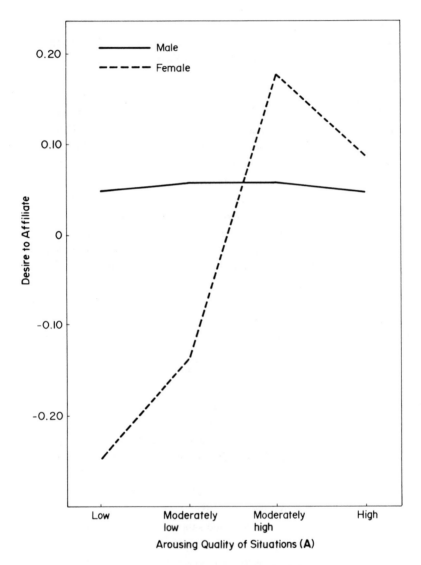

Figure 8.11.   The effect of the A × sex interaction of Experiment 1 on desire to affiliate*

*These are adjusted cell means, with the effect of **P** partialed out.

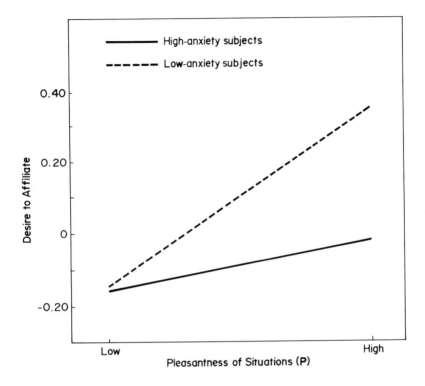

Figure 8.12.   The effect of the P X trait anxiety interaction of Experiment 1 on desire to affiliate*

*These are unadjusted cell means. Based on *t*-tests, only the pair of cell means corresponding to pleasant situations differ significantly at the 0.05 level.

to physical proximity, eye contact, direct bodily orientation, or conversation) is correlated with arousal level. A high-arousal seeker's greater desire for affiliation is thus part of his attempt to increase his arousal to a desired level with increased exposures to interpersonal cues.

The final two effects in equation 3 show that the desire to affiliate was a direct correlate of affiliative tendency and an inverse correlate of sensitivity to rejection. This finding is in accord with the predictions of Mehrabian and Ksionzky (1970). The rationale for their model, as it related to personality variables, was that affiliative behavior is encouraged by generalized positive expectations (i.e., affiliative tendency) and is discouraged by generalized

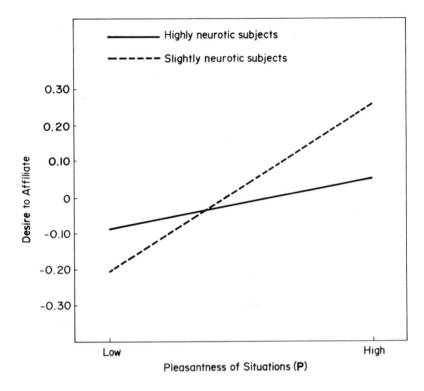

Figure 8.13.   The effect of the **P** X neuroticism interaction of Experiment 1 on desire
to affiliate*
*These are unadjusted cell means. Based on *t*-tests, only the pair of cell means corresponding to pleasant situations differ significantly at the 0.05 level.

negative expectations (i.e., sensitivity to rejection), and the present findings
supported that view.

Desire to Work

In Experiment 1, trait anxiety was the only personality variable that interacted significantly to affect the subject's desire to solve problems. The cell
means for this **P** X **A²** X trait anxiety interaction of equation 4, given in
Figure 8.14, show that, in the unpleasant situations, both high- and low-
anxiety persons exhibited similar patterns of desire to solve problems. However, in pleasant situations, different patterns were obtained for these two
groups of subjects: There was a more rapid decline of the more anxious
subjects' desire to solve problems as the arousing quality of situations in-

creased. The findings for the pleasant, but not those for the unpleasant, situations supported the proposed summary equation 2 of Chapter 6. In that equation, performance was hypothesized to be an inverted-U-shaped function of the weighted sum of information rate from the task setting and trait arousal of the subject. On the basis of that hypothesis, the (desire for) performance of all subjects rises initially with increases in the arousing quality of a work situation and then begins to decline beyond the optimum information-rate value. Further, this optimum information-rate value is lower for the more aroused subjects. Since trait anxiety is a correlate of trait arousal (Table 3.4) and since the tasks of Experiment 1 were complex, data for the pleasant situations in Figure 8.14 support the hypothesized relations in equation 2 of Chapter 6.

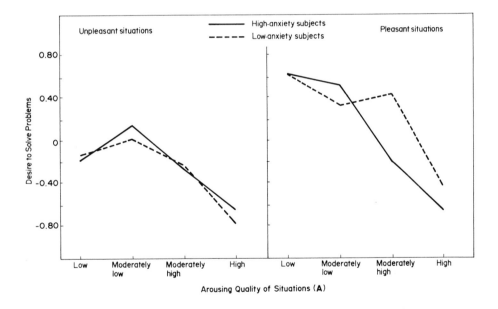

Figure 8.14. The effect of $P \times A^2 \times$ trait anxiety interaction of Experiment 1 on desire to solve problems

Figure 8.15 illustrates the cell means for the **P** X **A** X neuroticism interaction of equation 6. In unpleasant situations, highly and slightly neurotic
subjects showed similar continued decrements in desire to work with the increases in the arousing quality of the situations; however, this decrease in desire to work was more accelerated for the more neurotic subjects. Since neuroticism is a correlate of arousal (Table 3.4), this finding is consistent with the
hypotheses of equation 2 in Chapter 6.

For the pleasant situations of Figure 8.15, slightly neurotic subjects' desire
to work as a function of the arousing quality of the situation was consistent
with the inverted-U hypothesis; for highly neurotic subjects, the graph resembles the right-hand side of the inverted-U-shaped curve. In other words,

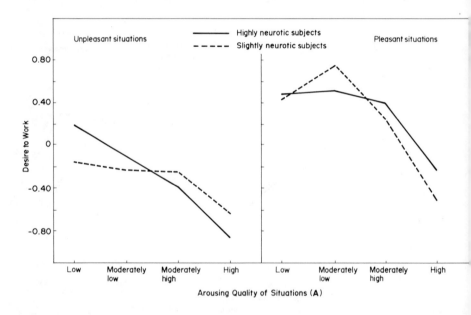

Figure 8.15. The effect of the **P** X **A** X neuroticism interaction of Experiment 3 on
desire to work

for the more neurotic (more aroused) subjects, the decrement in (desire for) performance began at a lower information rate from the task settings, and this again supports equation 2 of Chapter 6. One aspect of Figure 8.15 was discrepant with expectations, however. In pleasant and highly arousing situations, the slightly neurotic subjects expressed a lower desire to work than the highly neurotic subjects.

Preference and Desire to Explore

In Experiment 1, the dependent measure of preference was a composite of tendencies to seek, explore, prefer, and not leave a situation. In Experiments 2 and 3, the corresponding dependent measures of desire to explore and desire to stay were analyzed separately. In this section, we shall consider the preference measure of Experiment 1 and the desire to explore measure of Experiments 2 and 3.

The adjusted cell means for the $A \times D \times$ trait anxiety interaction in equation 7 are given in Figure 8.16. In general, the results for slightly, compared to highly, anxious individuals were in the expected direction; that is, more anxious subjects had less preference for the more arousing situations. For instance, of the two curves in Figure 8.16 that correspond to dominance-eliciting situations, the one for the more anxious subjects has a smaller positive slope. On the other hand, for the submission-eliciting situations, the curve for the high-anxiety subjects peaks at moderately arousing settings, whereas that of the low-anxiety subjects drops sharply only for highly arousing situations. In addition to these results, comparison of the pairs of curves corresponding to dominance- and submission-eliciting situations in the two halves of Figure 8.16 shows a $D \times A^2$ effect that was already noted in Figure 8.7.

The results for extroversion and sex differences described in Figures 8.17 through 8.19 do not bear directly on any of our hypotheses but are of incidental interest for understanding how these two aspects of personality affect preference and exploration of situations. The unadjusted cell means for the $P \times D \times$ extroversion effect of equation 7 are given in Figure 8.17. The only significant difference in the preferences of extroverts and introverts was found in pleasant and submission-eliciting settings: The introverts preferred such situations more than the extroverts, although these situations were not necessarily repugnant to extroverts.

Figure 8.18 presents the unadjusted cell means for the $D \times$ sex effect on

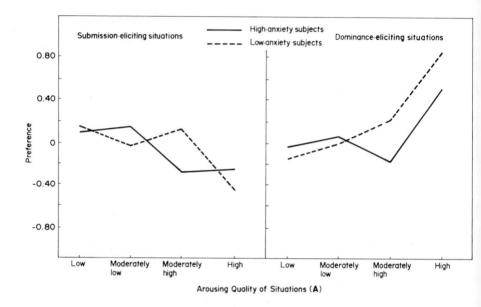

Figure 8.16. The effect of the A × D × trait anxiety interaction of Experiment 1 on preference*
*These are adjusted cell means, with the effect of **P** partialed out.

desire to explore given in equation 8. Although females and males did not differ significantly in their desire to explore dominance-eliciting situations, females were particularly hesitant to explore situations that elicited submissiveness. This finding is consistent with the well-documented greater aggressiveness of males relative to females (Anastasi, 1958). A similar interpretation applies to the **P** × sex effect of equation 9 shown in Figure 8.19. Whereas males and females did not differ in their desire to explore pleasant situations, females reported less desire to explore in the unpleasant situations than males.

Two additional main effects in equation 9 show that higher arousal seekers and more affiliative persons were more desirous of exploring situations.

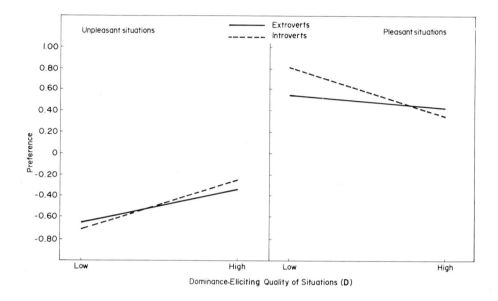

Figure 8.17. The effect of the **P** × **D** × extroversion interaction of Experiment 1 on preference*
*These are unadjusted cell means. Based on *t*-tests, only the pair of cell means corresponding to pleasant and submission-eliciting situations differ significantly at the 0.05 level.

Since exploration increases stimulation, and thereby arousal level, higher arousal seekers' greater desire for exploration is readily understood. The corresponding result for affiliative tendency confirmed the evidence in Chapter 3, showing a novel aspect of this personality trait. The data of Experiment 3 of Chapter 3 had shown a 0.32 correlation between arousal seeking and affiliative tendency and a –0.30 correlation between arousal seeking and sensitivity to rejection. It will also be recalled that in Table 3.4 the more affiliative persons were portrayed not only as more pleasant but also as more aroused. Thus, affiliative persons seek interpersonal cues not only because they expect positive reinforcement from such interchanges but

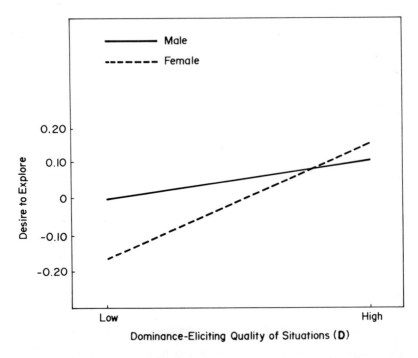

Figure 8.18.   The effect of the **D** × sex interaction of Experiment 2 on desire to explore*
*These are unadjusted cell means. Based on t-tests, only the pair of cell means corresponding to submission-eliciting situations differ significantly at the 0.05 level.

also because they prefer a higher arousal level. On the other hand, those who are sensitive to rejection show a slight avoidance of interpersonal cues because they expect negative reinforcers and because they find such exchanges overly arousing.

Desire to Stay

Equation 10 shows three related interactions involving the sex difference variable, and the **A** × **D** × sex interaction provides the necessary information for understanding all three effects. The adjusted cell means of this interaction (for which a figure is not necessary) showed that in submission-eliciting situations, males' and females' desires to stay in the situation were similar for all four situations differing in arousing quality. However, in dominance-eliciting situations, a difference in their desires to stay was observed only

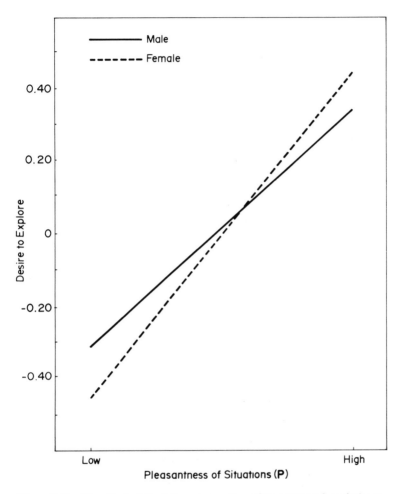

Figure 8.19. The effect of the P × sex interaction of Experiment 3 on desire to explore*

*These are unadjusted cell means. Based on *t*-tests, only the pair of cell means corresponding to unpleasant situations differ significantly at the 0.05 level.

when the situations were highly arousing; in such settings, males showed a significantly greater desire to stay than females.

Two related effects of arousal-seeking tendency were obtained in equation 11. The adjusted cell means in Figure 8.20 for the A × arousal-seeking

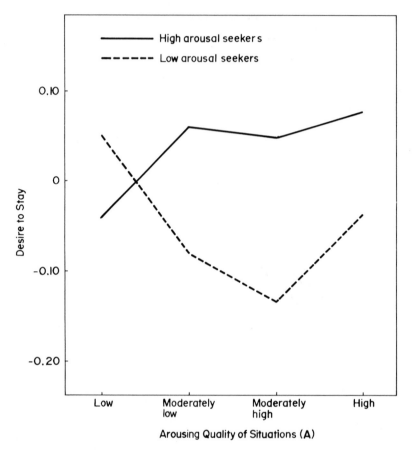

Figure 8.20.   The effect of the **A** × arousal-seeking tendency interaction of Experiment 3 on desire to stay*
*These are adjusted cell means, with the effect of **P** partialed out.

tendency interaction show that high-arousal seekers' desire to stay in a situation increased as a function of the arousing quality of the setting. In contrast, low-arousal seekers expressed a significantly lower desire to stay in the more arousing situations. This finding provided validation for the measure of Appendix C.

State Pleasure

In this section and the following two sections, we investigate interactions of the emotion-eliciting qualities of situations (i.e., **P, A, D**) with personality

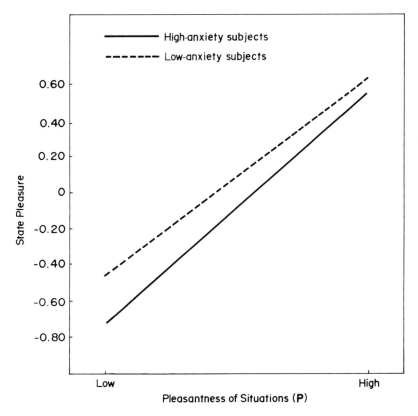

Figure 8.21.   The effect of the **P** X trait anxiety interaction of Experiment 3 on state pleasure*
*These are unadjusted cell means. Based on *t*-tests, only the pair of cell means corresponding to unpleasant situations differ significantly at the 0.05 level.

attributes in determining state emotions. The data of Experiments 2 and 3 were used, and the results are summarized in equations 12 through 17 of Table 8.9.

The unadjusted cell means for the **P** X trait anxiety interaction of equation 13 are given in Figure 8.21. It was seen that more anxious subjects generally felt less pleasant (i.e., had lower state pleasure)—findings that are consistent with their characteristic feelings of displeasure noted in Table 3.4. Moreover, Figure 8.21 shows that these differences in state pleasure of high- and low-anxiety persons were most pronounced in the unpleasant situations.

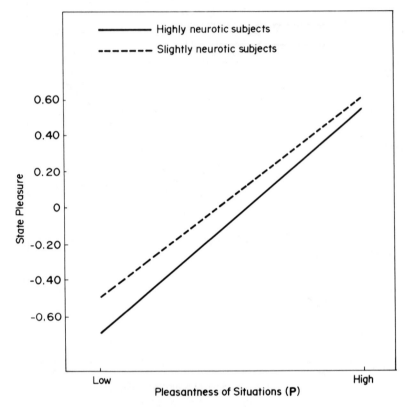

Figure 8.22.   The effect of the **P** X neuroticism interaction of Experiment 3 on state pleasure*
*These are unadjusted cell means. Based on *t*-tests, only the pair of cell means corresponding to unpleasant situations differ significantly at the 0.05 level.

The unadjusted cell means for the **P** X neuroticism interaction of equation 13, given in Figure 8.22, show a similar pattern of results; that is, the more neurotic persons felt even more displeasure in the more unpleasant situations.

We can extrapolate from the results in Figure 8.21 and 8.22 and state the "personality-emotional sensitivity" hypothesis. Each personality attribute is associated with certain heightened emotional sensitivities (e.g., displeasure in the case of trait anxiety and neuroticism), and situations that generally elicit a certain emotion (e.g., unpleasant situations) have the strongest effect on persons who possess a related emotional sensitivity (e.g., anxious persons and neurotics). This hypothesis not only subsumes the phenomena reported in Figures 8.21 and 8.22 but is also useful in understanding many of the interactions reported later in this chapter.

The adjusted cell means for the A X arousal-seeking tendency interaction in equation 13 are given in Figure 8.23. For high-arousal seekers, state pleasure increased monotonically with the arousing quality of settings. For low-arousal seekers, state pleasure decreased in the more arousing settings, although there was a nonsignificant reversal of the trend for the highly arousing situations. This interaction of Figure 8.23 had not been hypothesized but was consistent with the definition of arousal-seeking tendency. Higher arousal seekers seek more arousing stimulation, and, understandably,

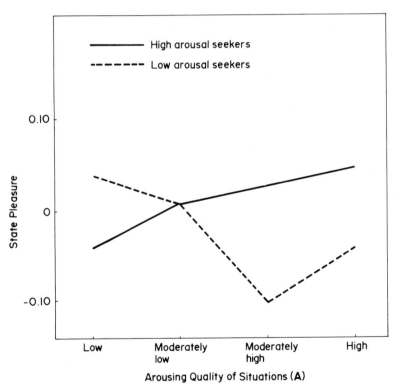

Figure 8.23. The effect of the A X arousal-seeking tendency interaction of Experiment 3 on state pleasure*
*These are adjusted cell means, with the effect of P partialed out.

more arousing situations are more pleasing to them, whereas the reverse is true for low-arousal seekers.

The last effect in equation 13 shows an inverse correlation between state pleasure and sensitivity to rejection and is consistent with data already reported in Table 3.4.

State Arousal

The unadjusted cell means for the **A** X sex effect of equation 14 are given in Figure 8.24. As shown in this figure, compared to males, females' state arousal as a function of the arousing quality of settings had a larger positive slope. Since females are characteristically more aroused than males (Table 3.4), this finding is a confirmation of the personality-emotional sensitivity hypothesis.

A similar **A** X sex interaction was obtained in Experiment 3, and the unadjusted cell means for this effect of equation 15 are given in Figure 8.25. Once again, the slope for state arousal as a function of the increasingly arousing quality of settings was greater for females than for males.

Figure 8.26 shows the unadjusted cell means for the **A** X neuroticism interaction of equation 15. Here again, consistent with the personality-emotional sensitivity hypothesis, the slope for state arousal as a function of the arousing quality of settings was greater for the more neurotic persons. A similar result is observed in Figure 8.27, which shows that the state arousal of more extroverted persons increased faster with increases in the arousing quality of settings. Again, unadjusted cell means for the **A** X arousal-seeking tendency interaction in equation 15, as given in Figure 8.28, show that higher arousal seekers' state arousal increased more with increases in the arousing quality of settings. Finally, the unadjusted cell means for the **A** X affiliative tendency interaction of equation 15, given in Figure 8.29, show that more affiliative persons' state arousal increased more with increases in the arousing quality of the various situations.

Since characteristically high arousal levels are associated with neuroticism, extroversion, arousal-seeking tendency, and affiliative tendency (note the positive trait arousal components for these traits in the equations of Table 3.4), it follows that the results in Figures 8.26 through 8.29 are all consistent with the personality-emotional sensitivity hypothesis.

State Dominance

The few significant effects on state dominance are reported in equations 16

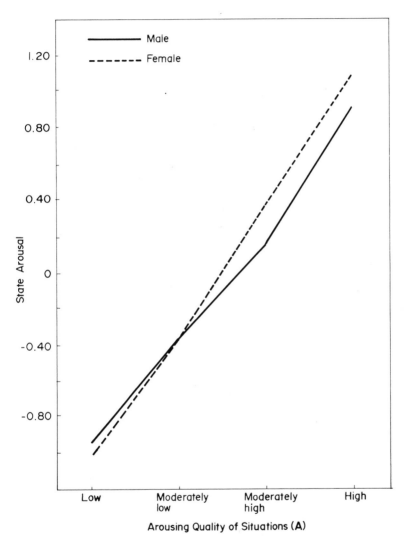

Figure 8.24. The effect of the A X sex interaction of Experiment 2 on state arousal*
*These are unadjusted cell means. According to *t*-tests, the state-arousal levels of males
and females differ significantly at the 0.05 level in only the moderately high and highly
arousing situations.

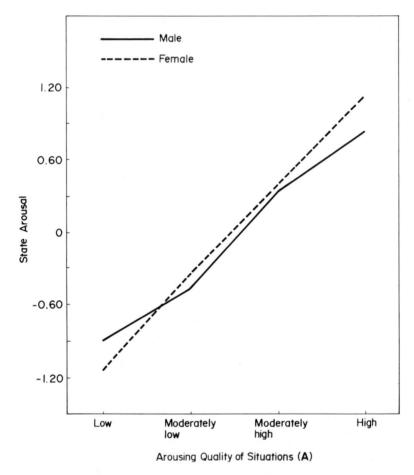

Figure 8.25.   The effect of the **A** × sex interaction of Experiment 3 on state arousal*
*These are unadjusted cell means. According to *t*-tests, the state-arousal levels of males and females differ significantly at the 0.05 level in only low and highly arousing situations.

and 17 of Table 8.9. The unadjusted cell means for the **P** × sex interaction of equation 16 are given in Figure 8.30 and show that in the pleasant (but not the unpleasant) situations, males felt more dominant than females. The unadjusted cell means for the **D** × sex interaction, given in Figure 8.31, show that in submission-eliciting (but not in dominance-eliciting) situations males

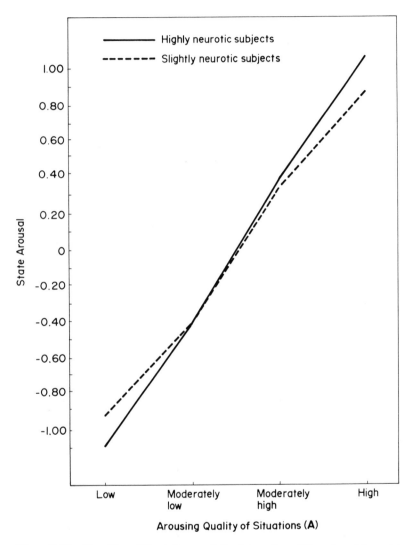

Figure 8.26. The effect of the A × neuroticism interaction of Experiment 3 on state arousal*
*These are unadjusted cell means. Based on *t*-tests, the state-arousal levels of highly and slightly neurotic subjects differ significantly at the 0.05 level only in highly arousing situations.

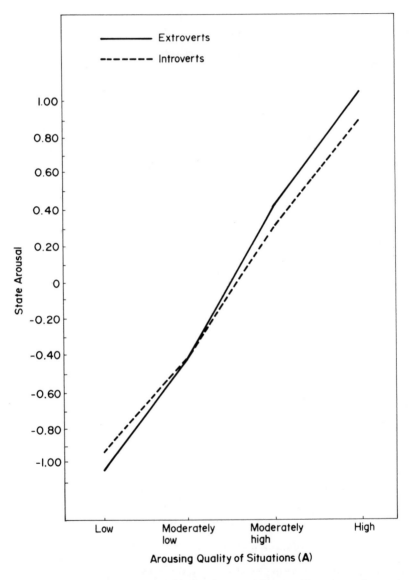

Figure 8.27.   The effect of the A × extroversion interaction of Experiment 3 on state arousal*
*These are unadjusted cell means. Based on t-tests, the state-arousal levels of extroverts and introverts differ significantly at the 0.05 level only in highly arousing situations.

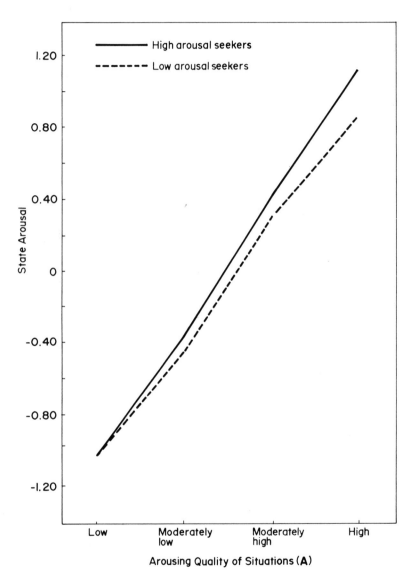

Figure 8.28. The effect of the A × arousal-seeking tendency interaction of Experiment 3 on state arousal*

*These are unadjusted cell means. Based on *t*-tests, the arousal levels of high- and low-arousal seekers differ significantly at the 0.05 level only in highly arousing situations.

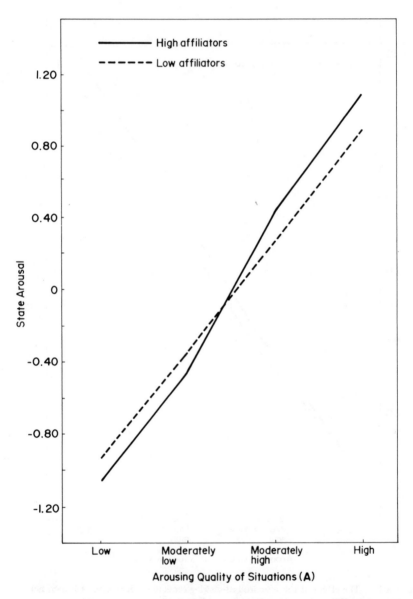

Figure 8.29.   The effect of the A × affiliative tendency interaction of Experiment 3 on state arousal*

*These are unadjusted cell means. Based on *t*-tests, the state-arousal levels of high and low affiliators differ significantly at the 0.05 level only at moderately highly and highly arousing situations.

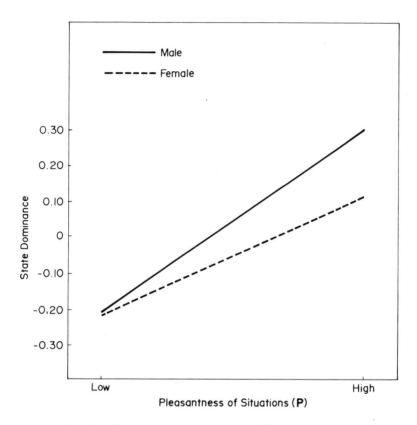

Figure 8.30.   The effect of the P X sex interaction of Experiment 2 on state dominance*
*There are unadjusted cell means. Based on t-tests, only the pair of cell means corresponding to pleasant situations differ significantly at the 0.05 level.

felt more dominant than females. Thus, even though males generally feel more dominant than females (note the main effect for sex in equation 17 of Table 8.9 and the equations describing sex differences in Table 3.4), this difference is more likely in situations that are pleasant and/or in situations that tend to elicit a submissive feeling from most people.

The two main effects in equation 17 of Table 8.9 simply indicate that more anxious persons and those who were more sensitive to rejection felt less dominant in general.

Summary and Some Implications
The experiments reported in this chapter were designed to yield preliminary,

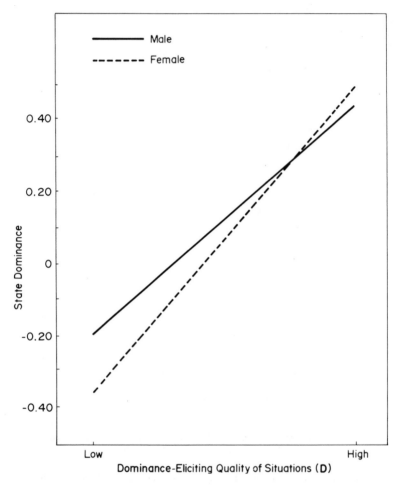

Figure 8.31.   The effect of the **D** × sex interaction of Experiment 2 on state dominance*
*These are unadjusted cell means. Based on t-tests, only the pair of cell means cor-
responding to submission-eliciting situations differ significantly at the 0.05 level.

but extensive, data bearing on all the facets of the proposed theory of environmental psychology. In the first section of this chapter, data on approach-
avoidance responses to a variety of everyday situations, described in Appendix A, were analyzed. The resulting verbal measures of approach-avoidance are given in Appendix E. When precise experimental results are required, it is suggested that the four measures of Appendix E be used sep-

arately. However, when a more general approach-avoidance index is desired, a combination of the first three measures of Appendix E for desire to stay, explore, and work in situations should suffice. A series of regression equations (Table 8.7) summarizes the results from the second section of this chapter. Each equation expresses a category of approach-avoidance as a function of the significant main and interactive effects of average pleasure-eliciting (P), arousal-eliciting (A), and dominance-eliciting (D) qualities of various situations. The significant positive P component in each of the equations provides strong confirmation for the hypothesized direct relationship between approach-avoidance and pleasure. The data on desire to affiliate provided the weakest support for the inverted-U-shaped hypothesis relating approach-avoidance to arousal. The data for desire to work and for preference and exploration of situations were generally consistent with the hypothesis. The desire for affiliation was unexpectedly high in those highly arousing situations that elicited either a submissive or an unpleasant feeling. These exceptions were interpreted in terms of Schachter's (1959) analysis of affiliation: Desire to affiliate increases in stressful (arousing, unpleasant, and submission-eliciting) situations. Related results from the individual differences section of this chapter, reported in Figure 8.11, showed that females' desire for affiliation increased with the arousing quality of a setting, whereas males' desire for affiliation was not significantly affected. Since females are characteristically more submissive than males, it follows that a combination of high arousal (elicited by the situation) and submissive feelings (elicited by the situation in Figure 8.1 and associated with a sex difference in Figure 8.11) leads to a heightened desire for affiliation.

The findings summarized in the preceding paragraph suggested other determiners for affiliation in addition to those hypothesized for the study of the generic class of approach-avoidance behaviors. It is therefore not surprising that the factor analytic findings have shown desire for affiliation to be a somewhat independent factor of approach-avoidance relative to the desires to stay, explore, and work in a setting.

Another exception to the inverted-U-shaped hypothesis was that there was an unexpectedly high preference for highly arousing situations that also elicited a dominant feeling. In contrast, the expected low level of preference was obtained for highly arousing but submission-eliciting situations (Figure 8.7). Even though there is some intuitive appeal to these findings, no similar effect has been identified in other research, and thus it is difficult to interpret this result. The results of Figure 8.7 do, however, suggest that a person should be able to tolerate (or is likely to desire) higher information rates when he is in his own territory rather than in another's.

Additional results were independent of the proposed hypotheses. For instance, the desire to work attained a maximum value for the higher information rate work settings when the place of work was more pleasant (Figure 8.5). Further differentiation of this finding was reported in Figure 8.6, which showed that this effect was true only for pleasant and submission-eliciting work situations. In other words, for most employees (who have submissive roles), performance is not hindered because of excessive levels of information rate from the job and the situation, provided the situation is pleasant. A similar result was reported for desire to explore, which was maximized at a higher level of information rate when the situation was more pleasant (Figure 8.8).

These findings for work and exploration provide a novel perspective for the reexamination of one of the earlier concerns of industrial psychology, the identification of environmental conditions that enhance work performance. It is seen that the pleasantness of a work setting is in itself of considerable appeal to the workers and their motivation to perform. In addition, the more pleasant work settings can particularly help to increase the motivation to perform complex tasks because the optimum information rate is higher for more pleasant situations.

Additional results, which were not hypothesized, showed that there was a significant drop in both the desire for affiliation and for exploration in unpleasant situations that also elicited a more dominant feeling (Figures 8.3, 8.10). No corresponding effect of dominance was noted in the pleasant situations. This pair of findings is of interest for studies of territoriality. Thus, these results suggest that a person avoids affiliation and exploration in his own territory (dominance-eliciting situation) when it is unpleasant. When his territory is a pleasant one or he is in another's territory, there is no such extreme avoidance of affiliation and exploration.

The third section of this chapter provided extensive data on how approach-avoidance behaviors and state emotions were affected by interactions of personality traits and the pleasure, arousal, and dominance-eliciting qualities of situations. We focused primarily on the interactions involving traits, since the main effects relating emotional states to traits were similar to those already reported in Chapter 3.

The results for sex differences showed that the desire for affiliation of females increased directly with the arousing quality of the environment, whereas that of males was not affected (Figure 8.11). The same results also showed that females' desire for affiliation was significantly lower than that of males in the low and moderately low arousing situations. Females, relative to males, expressed a significantly lower desire to explore situations that elicited submissive feelings (Figure 8.18) and to explore situations that were unpleasant (Figure 8.19). Also, females had less desire than males to stay in highly arousing and dominance-eliciting situations.

The results generally showed that the approach-avoidance reactions of females were affected to a greater degree than those of males by the variations in the pleasant and arousing qualities of situations. Support for these sex differences was provided in Table 3.4 and in Figures 8.24 and 8.25, which showed that the state arousal of females relative to that of males was influenced to a greater degree by variations in the arousing quality of environments. In addition, state dominance of females varied to a greater degree than that of males as a function of the dominance-eliciting quality of situations (Figure 8.31). The only exception to the observed pattern was that females reported smaller fluctuations in state dominance as a function of pleasantness of situations (Figure 8.30).

These results for sex differences showed that the emotional impact of environments was greater for females than for males. Further corroboration for this conclusion was obtained by Mehrabian and Epstein (1972), whose female subjects, relative to the male subjects, scored significantly higher on a measure of emotional empathy. Their measure of emotional empathy had been constructed to assess emotional sensitivity to both pleasant and unpleasant interpersonal cues. Findings from these various sources have consistently shown that females have greater emotional reactivity than males to the same situation and that, as a consequence, their approach-avoidance reactions are affected to a greater degree by the emotion-arousing qualities of situations.

The results for trait anxiety showed that in the pleasant situations high-anxiety persons were less desirous of affiliation than low-anxiety persons (Figure 8.12). Also, in pleasant situations the more anxious persons' desire to solve problems declined more rapidly with the arousing quality of the work settings (Figure 8.14). In dominance-eliciting situations, more anxious subjects showed a less rapidly increasing preference for more arousing settings

(Figure 8.16). In unpleasant situations, more anxious subjects felt more displeasure (Figure 8.21).

The results for neuroticism were similar to those for trait anxiety and showed an attenuation of approach behaviors for more neurotic persons. More neurotic persons showed a lower desire to affiliate in pleasant situations (Figure 8.13). Their desire to work was discouraged to a greater extent by increases in the arousing quality of unpleasant work settings (Figure 8.15). They felt more displeasure in unpleasant situations (Figure 8.22). And finally, their state arousal was affected to a greater degree by variations in the arousing quality of situations (Figure 8.26).

The combined results for trait anxiety and neuroticism showed that persons who are more psychologically disturbed are affected to a greater extent by the unpleasant and arousing qualities of the environments in which they function. They feel more displeasure in unpleasant situations and are also more aroused in the more arousing situations. Their heightened emotional reactivity to these environmental qualities tends to discourage their approach behaviors. They desire less affiliation in pleasant situations and have less preference for, and less desire to work in, the more arousing situations.

The results for extroversion showed that introverts had an especially high preference for pleasant, but submission-eliciting, situations; however, extroverts did not seek to avoid such situations (Figure 8.17). Also, the state arousal of extroverts varied more than that of introverts as a function of variations in the arousing quality of environments (Figure 8.27).

The results for arousal-seeking tendency provided strong validation for the measure of Appendix C. Whereas low-arousal seekers' desire to stay in a situation decreased, that of high-arousal seekers increased as the arousing quality of environments increased (Figure 8.20). Consistent with these results, a similar reversal of state pleasure was observed: High-arousal seekers felt more pleasure in more arousing settings and low-arousal seekers felt less pleasure (Figure 8.23). State arousal of the higher-arousal seekers increased to a larger degree as a function of increases in the arousing quality of the environment (Figure 8.28). This result provides direct confirmation for the relationship between arousal-seeking tendency and state arousal hypothesized in Chapter 3. Finally, the state arousal of more affiliative persons, as of high-arousal seekers, was influenced to a greater degree by variations in the arousing quality of environments (Figure 8.29).

Many of the interactions involving the personality traits were also consistent in providing support for the proposed personality-emotional sensitivity hypothesis. According to this hypothesis, each personality attribute is associated with certain heightened emotional sensitivities, and situations that generally elicit a certain emotion are likely to have the strongest effect on persons who possess a related emotional sensitivity. The results, summarized in Figures 8.24 and 8.25 for sex differences, in Figures 8.21 for trait anxiety, in Figures 8.22 and 8.26 for neuroticism, in Figure 8.27 for extroversion, in Figure 8.28 for arousal-seeking tendency, and in Figure 8.29 for affiliative tendency, all consistently support that hypothesis. Although there was an absence of a number of additional interactive effects that would have been predicted from the personality-emotional sensitivity hypothesis, nevertheless, in all cases where significant results were obtained, the results were consistent with this hypothesis.

It is important to note that the personality-emotional sensitivity hypothesis is a nontrivial one in the sense that alternative outcomes are possible. For instance, high-anxiety persons could show the same decrement in state pleasure relative to low-anxiety persons across situations differing in pleasantness. Further, this hypothesis was proposed when extroversion did not relate significantly to trait arousal in one of the two relevant equations of Table 3.4. Without the hypothesis, there would have been little motivation to explore the relative state arousal levels of extroverts and introverts as a function of the arousing quality of situations. Thus, the hypothesis not only led to the identification of the latter phenomena but also had considerable heuristic value for discovering related phenomena for other personality traits.

Notes

1. It is important to note that the correlations on the basis of which these regression equations were computed employed within-subject and between-subject data, but the degrees of freedom that were used in the assessment of significance levels were based on the assumption that the observations were independent. In general, such an assumption is not valid, since within-subject variance is often smaller than between-subject variance, and the assumption would normally lead to an inflated estimate of significance. However, for the data presented in this chapter, specific comparisons of within-subject and between-subject variance for each dependent measure showed that within-subject variance was *larger* than between-subject variance. As a consequence, our estimates of significance tend to be conservative. The within-subject variance was greater than between-subject variance in the data of this and the next two experiments because a

subject's reading of different situations tended to enhance his discrimination of his reactions to the differences in the situations.

2. Since P also interacted with A in this equation, one assumption of the analysis of covariance was violated. However, we proceeded with the use of this method since the confounding effects of P shown in Table 8.7 were too large to be ignored.

9 Conclusions

The definition of environmental psychology has been especially difficult because, if it is viewed as the study of human reactions to environments, then there is the difficulty of distinguishing it from the general stimulus-response approach to psychology itself. Thus, there is a temptation to attempt to define the field in terms of a specific list of problem areas (i.e., use an omnibus definition) or to define the field implicitly by identifying it with a certain method (e.g., Barker, 1960; 1965). Such definitions are inadequate. A survey or an omnibus definition cannot on an *a priori* basis exhaustively delineate the potential issues that will be the subject of a field of study. For instance, since there is no general principle relating the items included in such a definition, there is no criterion for including or excluding additional items from that list. As for the second approach, an experimental method is only an instrument to be used for answering a question and thus logically cannot be the basis for developing the questions or hypotheses that would help define an area of investigation.

Preoccupation with defining environmental psychology is only part of the more general concern with the absence of a theory for this field. Without a theory, it is not possible to identify general concepts and measures that can be the basis for the analysis and description of the phenomena in a field; as a consequence, it is difficult to develop and test hypotheses that would relate these concepts. As was evident from the reviews, in the preceding chapters, of various phases of research in environmental psychology, the absence of general concepts and hypotheses has been a deterrent to efficient research. Investigators frequently used new and varied measures for their studies that were usually particular to their experimental needs. Thus, because of the absence of information on the relationships among the large variety of measures, it was difficult to extract generalizations from the work of different investigators. Also, differentiated hypotheses were not available for characterizing the interactions among stimulus variables in determining human emotions and approach-avoidance reactions. As a consequence, experimental studies failed to measure or control the effects of certain independent variables that, although of no interest to a particular study, should have been controlled to allow an adequate test of its hypothesis.

In the present approach, the problem of the absence of a definition for environmental psychology was resolved by providing a theory for it. As reviews of the available literature and reports of our own findings hopefully showed, the availability of a theory such as this one helps to delineate the phenomena that are the primary focuses of that theory. A similar approach to the definition of a field of study was advanced by Kelly (1955) in terms of his concept of "range of convenience of a theory." This range of convenience can correspond to any one of a series of larger (and more inclusive) sets of phenomena, which defines that field. The idea, however, is that the most convenient focuses of the theory (and implied defining limits of the corresponding field) are the smaller sets of phenomena that are most readily characterized with the concepts and measures of the theory. In the present theory, the phenomena corresponding to these less inclusive sets are the emotional and approach-avoidance reactions of persons to any combination of physical and/or interpersonal stimuli. The specific measures that were developed for assessing emotional and approach-avoidance reactions helped to further delineate this more inclusive set of phenomena.

However, the development of the specific measures reported in this volume was motivated by even more important considerations than their role in defining the field. To test the validity of the hypotheses of a theory and to modify them, an essential step is to define clearly and measure its major concepts (Mehrabian, 1968). As a consequence, one major objective in the present volume was to develop a rationale for the selection of concepts, review available measures in the literature, and extract the most useful aspects of available work to provide measures of general applicability. The end result of these efforts is the set of measures reported in some tables and the appendixes of this volume.

In the search for major dependent variables for studies of environmental psychology, the general idea of approach-avoidance was initially and tentatively used as the basic dependent measure in Chapter 6. It included several specific behaviors such as physical approach, exploration, nonverbal indexes of interest, verbal expressions of preference, level of performance at work, and the desire to affiliate with others. The next step was to define and examine the relationships among the various behaviors subsumed in this category. Accordingly, verbal questionnaire measures of approach-avoidance were developed and investigated in the first part of Chapter 8. The assumed relations among the various approach-avoidance behaviors were confirmed in that significant positive correlations were obtained among measures of expressed desire to affiliate in a situation, general preference for it as indexed by desire to explore it, stay there, seek it rather than avoid it, and work in it. It was also shown that the desire to affiliate in a situation was most distinct from the remaining measures. In particular, for the measures of Appendix E, the first three indexes of desire to stay, explore, and work in a situation were interrelated and defined one factor, whereas desire to affiliate defined a second factor. Additional findings showed that some determinants of desire for affiliation were quite distinct from those generally hypothesized for approach-avoidance behavior. Examination of the specific results for each of the first three indexes in Appendix E also showed that it is helpful to distinguish among them when attempting to obtain precise estimates of the ways in which these behaviors are differentially affected in different situations. However, the factor-analytic results suggested that when the distinction between desire to stay, explore, and work in a situation is not critical, a composite of these three indexes can serve as a comprehensive measure of approach-avoidance.

Appendix B, in turn, provides measures for the major intervening variables of the proposed theory. It consists of a series of semantic differential scales that can be used to measure emotional reactions to any environment, whether that environment is described verbally (as in the situations of Appendix A) or shown to subjects with the use of photographs, video recordings, movies, or face-to-face confrontations. The rationale for the selection of pleasure, arousal, and dominance as three basic human emotional reactions was reviewed in Chapter 2. The measures of Appendix B were obtained from three experiments where emotional reactions to a diversity of settings were factor analyzed. These measures can be used to assess state emotions by instructing the subject to report his particular emotional reactions at a given time to a given situation. With a second set of instructions, the same measures can be used by a subject to describe his trait emotions, namely his characteristic levels of pleasure, arousal, and dominance.

A person's approach-avoidance responses to a situation are determined not only by the emotional responses that the situation typically elicits but also by the emotions with which he enters that situation. It is therefore important to be able to specify the emotional correlates of various personality attributes. Thus, the measures of trait emotions given in Appendix B are useful in studying individual differences in approach-avoidance to different environments.

These measures provide a parsimonious means of characterizing personality variables as differences in individual predispositions to react with certain emotions. The series of regression equations of Table 3.4 exemplify this particular approach to personality measurement. Each equation specifies the characteristic emotional correlates of each of the personality attributes that have been of concern in environmental psychology. The personality measures described in this way were various measures of trait anxiety and measures of arousal-seeking tendency, neuroticism, extroversion, affiliative tendency, sensitivity to rejection, and sex.

The measure of arousal-seeking tendency was of special significance, since individual differences in trait arousal or arousal-seeking tendency can interact with information rate from a setting in determining approach-avoidance responses to it. As a consequence, an effort was made to develop a comprehensive measure of arousal-seeking tendency. A combination of items from available verbal questionnaire measures constituted an initial 312-item questionnaire. Through a series of three successive factor-analytic and validating experiments reported in Chapter 3, the forty-item questionnaire measure given in Appendix C was obtained. This measure consists of a set of positively intercorrelated factors, each of which measures a slightly different aspect of arousal-seeking tendency. Thus, the measure has considerably more generality than would have been possible if the item analyses had focused solely on maximizing the homogeneity of that scale. Despite its generality, the measure was found to have very satisfactory internal reliability (homogeneity) and test-retest reliability.

The development of measures for the description of the environments themselves, as distinct from behavioral responses to the environments, presented many problems. Some of the proposed alternatives in earlier research were: (1) the everyday language descriptors, such as "chair" and "room," (2) the terms used in the physical sciences, such as "temperature," "distance," and "altitude," and (3) the variables of perception studies, which are defined in terms of sense modalities, such as sound and odor. These approaches provided neither a parsimonious list of descriptors nor a useful method for concisely relating environments to the behaviors that characteristically occur in them.

In developing our alternative list of categories for describing environments, it was important to recognize that in traditional psychological research, stimulus categories are frequently distinguished on the basis of different reactions to them. Notable examples of this approach to the characterization of stimuli are studies of perception in which different stimuli (e.g., visual, auditory, kinesthetic, and tactual) are distinguished simply on the basis of their differential impact on the various sense organs. Other approaches to stimulus description are illustrated by concepts such as "reinforcing" or "stressful," which are response-defined. In the work of Osgood, Suci, and Tannenbaum (1957), and related studies summarized in Snider and Osgood (1969), stimulus categories are distinguished in terms of three basic response factors of evaluation, potency, and activity.

In the present approach, the stimulus categories were also response-defined. Since the three basic emotional factors of pleasure, arousal, and dominance were identified as providing a comprehensive classification base, these categories were used to describe the various environments of the studies in Chapter 8. Thus, in this case, stimuli were distinguished on the basis of their differential impacts on human feelings. The mean level of pleasure elicited from a representative sample of people in an environment defined its "pleasantness." The mean level of arousal elicited in an environment defined its "arousing quality." A similar average dominance response defined a situation's "dominance-eliciting quality." These emotion-defined characterizations of environments provide a parsimonious means to describe and measure differences among situations.

Given the proposed set of categories for describing environments, Chapter 4 reviewed the existing literature to abstract the major consistent relations that have been identified between various stimulus dimensions (e.g., hue, sound intensity, temperature) and each of the three basic emotion factors. Also, Table 4.1 provided the results of a factor analysis of verbal environmental descriptors (e.g., hot-cold, ordinary-distinctive, large-small). The regression equations of Table 4.4 expressed each of the obtained nine factors in terms of pleasure, arousal, and dominance. Thus, when differences in the physical attributes of situations are either experimentally measured or verbally described along one- or two-stimulus dimensions, the review and experimental data of Chapter 4 make it possible to characterize differences in the pleasure- (P), arousal- (A), and dominance-eliciting (D) qualities of the situations.

It was recognized, however, that most of the earlier studies reviewed in

Chapter 4 dealt with single-stimulus dimensions and that everyday environments usually consist of elaborate combinations of stimuli in various sense modalities. It was important therefore to identify an attribute of physical environments that would be useful for characterizing the relationships among stimulus dimensions and that would also relate to the emotional categories. The review of available literature in Chapter 5 drew on information theory to specify one such attribute—information rate. This concept was used to characterize variations in simplicity-complexity of stimulation within and across sense modalities, including temporal variations. It thus helped to describe and interrelate a large number of familiar concepts used in studies of environmental psychology (e.g., scale, complexity, novelty, good form, density, patterning, and crowding). Final sections of Chapter 5 were devoted to a review of the literature that employed measures relating to this concept and culminated in (1) the measure of information rate given in Appendix D and (2) a strong confirmation of the hypothesized relation between information rate and arousal in the following form:

Total information rate (Appendix D) = 0.57 arousal state.

The concept of information rate is also of considerable importance in evaluating the significance of the results that are obtained with particular experimental methods. Craik (1970a) provided a thorough discussion of methodologies in environmental psychology. He described methods such as actual confrontation with a specific physical environment, video recordings of the setting taken by someone moving through various parts of it, slides, and verbal descriptions. This series of methods presents a monotonic decrease in the immediacy of, and the information rate from, the environment being studied. Such differences in information rate (and correlated differences in arousal levels that are elicited from subjects) are due to different methods and must be taken into account in interpreting (possibly inconsistent) findings from different experiments.

To summarize, wherever possible, the relevant literature was examined, its implications for measurement were considered, and measures were developed. The proposed measures are general enough to be applied in the many different contexts of research that were considered in developing them; moreover, they can also be used in related areas of research that are as yet unexplored.

The survey of the available literature in Chapters 6 and 7 for developing hypotheses among the measures of Appendix E presented numerous difficulties. Differences in methods and measurement procedures (e.g., the diversity of dependent and independent variables used and the lack of comparability of measures across experiments) and absence of controls for certain critical variables had led to frequently contradictory results that were difficult to reconcile. Nevertheless, the proposed framework facilitated the identification, in Chapter 6, of some consistent patterns among the data on approach-avoidance responses to physical environments.

As already noted, affiliative behavior, which is the approach response to interpersonal stimuli, is somewhat independent of the remaining aspects of approach-avoidance behavior. Thus, it was treated separately in Chapter 7, where the significance of others as part of the environment was of central concern. The consideration of this literature led to the development of some simple, but general, hypotheses for describing the combined effects of physical and interpersonal cues on social interaction. For instance, the spatial organization of persons, as determined by building and urban design and even interior design, has a considerable influence on interpersonal exchanges. Findings showed that environments that facilitate immediacy and contacts among their residents (although allowing privacy when this is desired) are conducive to decreased prejudicial attitudes and increased interpersonal approach behaviors (i.e., increased affiliation, cooperation, liking, and friendship).

The hypotheses that were developed from a review of the determinants of approach-avoidance behavior in Chapters 6 and 7 were tested directly in a series of three experiments reported in Chapter 8. These experiments consistently confirmed the first hypothesis, which asserted a direct correlation between approach-avoidance behaviors and the pleasantness of environments. They also provided support for the inverted-U-shaped relationship between approach-avoidance and arousing quality (information rate) of situations. The majority of hypotheses regarding the interactive effects of personality measures were also confirmed. However, a number of unexpected, though consistent, results were obtained that have interesting pragmatic implications. A detailed summary of these findings of Chapter 8 has been provided in the final section of that chapter and will not be repeated here.

One conclusion from our own findings and reviews of available studies is that too much emphasis has been placed on the pleasant-unpleasant aspects of environments. There is little available work relating to dominance and, for instance, its relation to territorial behavior (e.g., Mehrabian, 1971a). Also, the implications of some findings involving arousal have been neglected. For instance, the prevalent use of alcohol and especially the rapidly increasing use of other tranquilizing drugs in Western cultures can be understood partially as owing to increases in the variability and novelty of modern urban environments. Toffler's (1970) analyses of the developmental trends in human civilization showed that almost every aspect of human life is changing at an accelerating rate. Examples of this change include population growth, the increasing speeds at which man is capable of traveling, higher rates of new discoveries, and the increased production of mass communication materials (e.g., televised messages, magazines, books). Thus, humans today are being inundated with an accelerated increase in information rate.

Present-day environments, then, tend to be excessively arousing and are certainly more arousing than the environments of a few decades ago. This is especially the case in urban areas where a high concentration of varied physical and social stimuli constantly impinge on the individual. City odors, chemicals, noises, billboards, lights, and crowding (which forces excessive exposure to strangers) are far in excess of those found in the more natural and less congested rural areas.

This accelerating rate of informational input is reminiscent of the stressful stimuli (including toxins, difficult and prolonged work) that according to Selye (1956) trigger the General Adaptation Syndrome. The syndrome starts with physiological arousal and a concomitant feeling of displeasure (i.e., anxiety), leads to depression, various diseases of adaptation (e.g., psychosomatic illnesses) and finally fatigue and exhaustion. One reason why people resort to drugs, then, is their attempt to control intolerable levels of arousal. Also, understandably, those residing in congested urban areas express unrelenting desires to visit simple and rural settings such as the national parks and to live in isolated suburbs, which tend to be less congested and polluted than the city centers.

Besides the psychological and physical harm that is caused by the persistent, highly arousing quality of congested urban environments, there is also a subtle generalization of the negative effect from the high-arousal state to social interactions, with associated detrimental effects in work settings.

Recent findings have clearly substantiated the earlier results of Calhoun (1962b) with rats. These findings, reviewed in Chapter 7 and supported by additional new evidence bearing on hostility, showed that persons in crowded and unpleasant places indiscriminantly generalize the negative feelings from the settings to the others who are present. Such findings are of considerable social importance because they partly explain the violent excesses in today's urban centers and particularly in the lower socioeconomic areas. Higher rates of violence in these areas are partly due to the financial limitations of the residents that force them to remain in these unpleasant and crowded settings.

A brief review was also included on the significance of experiments that have demonstrated the synchronous quality of internal-behavioral and external rhythms. This relationship suggests mechanisms that directly relate arousal to information rate from the environment. In this context, it is not surprising that the tempo of work and even recreational activity in urban settings far exceeds that in rural environments. The many diverse sources of arousal in the environment, and particularly their combined effects, which are much stronger than the individual components taken singly, play an important role in increasing the general tempo of living. Kelley (1967) showed that people are more likely to attribute the changes in their behaviors to themselves than to external stimuli. It is thus easy to overlook these strong environmental factors in urban centers and their possible future dangers.

Appendix A
A Varied Set of Verbally Described Situations*

1. (+2.12, +0.54, –0.04)
You are sitting on the top of a huge rock that rises up out of a sandy beach. The waves are loudly crashing below you, and you are watching them from far above. Seagulls are swimming in the water below and hopping along the sand. Other people are exploring the smaller rocks down on the beach.

2. (+1.70, +0.46, –0.36)
You are sitting on a deserted beach in the late afternoon. The water is dark blue, and the waves are crashing loudly. The whole beach is hidden completely from the outside by the sand dunes behind it.

3. (–0.04, +0.55, –0.37)
You are attending a reception in a large room in a hotel. There is a long table down one side of the room. On it are hors d'oeuvres and champagne glasses. Many of the guests have arrived and are milling about. Several white-coated waiters are in attendance.

4. (+1.57, –0.39, –0.17)
You are camping by yourself in the woods and are lying in a sleeping bag in the early morning just before dawn. It is dark all around, and everything is still. The ground is slightly damp.

5. (–1.20, +2.40, –0.90)
From a nearby hill you can see a raging brush fire in progress. Clouds of black smoke billow up until the sky is darkened. The flames are a contrastingly bright red, and you can hear them crackling. They seem to be spreading quickly, and the brisk wind helps them to leap from one spot to another. The sound of sirens can be heard in the distance.

6. (–1.48, +0.62, –0.47)
You are looking at the blackened remains of a burned-out house. There are only a few parts of walls standing, and the roof is gone. Evidently most of the rubble has been cleared away, for there is no trace of anything left inside. Everything is a dull charred color.

*The three consecutive numbers preceding the description of each situation refer to normalized values of elicited pleasure, arousal, and dominance, respectively.

7. (−1.46, +1.12, −0.30)

You are sitting in your own room, studying. There are several other people there, and music is playing on the stereo. The whole room is humming with the vibration. There is also some talking and shouting going on, and the room is filled with cigarette smoke.

8. (+2.48, +2.26, +1.22)

You are water-skiing behind a speedboat on a mountain lake. As you go by, you watch the sun glinting on the water and look at the thickly wooded shore of the lake as it quickly passes. There are only a few other boats out, and they are down near the other shore of the lake. The water is smooth and glassy, and the air is fairly warm with a slight breeze.

9. (+0.58, −1.20, +0.18)

You have been on a trip and are sitting alone in your camper late at night in a roadside rest stop.

10. (+0.97, +2.82, −1.22)

You are taking a ride on a roller coaster. First it moves up a high hill, then comes speeding down, and makes a series of sharp turns during the descent. All around are brightly colored booths and other rides decorated with flashing lights. Carnival music is playing in the background as the roller coaster carries its screaming passengers along the winding course.

11. (+1.19, −0.35, −0.36)

You have been sitting beneath a tall tree in the middle of a heavily wooded area. There is nothing but trees all around, and a heavy blanket of fallen leaves is covering the ground. It is late in the afternoon and kind of quiet. It is getting very cold.

12. (−1.51, +0.16, −0.72)

You are in the mountains and are looking down over the Los Angeles basin. You see the whole area covered by a thick blanket of brown haze. It is difficult to make out any specific details of the city far below you. In the other direction giant mountains tower above you.

13. (+0.17, +1.11, −0.68)

It is a blazing July day. A powerful dry wind from the steppes is driving clouds of black dust and pressed hay across the field in which you are standing. The dust is swirling all around, the sky is an unusual metallic hue, and the sunset is blood red.

14. (+0.57, −1.84, +0.13)

Imagine yourself sitting alone in your own back yard on a quiet day when there isn't much of anything going on.

15. (+1.91, −0.62, −0.14)

You are sitting in a small boat out on the ocean beyond the waves. The water is smooth and clear and quiet. White clouds are moving by very slowly overhead, and the air is still. The sun beats down very intensely.

16. (+1.07, +0.50, −0.71)

You are standing right under a land formation in a dry, desertlike area. It is a barren, elliptical mound that rises high in the air. It has a strange appearance: Its top plateau is quite flat, as if a giant hand had smoothed it down; and the sides of the mound are perfect earthen slopes, each making an angle of forty-five degrees with the ground, as if the same hand had put out a finger to round off the edges. It is backed up by hills and by the rugged mountains behind them.

17. (−0.32, −1.22, −0.21)

You are sitting alone and reading in one of the cubicles in a library. It is about five by six feet in size, and the walls are made of gray metal. It is quiet except for the occasional muffled sound of distant footsteps. The cubicle is in a remote corner of the library and is almost completely closed off from the outside.

18. (−0.15, +1.92, −1.05)

You are on a ship at sea during a rainstorm. The waves have become fairly high and are causing the ship to rock more than it usually does, but not dangerously. The wind is howling around the deck, and the rain is beating down hard.

19. (−1.12, +0.85, −0.22)
You are driving a new and very fast sportscar. It is a clear sunny day, and the top is down. The street you are driving on is very crowded with cars moving in the same direction, and the traffic is moving slowly.

20. (+2.06, −1.22, −0.51)
You are lying on the grass in a botanical garden, with hardly any people around. The sunlight is filtering down through the trees, but it is mainly shady all around you.

21. (+1.61, −0.33, −0.74)
It has been a clear day on the desert, and now you are watching the sun settle down near the horizon. The sky is streaked with color, and the few clouds in the west have a rosy glow. Everything is silent and still, and there is no one else around.

22. (−1.39, −1.40, −0.61)
You are sitting alone in the waiting room of a business office. The walls are a pale beige color, and the desk and chairs are a slightly darker tan. The carpeting also is a tan color. There are no windows; the indirect lighting comes from fluorescent lights on the ceiling. There are a few pictures on the walls, framed in brown wood, depicting quiet, pastoral scenes.

23. (−1.15, +0.14, −0.15)
You are visiting the county fair and are standing in the building where the pigs are displayed. The building is filled with long rows of pens. The air is filled with the squealing and grunting of the animals. There is also a definite farmlike odor in the air. It is hot and there are naturally quite a number of flies around.

24. (+0.19, +0.44, −0.72)
You have just entered a formal living room and are looking around. There are massive red sofas covered in red damask, ranged against the walls. The window curtains are also heavy red damask. In each corner is a tall gilt candelabrum with eight flaming candles, besides those in silver sconces on the table. These form moving shadows on the walls. Tapestries cover almost all the walls and add to the reddish glow of the room.

25. (+1.26, +1.83, –0.01)
You are in a fairly large room with a few other people listening to a rock band practicing. The beat is driving, and the music is loud, featuring an emphatic lead vocal. Every part is being performed with abandon, and the musicians seem completely absorbed in their playing.

26. (+0.92, –0.56, –0.28)
It is evening, and you are sitting at a window, looking out over the lights of the city. It is a misty, cold night, and everything looks small and far away.

27. (+2.11, +1.34, –0.10)
You are standing at the base of a high waterfall. The water is loudly crashing down and foaming into a large pool at the bottom. Everything is surrounded by heavy green foliage and large damp moss-covered rocks. The water flows away into a brook with a tinkling sound.

28. (+1.01, –1.09, –0.15)
You are the passenger in a car, out for an afternoon drive. The land around is gently hilly and covered with pasture marked by an occasional tree. A few cows are out eating the grass, but otherwise the scene is fairly unchanging. The road can be seen stretching on and on for miles.

29. (–0.47, +0.69, –0.67)
It is pouring rain, and you have been walking across a field on your way somewhere. The ground has completely turned to mud, and it is very soft and slippery. The sky is a dark gray, and the only sound is the constant drumming of the rain.

30. (+0.34, –0.95, –0.17)
Try to picture yourself sitting and studying in the place where you study most of the time. Although it is very cold outside, it is warm here inside.

31. (+2.32, +0.54, –0.05)
You have stopped your car by the side of a country road near an old wooden fence. You can see a beautiful black mare nursing her little colt, who stands on delicate legs.

32. (+1.04, +1.72, +0.64)
You are dancing in an old country barn. A live group is playing fast and loud. A lot of laughing and screaming can be heard. The place is dark, but a strobe light randomly flashes and brightens small sections. The people around you are in colorful bright clothes. Their body odors are sometimes noticeable along with the smell of cigarettes and good food.

33. (−0.69, +0.84, −0.03)
You are walking home from work on a blistery cold day. The freezing wind stings your face and penetrates your clothes. You only have one more block to go. Little children are shouting and running around you.

34. (−1.88, +0.45, +0.01)
You have just walked into your apartment. Piles of trash and dirty dishes stare at you. Music is playing and the TV going.

35. (−1.22, +1.73, −0.86)
You are walking on a barren country road when suddenly the rain pours down. There is no shelter in sight.

36. (−1.11, −0.77, +0.06)
You are in your office alone. There are piles of books and paper lying around that you have been working on all day. Other than your equipment (telephone, typewriter, etc.), the room is almost barren.

37. (+0.46, +1.54, −0.22)
You are with a scientific expedition in the Amazon jungle. Thick vines climb into the tall trees. The lush vegetation is so tall and thick you must fight for every step. Occasionally you glimpse the towering mountains.in the distance. It is warm, and the wild birds chirp merrily.

38. (+0.02, +1.10, +0.37)
You have just plunged into a cool pool at a public park on an extremely hot summer day. The pool is crowded. Many of the people around you are playing with a large rubber beach ball. The ball hits your head and bounces off a couple of times.

39. (−0.75, +1.52, +0.84)
You are teaching in a children's day care center. All the boys are running, hitting each other, and screaming; a little girl sits a few feet away from them, banging on a drum.

40. (+0.63, −1.94, −0.15)
You are lying in your bed in the afternoon. The television and the stereo are silent. Your books and sporting equipment sit on a desk.

41. (−0.53, −0.40, −0.80)
You are the only passenger in a big, old bus. The bus moves slowly because of the driving snow. You see nothing out the window but white. The seat is hard and the bus chilly.

42. (−1.03, +1.29, +0.72)
You are in your kitchen—a hot, steamy, and smelly room. You have things cooking on the stove. Little children are around you, playing and shouting for your attention.

43. (−1.42, −0.30, −0.36)
You are in the rest room of an old building. You are sitting in a small, barren, wooden stall. There is a slightly unpleasant odor.

44. (+1.85, +1.68, +0.03)
You are sitting in a new, gigantic, beautiful concert hall, watching and listening to fantastic music. The music is loud, the rhythms are driving and sensuous, but the people around you are quiet and still.

45. (+2.31, −1.73, −0.16)
You are quietly floating in a pool of water. There is nothing in sight, and all is silent. The water temperature is such that you can't feel it.

46. (−0.99, −0.61, −0.39)
You are alone in your own apartment. You have just finished eating a large meal, and the dirty dishes are piled up. At another table is spread out your work—some papers and books. Both the television and the stereo are on in the other room.

47. (−0.17, −1.76, −0.44)
It is an evening during a hot spell—the heat has yet to subside. You are
lying on the couch in your living room. It is absolutely dark and quiet.

48. (−1.02, −0.08, −0.47)
You are sitting in a narrow alley. The buildings on either side tower above
you. There is some litter and pieces of large, old machinery near you.

49. (−1.36, −0.17, −0.64)
You are walking through a soap-manufacturing factory on a hot day. The
machines around you are crackling and sputtering, emitting a pungent odor.

50. (+0.44, −0.23, +0.03)
You are sitting on a small wooden bench in a cold, deserted classroom. You
had attended first grade here. You have been sitting here for a few hours.

51. (−1.82, −0.68, −0.07)
You are in a room—cold, barren, and empty, except for a large steel cage of
rats. You are taking notes on their behavior and have been doing this all
day. The urine smell is very strong.

52. (−0.69, +0.06, −0.38)
You are walking through a series of long corridors. No one else is in sight.
Every ten yards there is a closed door with a small name plaque on it.

53. (−0.95, −1.56, −0.20)
You are in the back of a concert hall. The lights are very dim. The music
is slow, faint, and unappealing. No one is sitting near you.

54. (+0.46, +0.42, −0.13)
For the first time, you are in a lobby of an old fashionable hotel. It is large
and ornate, full of antique furnishings. There are expensive shops and uni-
formed bellboys. Most guests are elderly and very well-dressed.

55. (−2.19, −1.21, −1.14)
You are at the funeral of a distant relative. It takes place at the funeral
home, and everyone is dressed in dark colors. The minister's voice drones

on in the service. The casket up in front is the only decoration in the otherwise plain room.

56. (+1.70, +0.32, +1.54)
You are driving home in a car on the freeway. It is not crowded at all, and
there is no trouble in moving along.

57. (+0.93, +0.45, +0.63)
You are shopping for the first time in a supermarket you have never been
inside before. All around are brightly colored packages and signs in red
letters telling the specials of the day. The fruit and vegetable corner is very
colorful with its mounds of oranges, grapefruit, apples, lettuce, carrots,
and many other items. There are no other people around.

58. (+2.32, +1.91, +1.51)
You are on a winding country road, riding a powerful motorcycle in the
early morning hours. The sun is just coming up over the horizon, and there
is almost no other traffic.

59. (+1.16, −1.05, +0.90)
Imagine sitting by yourself in your own room, when it is quiet.

60. (−1.80, +1.31, −0.92)
While going down the freeway you must pass a wreck that has recently occurred. The dividing fence is twisted and broken, and the bodies of two
crumpled cars with broken windshields are smashed up against it. The traffic
is moving slowly by and speeding up markedly after passing the spot.

61. (+1.59, −0.52, +0.82)
It's the end of a long day, and you've just finished repainting your apartment. All the furniture is covered with white canvas, and you've been
painting the whole place a solid off-white.

62. (+2.39, −0.46, +0.72)
You are sitting in your clean kitchen. The pie in the oven smells very good.

63. (−1.79, −0.70, −1.02)

You are lying on a large, soft cot, the only piece of furniture in a small room (about six feet by six feet). There is no window, just a wooden door and gray walls. The only light comes from a dim bare light bulb in the ceiling.

64. (+1.83, +0.13, +1.34)

You are walking around your vegetable garden in which rows of carrots, tomatoes, cabbage, and onions grow. A flock of birds fly over your head in a neat formation.

65. (+1.71, +2.95, +2.54)

You are a champion auto racer at the Indianapolis 500 (where you go round and round the course). The competition is right up with you. The heat is very intense, and so are the gas fumes. You watch the dials and the road very carefully.

Appendix B
Semantic Differential Measures of Emotional State or Characteristic (Trait) Emotions

Instructions to Subjects

When these scales are used as measures of EMOTIONAL STATE in a particular setting, the instructions are as follows:

Take about two minutes to really get into the mood of the situation; then rate your feelings in the situation with the adjective pairs below. Some of the pairs might seem unusual, but you'll probably feel more one way than the other. So, for each pair, put a check mark (Example: - - - -:- - - -:- -✓- -:- - - -) close to the adjective which you believe to describe your feelings better. The more appropriate that adjective seems, the closer you put your check mark to it.

When the scales are used as TRAIT measures, that is, as measures of a person's characteristic emotions over time, the instructions are as follows:

Each pair of words below describes a feeling dimension. Some of the pairs might seem unusual, but you may generally feel more one way than the other. So, for each pair, put a check mark (Example: - - - -:- - - -:- -✓- -:- - - -) to show how you feel IN GENERAL, that is, most of the time. Please take your time so as to arrive at a real characteristic description of your feelings.

Pleasure

Happy	- - - -:- - - -:- - - -:- - - -:- - - -:- - - -:- - - -:- - - -	Unhappy
Pleased	- - - -:- - - -:- - - -:- - - -:- - - -:- - - -:- - - -:- - - -	Annoyed
Satisfied	- - - -:- - - -:- - - -:- - - -:- - - -:- - - -:- - - -:- - - -	Unsatisfied
Contented	- - - -:- - - -:- - - -:- - - -:- - - -:- - - -:- - - -:- - - -	Melancholic
Hopeful	- - - -:- - - -:- - - -:- - - -:- - - -:- - - -:- - - -:- - - -	Despairing
Relaxed	- - - -:- - - -:- - - -:- - - -:- - - -:- - - -:- - - -:- - - -	Bored

Arousal

Stimulated	- - - -:- - - -:- - - -:- - - -:- - - -:- - - -:- - - -:- - - -	Relaxed
Excited	- - - -:- - - -:- - - -:- - - -:- - - -:- - - -:- - - -:- - - -	Calm
Frenzied	- - - -:- - - -:- - - -:- - - -:- - - -:- - - -:- - - -:- - - -	Sluggish
Jittery	- - - -:- - - -:- - - -:- - - -:- - - -:- - - -:- - - -:- - - -	Dull
Wide-awake	- - - -:- - - -:- - - -:- - - -:- - - -:- - - -:- - - -:- - - -	Sleepy
Aroused	- - - -:- - - -:- - - -:- - - -:- - - -:- - - -:- - - -:- - - -	Unaroused

Dominance

Controlling	- - - -:- - - -:- - - -:- - - -:- - - -:- - - -:- - - -:- - - -	Controlled
Influential	- - - -:- - - -:- - - -:- - - -:- - - -:- - - -:- - - -:- - - -	Influenced
In control	- - - -:- - - -:- - - -:- - - -:- - - -:- - - -:- - - -:- - - -	Cared-for
Important	- - - -:- - - -:- - - -:- - - -:- - - -:- - - -:- - - -:- - - -	Awed
Dominant	- - - -:- - - -:- - - -:- - - -:- - - -:- - - -:- - - -:- - - -	Submissive
Autonomous	- - - -:- - - -:- - - -:- - - -:- - - -:- - - -:- - - -:- - - -	Guided

A numerical scale of +4 to −4 is used for each dimension (e.g., +4 is assigned for extremely happy and −4 for extremely unhappy). Subjects' responses are averaged across the six dimensions of each of the three factors, such as for the data presented in Appendix A. In the actual administration of these measures, three scales within each factor are inverted, and all the scales are presented in a random order.

Appendix C
A Measure of Arousal-Seeking Tendency*

Instructions to Subjects

Please use the following scale to indicate the degree of your agreement or disagreement with each of the statements on the following pages. Record your answers in the spaces provided below.

+4 = very strong agreement
+3 = strong agreement
+2 = moderate agreement
+1 = slight agreement
 0 = neither agreement nor disagreement
−1 = slight disagreement
−2 = moderate disagreement
−3 = strong disagreement
−4 = very strong disagreement

(+) 1. Designs or patterns should be bold and exciting
(−) 2. I feel best when I am safe and secure
(+) 3. I would like the job of a foreign correspondent for a newspaper.
(−) 4. I don't pay much attention to my surroundings.
(−) 5. I don't like the feeling of wind in my hair.
(+) 6. I prefer an unpredictable life that is full of change to a more routine one.
(−) 7. I wouldn't like to try the new group-therapy techniques involving strange body sensations.
(+) 8. Sometimes I really stir up excitement.
(−) 9. I never notice textures.
(+) 10. I like surprises.
(−) 11. My ideal home would be peaceful and quiet.
(−) 12. I eat the same kind of food most of the time.
(+) 13. As a child I often imagined leaving home, just to explore the world.
(−) 14. I don't like to have lots of activity around me.
(−) 15. I am interested only in what I need to know.
(+) 16. I like meeting people who give me new ideas.
(−) 17. I would be content to live in the same town for the rest of my life.
(+) 18. I like continually changing activities.
(+) 19. I like a job that offers change, variety, and travel, even if it involves some danger.
(−) 20. I avoid busy, noisy places.

*Mean = 39; standard deviation = 34 for this scale. For further details see Chapter 3.

(+) 21. I like to look at pictures that are puzzling in some way.

(−) 22. I wouldn't enjoy dangerous sports such as mountain climbing, airplane flying, or sky diving.

(+) 23. I like to experience novelty and change in my daily routine.

(+) 24. Shops with thousands of exotic herbs and fragrances fascinate me.

(−) 25. I much prefer familiar people and places.

(+) 26. When things get boring, I like to find some new and unfamiliar experience.

(+) 27. I like to touch and feel a sculpture.

(−) 28. I don't enjoy doing daring, foolhardy things just for fun.

(−) 29. I prefer a routine way of life to an unpredictable one full of change.

(+) 30. I like to go somewhere different nearly every day.

(−) 31. I seldom change the decor and furniture arrangement at my place.

(+) 32. People view me as a quite unpredictable person.

(+) 33. I like to run through heaps of fallen leaves.

(+) 34. I sometimes like to do things that are a little frightening.

(−) 35. I prefer friends who are reliable and predictable to those who are excitingly unpredictable.

(+) 36. I am interested in new and varied interpretations of different art forms.

(−) 37. I seldom change the pictures on my walls.

(−) 38. I am not interested in poetry.

(−) 39. It's unpleasant seeing people in strange, weird clothes.

(+) 40. I am continually seeking new ideas and experiences.

Appendix D
A General Measure of Information Rate*

Instructions to Subjects

Please use the following adjective pairs to describe the situation shown (or described). Each of the following adjective pairs helps define the situation or the relation among the various parts of the situation. Put a check mark somewhere along the line (Example: - - - -:- - -:- -✓-:- - - -) to indicate what you think is an appropriate description.

(–) varied	- - -:- - -:- - -:- - -:- - -:- - -:- - -:- - -	redundant
(+) simple	- - -:- - -:- - -:- - -:- - -:- - -:- - -:- - -	complex
(–) novel	- - -:- - -:- - -:- - -:- - -:- - -:- - -:- - -	familiar
(+) small-scale	- - -:- - -:- - -:- - -:- - -:- - -:- - -:- - -	large-scale
(+) similar	- - -:- - -:- - -:- - -:- - -:- - -:- - -:- - -	contrasting
(–) dense	- - -:- - -:- - -:- - -:- - -:- - -:- - -:- - -	sparse
(–) intermittent	- - -:- - -:- - -:- - -:- - -:- - -:- - -:- - -	continuous
(+) usual	- - -:- - -:- - -:- - -:- - -:- - -:- - -:- - -	surprising
(–) heterogeneous	- - -:- - -:- - -:- - -:- - -:- - -:- - -:- - -	homogeneous
(+) uncrowded	- - -:- - -:- - -:- - -:- - -:- - -:- - -:- - -	crowded
(–) asymmetrical	- - -:- - -:- - -:- - -:- - -:- - -:- - -:- - -	symmetrical
(–) immediate	- - -:- - -:- - -:- - -:- - -:- - -:- - -:- - -	distant
(+) common	- - -:- - -:- - -:- - -:- - -:- - -:- - -:- - -	rare
(+) patterned	- - -:- - -:- - -:- - -:- - -:- - -:- - -:- - -	random

*In actual administration, the scoring direction signs to the left of each scale are omitted. Assign a score of –4 to checks placed in the farthest left space, –3 to the space next to it, on to +4 to checks placed in the farthest right space. To obtain a total score, change the signs of responses to the negatively signed items, and then sum over all responses. With this procedure for obtaining total scores, our sample yielded: Mean = –2.2, and standard deviation = 15.7.

Appendix E
Verbal Measures of Approach-Avoidance*

Desire to stay in the situation

(+) 1. How much time would you like to spend in this situation?

(–) 2. How much would you try to leave or get out of this situation?

Desire to explore the situtation

(+) 3. Once in this situation, how much would you enjoy exploring around?

(–) 4. How much would you try to avoid any looking around or exploration of this situation? (0 = no avoidance)

Desire to work in the situation

(+) 5. To what extent is this situation a good opportunity to think out some difficult task you have been working on?

(–) 6. How much would you dislike having to work in this situation? (0 = no dislike)

Desire to affiliate in the situation

(+) 7. To what extent is this a situation in which you would feel friendly and talkative to a stranger who happens to be near you?

(–) 8. Is this a situation in which you might try to avoid other people, avoid having to talk to them? (0 = no avoidance)

*The eight questions in this list are presented in a random order and without names (e.g., "desire to stay in the situation") with each situation. The subject answers question 1 by circling one of the following alternatives listed with the question: 0, none; 1, a few minutes; 2, half an hour; 3, one hour; 4, a few hours; 5, a day; 6, a few days; 7, many, many days. Questions 2 through 8 are answered by the subject using the following scale: 0, not at all; 1, very slight; 2, slight; 3, slight to moderate; 4, moderate; 5, much; 6, very much; 7, extremely so.

To compute scores on each of the four dimensions, the numerical responses to the negatively signed items are given minus signs and the scores for each pair are then summed.

The first three categories of approach-avoidance are highly intercorrelated and define a single factor called "preference." The latter has a low but significant correlation with the "desire to affiliate" factor.

References

Alexander, C., Hirshen, S., Ishikawa, S., Coffin, C., and Angel, S. *Houses generated by patterns.* Berkeley, California: Center for Environmental Structure, 1969.

Alexander, C., Ishikawa, S., and Silverstein, M. *A pattern language which generates multi-service centers.* Berkeley, California: Center for Environmental Structure, 1968.

Alexander, M., and Isaac, W. "Effect of illumination and d-amphetamine on the activity of the *Rhesus macaque.*" *Psychological Reports 16* (1965): 311–313.

Alexander, W. "Some harmful effects of noise." *Canadian Medical Association Journal 99* (1968): 27–31.

Allen, E. C., and Guilford, J. P. "Factors determining the affective values of color combinations." *American Journal of Psychology 48* (1936): 643–648.

Altman, I. "Territorial behavior in humans: An analysis of the concept." Paper presented at the Conference on Explorations of Spatial-Behavioral Relationships as Related to Older People, Ann Arbor, Michigan, May 1968.

Altman, I., and Haythorn, W. W. "The ecology of isolated groups." *Behavioral Science 12* (1967): 169–182.

Altman, I., Taylor, D. A., and Wheeler, L. "Ecological aspects of group behavior in social isolation." *Journal of Applied Social Psychology 1* (1971): 76–100.

Anastasi, A. *Differential psychology.* New York: The Macmillan Company, 1958.

Argyle, M., and Dean, J. "Eye contact, distance, and affiliation." *Sociometry 28* (1965): 289–304.

Attneave, F. "Physical determinants of the judged complexity of shapes." *Journal of Experimental Psychology 53* (1957): 221–227.

Attneave, F. *Applications of information theory to psychology: A summary of basic concepts, methods, and results.* New York: Holt, Rinehart & Winston, Inc., 1959. (a)

Attneave, F. "Stochastic composition processes." *Journal of Aesthetics and Art Criticism 17* (1959): 503–510. (b)

Attneave, F., and Arnoult, M. D. "The quantitative study of shape and pattern perception." *Psychological Bulletin 53* (1956): 452–471.

Auerbach, S. M. "Anxiety and time estimation." Unpublished master's thesis, Florida State University, 1969.

Ayres, L. P. "The influence of music on speed in the Six Day Bicycle Race." *American Physical Education Review 16* (1911): 321–324.

Azrin, N. H. "Some effects of noise on human behavior." *Journal of the Experimental Analysis of Behavior 1* (1958): 183–200.

Bakan, P. "Extraversion-introversion and improvement in an auditory vigilance task." *British Journal of Psychology 50* (1959): 325–332.

Baker, G., and Franken, R. "Effects of stimulus size, brightness and complexity upon EEG desynchronization." *Psychonomic Science 7* (1967): 289–290.

Bandura, A. *Principles of behavior modification.* New York: Holt, Rinehart & Winston, Inc., 1969.

Barker, R. G. "Ecology and motivation." In *Nebraska symposium on motivation,* ed. M. R. Jones, pp. 1–50. Lincoln, Nebraska: University of Nebraska Press, 1960.

Barker, R. G. "Explorations in ecological psychology." *American Psychologist 20* (1965): 1–14.

Barmack, J. E. "Studies on the psychophysiology of boredom: Part 2, the effect of a lowered room temperature and an added incentive on blood pressure, report of boredom, and other factors." *Journal of Experimental Psychology 25* (1939): 634–642.

Basowitz, H., Persky, H., Korchin, S. J., and Grinker, R. R. *Anxiety and stress: An interdisciplinary study of a life situation.* New York: McGraw-Hill Book Company, 1955

Bayes, K. *The therapeutic effect of environment on emotionally disturbed and mentally abnormal children.* Montreal: Society for Emotionally Disturbed Children, 1967.

Beard, R. R., and Grandstaff, N. "CO exposure and cerebral function." Paper presented at the New York Academy of Sciences, January 1970.

Beard, R. R., and Wertheim, G. A. "Behavioral impairment associated with small doses of carbon monoxide." *American Journal of Public Health and the Nation's Health 57* (1967): 2012–2022.

Bedford, T. "Researches on thermal comfort." *Ergonomics 4* (1961): 289–310.

Bell, C. R. "Time estimation and increases in body temperature." *Journal of Experimental Psychology 70* (1965): 232–234.

Bell, C. R., and Provins, K. A. "Effects of high temperature environmental conditions on human performance." *Journal of Occupational Medicine 4* (1962): 202–211.

Bentler, P. M. "Semantic space is (approximately) bipolar." *Journal of Psychology 71* (1969): 33–40.

Berlyne, D. E. *Conflict, arousal, and curiosity.* New York: McGraw-Hill Book Company, 1960.

Berlyne, D. E. "Complexity and incongruity variables as determinants of exploratory choice and evaluative ratings." *Canadian Journal of Psychology 17* (1963): 274–290.

Berlyne, D.E. "Arousal and reinforcement." In *Nebraska symposium on motivation,* ed. D. Levine, pp. 1–110. Lincoln, Nebraska: University of Nebraska Press, 1967.

Berlyne, D. E., and Borsa, D. M. "Uncertainty and the orientation reaction." *Perception and Psychophysics 3* (1968): 77–79.

Berlyne, D. E., Borsa, D. M., Hamacher, J. H., and Koenig, I. D. V. "Paired-associate learning and the timing of arousal." *Journal of Experimental Psychology 72* (1966): 1–6.

Berlyne, D. E., Craw, M. A., Salapatek, P. H., and Lewis, J. L. "Novelty, complexity, incongruity, extrinsic motivation, and the GSR." *Journal of Experimental Psychology 66* (1963): 560–567.

Berlyne, D. E., and Lawrence, G. H., II. "Effects of complexity and incongruity variables on GSR, investigatory behavior and verbally expressed preference." *Journal of General Psychology 71* (1964): 21–45.

Berlyne, D. E., and Lewis, J. L. "Effects of heightened arousal on human exploratory behavior." *Canadian Journal of Psychology 17* (1963): 398–411.

Berlyne, D. E., and McDonnell, P. "Effects of stimulus complexity and incongruity on duration of EEG desynchronization." *Electroencephalography and Clinical Neurophysiology 18* (1965): 156–161.

Berlyne, D. E., McDonnell, P., Nicki, R. M., and Parham, L. C. C. "Effects of auditory pitch and complexity on EEG desynchronization and on verbally expressed judgments." *Canadian Journal of Psychology 21* (1967): 346–367.

Berlyne, D. E., and Peckham, S. "The semantic differential and other measures of reaction to visual complexity." *Canadian Journal of Psychology 20* (1966): 125–135.

Berrien, F. K. "The effects of noise." *Psychological Bulletin 43* (1946): 141–161.

Berry, P. C. "Effect of colored illumination upon perceived temperature." *Journal of Applied Psychology 45* (1961): 248–250.

Berscheid, E., and Walster, E. H. *Interpersonal attraction.* Reading, Massachusetts: Addison-Wesley Publishing Co., Inc., 1969.

Bexton, W. H., Heron, W., and Scott, T. H. "Effects of decreased variation in the sensory environment." *Canadian Journal of Psychology 8* (1954): 70–76.

Bindra, D. *Motivation: A systematic reinterpretation.* New York: The Ronald Press Company, 1959.

Birren, F. "Color and psychotherapy." *Modern Hospital 67* (1946): 57–58.

Bishop, M. P., Elder, S. T., and Heath, R. G. "Attempted control of operant behavior in man with intracranial self-stimulation." In *The role of pleasure in behavior,* ed. R. G. Heath, pp. 55–81. New York: Harper & Row, Publishers, 1964.

Blake, R. R., Rhead, C. C., Wedge, B., and Mouton, J. S. "Housing architecture and social interaction." *Sociometry 19* (1956): 133–139.

Bliss, E. L., Migeon, C. J., Branch, C. H. H., and Samuels, L. T. "Reaction of the adrenal cortex to emotional stress." *Psychosomatic Medicine 18* (1956): 56–76.

Board, F., Persky, H., and Hamburg, D. A. "Psychological stress and endocrine functions: Blood levels of adrenocortical and thyroid hormones in acutely disturbed patients." *Psychosomatic Medicine 18* (1956): 324–333.

Boche, R. D., and Quilligan, J. J., Jr. "Effect of synthetic smog on spontaneous activity of mice." *Science 131* (1960): 1733–1734.

Boggs, D. H., and Simon, J. R. "Differential effect of noise on tasks of varying complexity." *Journal of Applied Psychology 52* (1968): 148–153.

Bolt Beranek and Newman Inc. *Noise environment of urban and surburban areas.* Washington, D.C.: United States Government Printing Office, 1967.

Bourne, P. G. *Men, stress and Vietnam.* Boston: Little, Brown and Company, 1970.

Braddock, J. C. "The effect of prior residence upon dominance in the fish *Platypoecilus maculatus.*" *Physiological Zoology 22* (1949): 161–169.

Bradley, P. B. "The central action of certain drugs in relation to the reticular formation of the brain." In *Reticular formation of the brain,* ed. H. H. Jasper, L. D. Proctor, R. S. Knighton, W. C. Noshay, and R. T. Costello, pp. 123–149. Boston: Little, Brown and Company, 1958.

Broadbent, D. E. "Some effects of noise on visual performance." *Quarterly Journal of Experimental Psychology 6* (1954): 1–5.

Broadbent, D. E. "Effects of noise on behavior." In *Handbook of noise control,* ed. C. M. Harris, pp. 10-1 to 10-34. New York: McGraw-Hill Book Company, 1957.

Broadbent, D. E. "Possibilities and difficulties in the concept of arousal." In *Vigilance: A symposium,* ed. D. N. Buckner and J. J. McGrath, pp. 184–198. New York: McGraw-Hill Book Company, 1963.

Brown, R. L., Galloway, W. D., and Gildersleeve, K. R. "Effects of intense noise on processing of cutaneous information of varying complexity." *Perceptual and Motor Skills 20* (1965): 749–754.

Burke, K. *A grammar of motives and a rhetoric of motives.* Cleveland, Ohio: World Publishing Company, 1962.

Burney, C. *Solitary confinement.* New York: St. Martin's Press, Inc., 1961.

Burnham, C. A., and Grimm, C. T. "Towards a rational aesthetic criterion for the selection of the visual properties of architectural surfaces." Unpublished manuscript, University of Texas at Austin, 1969.

Bush, L. E., II. "Individual differences multidimensional scaling of adjectives denoting feelings." *Journal of Personality and Social Psychology 25* (1973): 50–57.

Byrd, R. E. *Alone.* New York: G. P. Putnam's Sons, 1938.

Byrne, D. "The influence of propinquity and opportunities for interaction on class-room relationships." *Human Relations 14* (1961): 63–70.

Byrne, D. "Attitudes and attraction." In *Advances in experimental social psychology,* ed. L. Berkowitz, pp. 35–89. New York: Academic Press, Inc., 1969.

Byrne, D. *The attraction paradigm.* New York: Academic Press, Inc., 1971.

Byrne, D., and Buehler, J. A. "A note on the influence of propinquity upon acquaint-anceships." *Journal of Abnormal and Social Psychology 51* (1955): 147–148.

Calder, N. *The mind of man.* London: British Broadcasting Corporation, 1970.

Calhoun, J. B. "Population density and social pathology." *Scientific American 206,* no. 2 (1962): 139–148. (a)

Calhoun, J. B. *The ecology and sociology of the Norway rat.* Bethesda, Maryland: United States Public Health Service, 1962. (b)

Calhoun, J. B. "The role of space in animal sociology." *Journal of Social Issues 22* (1966): 46–58.

Calhoun, J. B. "Space and the strategy of life." Paper presented at the American Association for the Advancement of Science, Dallas, December 1968.

Campbell, K. I., Emik, L. O., Clarke, G. L., and Plata, R. L. "Inhalation toxicity of peroxyacetyl nitrate." *Archives of Environmental Health 20* (1970): 22–27.

Cantor, G. N., Cantor, J. H., and Ditrichs, R. "Observing behavior in preschool children as a function of stimulus complexity." *Child Development 34* (1963): 683–689.

Carlson, J. A., and Hergenhahn, B. R. "Effects of rock-n-roll and classical music on the learning of nonsense syllables." *Psychological Reports 20* (1967): 1021–1022.

Carpenter, C. R. "Territoriality: A review of concept and problems." In *Behavior and evolution,* ed. A. Roe and G. G. Simpson, pp. 224–250. New Haven: Yale University Press, 1958.

Carson, D. H. "Population concentration and human stress." In *Explorations in the psychology of stress and anxiety,* ed. B. P. Rourke, pp. 27–42. Don Mills, Canada: Longmans Canada Limited, 1969.

Castanada, A., McCandless, B. R., and Palermo, D. S. "The children's form of the Manifest Anxiety Scale." *Child Development 27* (1956): 317–326.

Cattell, R. B. "Anxiety and motivation: Theory and crucial experiments." In *Anxiety and behavior,* ed. C. D. Spielberger, pp. 23–62. New York: Academic Press, Inc., 1966.

Chapin, F. S. "The effects of slum clearance and rehousing on family and community relationships in Minneapolis." *American Journal of Sociology 43* (1938): 744–763.

Chapman, R. M., and Levy, N. "Hunger drive and reinforcing effect of novel stimuli." *Journal of Comparative and Physiological Psychology 50* (1957): 233–238.

Cheek, F. E., Maxwell, R., and Weisman, R. "Carpeting the ward: An exploratory study in environmental psychiatry. *Mental Hygiene 55* (1971): 109–118.

Cherry, C. *On human communication: A review, a survey, and a criticism.* Cambridge, Massachusetts: The M.I.T. Press, 1966.

Chombart de Lauwe, P. *Famille et habitation.* Paris: Editions du Centre National de la Recherche Scientifique, 1959.

Choungourian, A. "Introversion-extraversion and color preferences." *Journal of Projective Techniques and Personality Assessment 31* no. 4 (1967): 92–94.

Christian, J. J. "The roles of endocrine and behavioral factors in the growth of mammalian populations." In *Comparative endocrinology: Proceedings of the Columbia University symposium on comparative endocrinology,* ed. A. Gorbman, pp. 71–97. New York: John Wiley & Sons, Inc., 1959.

Christian, J. J. "Phenomena associated with population density." *Proceedings of the National Academy of Science 47* (1961): 428–449.

Christian, J. J., Flyger, V., and Davis, D. E. "Factors in mass mortality of a herd of sika deer, *Cervus nippon.*" *Chesapeake Science 1* (1960): 79–95.

Cohen, A. "Noise and psychological state." Technical Report RR-9, July 1968, Occupational Health Program, Cincinnati, Ohio. United States Department of Health, Education, and Welfare. (a)

Cohen, A. "Noise effects on health, productivity, and well-being." *Transactions of the New York Academy of Sciences,* series 2, *30* (1968): 910–918. (b)

Cohen, A., Hummel, W. F., Turner, J. W., and Dukes-Dobos, F. N. "Effects of noise on task performance." Technical Report RR-4, January 1966, Occupational Health Research and Training Facility, Cincinnati, Ohio. United States Department of Health, Education, and Welfare.

Cohen, J. "Multiple regression as a general data-analytic system." *Psychological Bulletin 70* (1968): 426–443.

Cohen, S. I. "Central nervous system functioning in altered sensory environments." In *Psychological stress: Issues in research,* ed. M. H. Appley and R. Trumbull, pp. 77–112. New York: Appleton-Century-Crofts, 1967.

Condon, W. S., and Ogston, W. D. "Sound film analysis of normal and pathological behavior patterns." *Journal of Nervous and Mental Disease 143* (1966): 338–347.

Corcoran, D. W. J. "Individual differences in performance after loss of sleep." Unpublished doctoral dissertation, University of Cambridge, 1963. (a)

Corcoran, D. W. J. "Doubling the rate of signal presentation in a vigilance task during sleep deprivation." *Journal of Applied Psychology 47* (1963): 412–415. (b)

Corcoran, D. W. J. "Changes in heart rate and performance as a result of loss of sleep." *British Journal of Psychology 55* (1964): 307–314.

Corcoran, D. W. J. "Personality and the inverted-U relation." *British Journal of Psychology 56* (1965): 267–273.

Costello, C. G., and Hall, M. "Heart rates during performance of a mental task under noise conditions." *Psychonomic Science 8* (1967): 405–406.

Craik, K. H. "Environmental Psychology." In *New directions in psychology 4,* ed. K. H. Craik, B. Kleinmuntz, R. L. Rosnow, R. Rosenthal, J. A. Cheyne, and R. H. Walters, pp. 1–121. New York: Holt, Rinehart & Winston, Inc., 1970. (a)

Craik, K. H. "The comprehension of the everyday physical environment." In *Environmental psychology: Man and his physical setting,* ed. H. M. Proshansky, W. H. Ittelson, and L. G. Rivlin, pp. 646–658. New York: Holt, Rinehart & Winston, Inc., 1970. (b)

Crane, R. R., and Levy, B. I. "Color scales in responses to emotionally laden situations." *Journal of Consulting Psychology 26* (1962): 515–519.

Crowne, D. P., and Marlowe, D. "A new scale of social desirability independent of psychopathology." *Journal of Consulting Psychology 24* (1960): 349–354.

Davies, D. R., and Hockey, G. R. J. "The effects of noise and doubling the signal frequency on individual differences in visual vigilance performance." *British Journal of Psychology 57* (1966): 381–389.

Davies, D. R., Hockey, G. R. J., and Taylor, A. "Varied auditory stimulation, temperament differences and vigilance performance." *British Journal of Psychology 60* (1969): 453–457.

Davies, R. C. "Motor effects of strong auditory stimuli." *Journal of Experimental Psychology 38* (1948): 257–275.

Davis, J. M., McCourt, W. F., and Solomon, P. "Sensory deprivation: (1) Effects of social contact, (2) effects of random visual stimulation." Paper read at the American Psychiatric Association, Philadelphia, April 1958.

Davis, R. T., Settlage, P.H., and Harlow, H. F. "Performance of normal and brain-operated monkeys on mechanical puzzles with and without food incentive." *Journal of Genetic Psychology 77* (1950): 305–311.

Day, H. I. "Looking time as a function of stimulus variables and individual differences." *Perceptual and Motor Skills 22* (1966): 423–428.

Day, H. I. "A subjective definition of complexity." *Perceptual and Motor Skills 25* (1967): 583–584. (a)

Day, H. I. "Anxiety, curiosity and arousal." *Ontario Psychological Association Quarterly 20* (1967): 11–17. (b)

Day, H. I. "The effects of increased arousal on attention in high- and low-anxious subjects." *Ontario Journal of Educational Research 9* (1967): 185-191. (c)

Day, H. I. "Preference: Interest or pleasure?" Paper read at 29th Annual Meeting of the Canadian Psychological Association, Calgary, June 1968. (a)

Day, H. I. "Some determinants of looking time under different instructional sets." *Perception and Psychophysics 4* (1968): 279-281. (b)

Day, H. I. "The importance of symmetry and complexity in the evaluation of complexity, interest and pleasingness." *Psychonomic Science 10* (1968): 339-340. (c)

Day, H. I. "The measurement of specific curiosity." In *Intrinsic motivation: A new direction in education,* ed. H. I. Day, D. E. Berlyne, and D. E. Hunt, pp. 99-112. New York: Holt, Rinehart & Winston, Inc., 1971.

Day, H. I., and Berlyne, D. E. "Human responses to complexity." Paper read at 27th Annual Meeting of the Canadian Psychological Association, Montreal, June 1966.

Day, H. I., and Crawford, G. "An examination of changes in attitudes to visual complexity with increasing age." Paper presented at the C.C.R.E., Victoria, British Columbia, January 1969.

Day, H. I., and Thomas, E. L. "Effects of amphetamine on selective attention." *Perceptual and Motor Skills 24* (1967): 1119-1125.

de Charms, R. *Personal causation.* New York: Academic Press, Inc., 1968.

Delgado, J. M. R., and Hamlin, H. "Spontaneous and evoked electrical seizures in animals and in humans." In *Electrical studies on the unanesthetized brain,* ed. E. R. Ramey and D. S. O'Doherty, pp. 133-158. New York: Hoeber Medical Division, Harper & Row, Publishers, 1960.

Dember, W. N., and Earl, R. W. "Analysis of exploratory, manipulatory and curiosity behaviors." *Psychological Review 64* (1957): 91-96.

Dement, W. C. "An essay on dreams: The role of physiology in understanding their nature." In *New directions in psychology 2,* pp. 135-257. New York: Holt, Rinehart & Winston, Inc., 1965.

Dennis, W. "A comparison of the rat's first and second explorations of a maze unit." *American Journal of Psychology 47* (1935): 488-490.

Dennis, W. "Spontaneous alternation in rats as an indicator of the persistence of stimulus effects." *Journal of Comparative Psychology 28* (1939): 305-312.

Dennis, W., and Sollenberger, R. T. "Negative adaptation in the maze exploration of albino rats." *Journal of Comparative Psychology 18* (1934): 197-206.

Denny, M. R. "Learning through stimulus satiation." *Journal of Experimental Psychology 54* (1957): 62-64.

Deutsch, M., and Collins, M. E. *Interracial housing: A psychological evaluation of a social experiment.* Minneapolis: University of Minnesota Press, 1951.

Diespecker, D. D., and Davenport, W. G. "The initial effect of noise on a simple vibro-tactile learning task." *Perception and psychophysics 2* (1967): 569–571.

DiMascio, A., Boyd, R. W., and Greenblatt, M. "Physiological correlates of tension and antagonism during psychotherapy: A study of 'interpersonal physiology.' " *Psychosomatic Medicine 19* (1957): 99–104.

Dollard, J., and Miller, N. E. *Personality and psychotherapy: An analysis in terms of learning, thinking, and culture.* New York: McGraw-Hill Book Company, 1950.

Domino, G. "A validation of Howard's test of change-seeking behavior." *Educational and Psychological Measurement 25* (1965): 1073–1078.

Dorfman, D. D., and McKenna, H. "Pattern preference as a function of pattern uncertainty." *Canadian Journal of Psychology 20* (1966): 143–153.

Duffy, E. "The psychological significance of the concept of 'arousal' or 'activation.' " *Psychological Review 64* (1957): 265–275.

Duffy, E. *Activation and behavior.* New York: John Wiley & Sons, Inc., 1962.

Efroymsen, M. A. Multiple regression analysis. In *Mathematical methods for digital computers,* Part V (17), ed. A. Ralston and H. S. Wilf, New York: John Wiley & Sons, Inc., 1960.

Ekman, G., Hosman, J., and Lindström, B. "Roughness, smoothness, and preference: A study of quantitative relations in individual subjects." *Journal of Experimental Psychology 70* (1965): 18–26.

Ekman, P., and Friesen, W. V. "Nonverbal leakage and clues to deception." *Psychiatry 32* (1969): 88–106.

Ellis, D. S., and Brighouse, G. "Effects of music on respiration- and heart-rate." *American Journal of Psychology 65* (1952): 39–47.

Emik, L. O., and Plata, R. L. "Depression of running activity in mice by exposure to polluted air." *Archives of Environmental Health 18* (1969): 574–579.

Erwin, C. W., Lerner, M., Wilson, N. J., and Wilson, W. P. "Some further observations on the photically elicited arousal response." *Electroencephalography and Clinical Neurophysiology 13* (1961): 391–394.

Eysenck, H. J. "A critical and experimental study of colour preferences." *American Journal of Psychology 54* (1941): 385–394.

Eysenck, H. J. *The biological basis of personality.* Springfield: Charles C. Thomas, Publisher, 1967.

Eysenck, H. J. *The structure of human personality.* London: Eyre Methuen, Ltd., 1970.

Eysenck, H. J., and Eysenck, S. B. G. *Manual: Eysenck Personality Inventory.* San Diego: Educational and Industrial Testing Service, 1968.

Fantz, R. L. "Pattern vision in young infants." *Psychological Record 8* (1958): 43–47. (a)

Fantz, R. L. "Visual discrimination in a neonate chimpanzee." *Perceptual and Motor Skills 8* (1958): 59–66. (b)

Farber, I. E. "Anxiety as a drive state." In *Nebraska symposium on motivation,* ed. M. R. Jones, pp. 1–46. Lincoln, Nebraska: University of Nebraska Press, 1954.

Feldman, S. M., and Waller, H. J. "Dissociation of electrocortical activation and behavioural arousal." *Nature 196* (1962): 1320–1322.

Felipe, N. J., and Sommer, R. "Invasions of personal space." *Social Problems 14* (1966): 206–214.

Festinger, L. "Architecture and group membership." *Journal of Social Issues 1* (1951): 152–163.

Festinger, L. "Group attraction and membership." In *Group dynamics: Research and theory,* ed. D. Cartwright and A. Zander, pp. 92–101. Evanston, Illinois: Row, Peterson, 1953.

Festinger, L., Pepitone, A., and Newcomb, T. "Some consequences of de-individuation in a group." *Journal of Abnormal and Social Psychology 47* (1952): 382–389.

Festinger, L., Schachter, S., and Back, K. *Social pressures in informal groups: A study of human factors in housing.* Stanford, California: Stanford University Press, 1963.

Fine, B. J., Cohen, A., and Crist, B. "Effect of exposure to high humidity at high and moderate ambient temperature on anagram solution and auditory discrimination." *Psychological Reports 7* (1960): 171–181.

Fishman, J. R., Hamburg, D. A., Handlon, J. H., Mason, J. W., and Sachar, E. "Emotional and adrenal cortical responses to a new experience." *Archives of General Psychiatry 6* (1962): 271–278.

Fiske, D. W., and Maddi, S. R. *Functions of varied experience.* Homewood, Illinois: Dorsey Press, 1961.

Fox, W. F. "Human performance in the cold." *Human Factors 9* (1967): 203–220.

Freeman, G. L. "Changes in tension-pattern and total energy expenditure during adaptation to 'distracting' stimuli." *American Journal of Psychology 52* (1939): 354–360.

Freeman, J., and Neidt, C. O. Effect of familiar background music upon film learning. *Journal of Educational Research 53* (1959): 91–96.

Freud, S. *The problem of anxiety.* New York: W. W. Norton & Company, Inc., 1936.

Fried, M. "Grieving for a lost home." In *The urban condition: People and policy in the metropolis,* ed. L. J. Duhl, pp. 151–171. New York: Basic Books, Inc., Publishers, 1963.

Fried, M., and Gleicher, P. "Some sources of residential satisfaction in an urban slum." *Journal of the American Institute of Planners 27* (1961): 305–315.

Fromkin, H. L. "Affective and valuational consequences of self-perceived uniqueness deprivations: III. The effects of experimentally aroused feelings of self-perceived similarity upon valuation of unavailable and novel experiences." Unpublished manuscript, Purdue University, 1969.

Frost, J. W., Dryer, R. L., and Kohlstaedt, K. G. "Stress studies on auto race drivers." *Journal of Laboratory and Clinical Medicine 38* (1951): 523–525.

Gale, A. " 'Stimulus hunger': Individual differences in operant strategy in a button-pressing task." *Behaviour Research and Therapy 7* (1969): 265–274.

Gans, H. J. *The urban villagers: Group and class in the life of Italian-Americans.* New York: Free Press of Glencoe, 1962.

Gans, H. J. *People and plans: Essays on urban problems and solutions.* New York: Basic Books, Inc., Publishers, 1968.

Garlington, W. K., and Shimota, H. E. "The change seeker index: A measure of the need for variable stimulus input." *Psychological Reports 14* (1964): 919–924.

Garner, W. R. *Uncertainty and structure as psychological concepts.* New York: John Wiley & Sons, Inc., 1962.

Gaviria, B. "Autonomic reaction magnitude and habituation to different voices." *Psychosomatic Medicine 29* (1967): 598–605.

Gibson, W. *The boat.* Boston: Houghton Mifflin Company, 1953.

Glanzer, M. "Curiosity, exploratory drive, and stimulus satiation." *Psychological Bulletin 55* (1958): 302–315.

Godin, G., Wright, G., and Shephard, R. "Urban exposure to carbon monoxide." *Archives of Environmental Health 25* (1972): 305–313.

Goffman, E. *Asylums: Essays on the social situation of mental patients and other inmates.* Chicago: Aldine Publishing Company, 1961.

Goldsmith, J. R. "Carbon monoxide research–Recent and remote." *Archives of Environmental Health 21* (1970): 118–120.

Goldsmith, J. R., and Rogers, L. H. "Health hazards of automobile exhaust." *Public Health Reports 74* (1959): 551–558.

Granger, G. W. "An experimental study of colour preferences." *Journal of General Psychology 52* (1955): 3–20. (a)

Granger, G. W. "Aesthetic measure applied to colour harmony: An experimental test." *Journal of General Psychology 52* (1955): 205–212. (b)

Granger, G. W. "An experimental study of colour harmony." *Journal of General Psychology 52* (1955): 21–35. (c)

Granger, G. W. "The prediction of preference for colour combinations." *Journal of General Psychology 52* (1955): 213–222. (d)

Griffitt, W. "Environmental effects on interpersonal affective behavior: Ambient effective temperature and attraction." *Journal of Personality and Social Psychology 15* (1970): 240–244.

Griffitt, W., and Veitch, R. "Hot and crowded: Influences of population density and temperature on interpersonal affective behavior." *Journal of Personality and Social Psychology 17* (1971): 92–98.

Grut, A., Astrup, P., Challen, P., Jr., and Gerhardsson, G. "Threshold limit values for carbon monoxide." *Archives of Environmental Health 21* (1970): 542–544.

Guilford, J. P. "The affective value of color as a function of hue, tint, and chroma." *Journal of Experimental Psychology 17* (1934): 342–370.

Guilford, J. P. "A study in psychodynamics." *Psychometrika 4* (1939): 1–23.

Guilford, J. P., and Smith, P. C. "A system of color–preferences." *American Journal of Psychology 72* (1959): 487–502.

Gullahorn, J. "Distance and friendship as factors in the gross interaction matrix." *Sociometry 15* (1952): 123–134.

Gunderson, E. K. E. "Emotional symptoms in extremely isolated groups." *Archives of General Psychiatry 9* (1963): 362–368.

Gunderson, E. K. E. "Mental health problems in Antarctica." *Archives of Environmental Health 17* (1968): 558–564.

Gutman, R. "Site planning and social behavior." *Journal of Social Issues 22* (1966): 103–115.

Haagen-Smit, A. J. "Carbon monoxide levels in city driving." *Archives of Environmental Health, 12* (1966): 548–551.

Haber, R.N. "Discrepancy from adaptation level as a source of affect." *Journal of Experimental Psychology 56* (1958): 370–375.

Hall, E. T. *The silent language.* Garden City, New York: Doubleday & Company, Inc., 1959.

Hall, E. T. "A system for the notation of proxemic behavior." *American Anthropologist 65* (1963): 1003–1026.

Hall, E. T. *The hidden dimension.* Garden City, New York: Doubleday & Company, Inc., 1966.

Hammes, J. A., and Wiggins, S. L. "Perceptual-motor steadiness, manifest anxiety, and color illumination." *Perceptual and Motor Skills 14* (1962): 59-61.

Harlow, H. F. "Learning and satiation of response in intrinsically motivated complex puzzle performance by monkeys." *Journal of Comparative and Physiological Psychology 43* (1950): 289-294.

Harlow, H. F. "Motivation as a factor in the acquisition of new responses." In *Current theory and research in motivation, a symposium,* ed. J. S. Brown, H. F. Harlow, L. J. Postman, V. Nowlis, T. M. Newcomb, and O. H. Mowrer pp. 24-29. Lincoln, Nebraska: University of Nebraska Press, 1953.

Harlow, H. F., and Harlow, M. K. "Social deprivation in monkeys." *Scientific American 207,* no. 5 (1962): 136-146.

Harlow, H. F., Harlow, M. K., and Meyer, D. R. "Learning motivated by a manipulation drive." *Journal of Experimental Psychology 40* (1950): 228-234.

Harlow, H. F., and McClearn, G. E. "Object discrimination learned by monkeys on the basis of manipulation motives." *Journal of Comparative and Physiological Psychology 47* (1954): 73-76.

Hazzard, F. W. "A descriptive account of odors." *Journal of Experimental Psychology 13* (1930): 297-331.

Heath, R. G., ed. *Studies in schizophrenia.* Cambridge, Massachusetts: Harvard University Press, 1954.

Heath, R. G. "Electrical self-stimulation of the brain in man." *American Journal of Psychiatry 120* (1963): 571-577.

Heath, R. G. "Pleasure response of human subjects to direct stimulation of the brain: Physiologic and psychodynamic considerations." In *The role of pleasure in behavior,* ed. R. G. Heath, pp. 219-243. New York: Harper & Row, Publishers, 1964. (a)

Heath, R. G., ed. *The role of pleasure in behavior.* New York: Harper & Row, Publishers, 1964. (b)

Heath, R. G., and Mickle, W. A. "Evaluation of seven years' experience with depth electrode studies in human patients." In *Electrical studies on the unanesthetized brain,* ed. E. R. Ramey and D. S. O'Doherty, pp. 214-247. New York: Hoeber Medical Division, Harper & Row, Publishers, 1960.

Hebb, D. O. "Drives and the C.N.S. (Central nervous system)." *Psychological Review 62* (1955): 243-254.

Heron, W. "Cognitive and physiological effects of perceptual isolation." In *Sensory deprivation,* ed. P. Solomon, J. H. Mendelson, P. E. Kubzansky, R. Trumbull, P. H. Leiderman, and D. Wexler pp. 6-33. Cambridge, Massachusetts: Harvard University Press, 1961.

Heron, W., Bexton, W. H., and Hebb, D. O. "Cognitive effects of a decreased variation in the sensory environment." *American Psychologist 8* (1953): 366.

Hershberger, R. G. "A study of meaning and architecture." Paper presented at the Environmental Design Research Association First Annual Conference, Chapel Hill, North Carolina, June 1969.

Hess, E. H. "Attitude and pupil size." *Scientific American, 212,* no. 4 (1965): 46–54.

Hetzel, B. S., Schottstaedt, W. W., Grace, W. J., and Wolff, H. G. "Changes in urinary 17-hydroxycorticosteroid excretion during stressful life experiences in man." *Journal of Clinical Endocrinology and Metabolism 15* (1955): 1057–1068.

Hill, S. R., Jr., Goetz, F. C., Fox, H. M., Murawski, B. J., Krakauer, L. J., Reifenstein, R. W., Gray, S. J., Reddy, W. J., Hedberg, S. E., St. Marc, J. R., and Thorn, G. W. "Studies on adrenocortical and psychological response to stress in man." *A.M.A. Archives of Internal Medicine 97* (1956): 269–298.

Hitchcock, M. "Health effects of photochemical oxidants." Unpublished manuscript, Yale University School of Medicine, 1969.

Hoagland, H. "Pacemakers of human brain waves in normals and in general paretics." *American Journal of Physiology 116* (1936): 604–615.

Hochberg, J., and Brooks, V. "An item analysis of physiognomic connotation." Unpublished manuscript, New York University, 1956.

Hochberg, J., and McAlister, E. "A quantitative approach to figural 'goodness.' " *Journal of Experimental Psychology 46* (1953): 361–364.

Hoffman, J. E. "The effect of noise on intellectual performance as related to personality and social factors in upper division high school students." Unpublished doctoral dissertation, University of Southern California, 1966.

Hogg, J. "A principal components analysis of semantic differential judgments of single colors and color pairs." *Journal of General Psychology 80* (1969): 129–140. (a)

Hogg, J. "The prediction of semantic differential ratings of color combinations." *Journal of General Psychology 80* (1969): 141–152. (b)

Hogg, J., ed. *Psychology and the visual arts.* Baltimore, Maryland: Penguin Books, Inc., 1969. (c)

Hollingshead, A. B., and Redlich, F. C. *Social class and mental illness: A community study.* New York: John Wiley & Sons, Inc., 1958.

Holt-Hansen, K. "Taste and pitch." *Perceptual and Motor Skills 27* (1968): 59–68.

Hopkinson, R. G., and Collins, J. B. "The prediction and avoidance of glare in interior lighting." *Ergonomics 6* (1963): 379–383.

Hopkinson, R. G., and Longmore, J. "Attention and distraction in the lighting of work-places." *Ergonomics 2* (1959): 321–334.

Horvath, S. M., Dahms, T. E., and O'Hanlon, J. F., Jr. "Carbon monoxide and human vigilance." *Archives of Environmental Health 23* (1971): 343–347.

Horvath, S. M., Raven, P. B., Drinkwater, B. L., O'Hanlon, J. F., Jr., and Dahms, T. E. "A brief literature search regarding the influence of air pollutants on work capacity and psychophysiological responses of man." Unpublished manuscript, Institute of Environmental Stress, University of California, Santa Barbara, 1970.

Houston, B. K. "Inhibition and the facilitating effect of noise on interference tasks." *Perceptual and Motor Skills 27* (1968): 947–950.

Houston, B. K., and Jones, T. M. "Distraction and Stroop color-word performance." *Journal of Experimental Psychology 74* (1967): 54–56.

Howard, K. I. "A test of stimulus-seeking behavior." *Perceptual and Motor Skills 13* (1961): 416.

Howard, K. I., and Diesenhaus, H. I. "Personality correlates of change-seeking behavior." *Perceptual and Motor Skills 21* (1965): 655–664.

Hull, C. L. *Essentials of behavior.* New Haven: Yale University Press, 1951.

Hull, C. L. *A behavior system: An introduction to behavior theory concerning the individual organism.* New Haven: Yale University Press, 1952.

Humes, J. F. "The effects of occupational music on scrappage in the manufacture of radio tubes." *Journal of Applied Psychology 25* (1941): 573–587.

Hunt, J. McV. "Experience and the development of motivation: Some interpretations." *Child Development 31* (1960): 489–504.

Hunter, E. *Brain-washing in Red China: The calculated destruction of men's minds.* New York: Vanguard Press, Inc., 1953.

Husek, T. R., and Alexander, S. "The effectiveness of the anxiety differential in examination stress situations." *Educational and Psychological Measurement 23* (1963): 309–318.

Institut de Médecine et de Chirurgie Expérimentales. Montréal: Université de Montréal, Faculté de Médecine, 1964.

Irish, D. P. "Reactions of Caucasian residents to Japanese-American neighbors." *Journal of Social Issues 8* (1952): 10–17.

Isaac, W., and DeVito, J. L. "Effect of sensory stimulation on the activity of normal and prefrontal-lobectomized monkeys." *Journal of Comparative and Physiological Psychology 51* (1958): 172–174.

Isaac, W., and Kendall, N. P. "Sensory stimulation and timing behavior." *Psychonomic Science 8* (1967): 41–42.

Isaac, W., and Reed, W. G. "The effect of sensory stimulation on the activity of cats." *Journal of Comparative and Physiological Psychology 54* (1961): 677–678.

Ittelson, W. H., Proshansky, H. M., and Rivlin, L. G. "The environmental psychology of the psychiatric ward." In *Environmental psychology: Man and his physical setting,* ed. H. M. Proshansky, W. H. Ittelson, and L. G. Rivlin, pp. 419–439. New York: Holt, Rinehart & Winston, Inc., 1970.

Ittelson, W. H., Rivlin, L. G., and Proshansky, H. M. "The use of behavioral maps in environmental psychology." In *Environmental psychology: Man and his physical setting,* ed. H. M. Proshansky, W. H. Ittelson, and L. G. Rivlin, pp. 658–668. New York: Holt, Rinehart & Winston, Inc., 1970.

Izumi, K. "Psychosocial phenomena and building design." *Building Research,* July–August (1965): 9–11.

Jackson, D. N. *Personality Research Form Manual.* Goshen, New York: Research Psychologists Press, 1967.

Jahoda, M., and West, P. S. "Race relations in public housing." *Journal of Social Issues* 7 (1951): 132–139.

James, J. P., and Hughes, G. R. "Generalization of habituation of the GSR to white noise of varying intensities." *Psychonomic Science 14* (1969): 163–164.

James, W. T., and Domingos, W. R. "The effect of color shock on motor performance and tremor." *Journal of General Psychology 48* (1953): 187–193.

Janis, I. L., Kaye, D., and Kirschner, P. "Facilitating effects of 'eating-while-reading' on responsiveness to persuasive communications." *Journal of Personality and Social Psychology 1* (1965): 181–186.

Jarvik, M. E. "Drugs and arousal." In *Explorations in the psychology of stress and anxiety,* ed. B. P. Rourke, pp. 43–48. Don Mills, Canada: Longmans Canada Limited, 1969.

Johnson, E., III, and Myers, T. I. "The development and use of the primary affect scale (PAS)." Research report of the Naval Medical Research Institute, 1967.

Jones, A. "Drive and incentive variables associated with the statistical properties of sequences of stimuli." *Journal of Experimental Psychology 67* (1964): 423–431.

Jones, A. "Information deprivation in humans." In *Progress in experimental personality research,* Vol. 3, ed. B. A. Maher, pp. 241–307. New York: Academic Press, Inc., 1966.

Kansaku, J. "The analytic study of affective values of color combinations: A study of color pairs." *Japanese Journal of Psychology 34* (1963): 11–12.

Karwoski, T. F., and Odbert, H. S. "Color-music." *Psychological Monographs, 50* (1938) (2, Whole No. 222).

Karwoski, T. F., Odbert, H. S., and Osgood, C. E. "Studies in synesthetic thinking: II. The role of form in visual responses to music." *Journal of General Psychology 26* (1942): 199–222.

Kasmar, J. V. "The development of a usable lexicon of environmental descriptors." *Environment and Behavior 2* (1970): 153–169.

Kearney, G. E. "Hue preferences as a function of ambient temperatures." *Australian Journal of Psychology 18* (1966): 271–275.

Keeling, C. D. "A chemist thinks about the future." *Archives of Environmental Health 20* (1970): 764–777.

Kelley, H. H. "Attribution theory in social psychology." In *Nebraska symposium on motivation*, ed. D. Levine, pp. 192–240. Lincoln, Nebraska: University of Nebraska Press, 1967.

Kelly, G. *The psychology of personal constructs*. 2 vols. New York: W. W. Norton & Company, Inc., 1955.

Kendon, A. "Some observations on interactional synchrony." Unpublished manuscript, Western Psychiatric Institute and Clinic, Pittsburgh, Pennsylvania, 1967.

Kimble, G. A. *Hilgard and Marquis' conditioning and learning*. New York: Appleton-Century-Crofts, 1961.

Kimura, T. "Apparent warmth and heaviness of colours." *Japanese Journal of Psychology 20* (1950): 33–36.

Kipnis, D. M. "Interaction between members of bomber crews as a determinant of sociometric choice." *Human Relations 10* (1957): 263–270.

Kirk, R. E., and Hecht, E. "Maintenance of vigilance by programmed noise." *Perceptual and Motor Skills 16* (1963): 553–560.

Kish, G. B. "Learning when the onset of illumination is used as reinforcing stimulus." *Journal of Comparative and Physiological Psychology 48* (1955): 261–264.

Koffka, K. *Principles of Gestalt psychology*. New York: Harcourt, Brace & World, Inc., 1935.

Konz, S. A. "The effect of background music on productivity of four tasks." Unpublished doctoral dissertation, University of Illinois, 1964.

Korchin, S. J., Basowitz, H., Grinker, R. R., Hamburg, D. A., Persky, H., Sabshin, M. A., Heath, H., and Board, F. A. "Experience of perceptual distortion as a source of anxiety." *A.M.A. Archives of Neurology and Psychiatry 80* (1958): 98–113.

Kryter, K. D. "The effects of noise on man." *Journal of Speech Disturbance,* 1950 (Monogr. Suppl. 1).

Kryter, K. D. "Laboratory tests of physiological-psychological reactions to sonic booms." *Journal of the Acoustical Society of America 39* (1966): S65–S72. (a)

Kryter, K. D. "Psychological reactions to aircraft noise." *Science 151* (1966): 1346–1355. (b)

Kubzansky, P. E. "The effects of reduced environmental stimulation on human behavior: A review." In *The manipulation of human behavior*, ed. A. D. Biderman and H. Zimmer, pp. 51–95. New York: John Wiley & Sons, Inc., 1961.

Kuder, G. F., and Richardson, M. W. "The theory of estimation of test reliability." *Psychometrika 2* (1937): 151–160.

Kumata, H. "A factor analytic study of semantic structures across three selected cultures." Unpublished doctoral dissertation, University of Illinois, 1957.

Kumata, H., and Schramm, W. "A pilot study of cross-cultural meaning." *Public Opinion Quarterly 20* (1956): 229–238.

Lacey, J. I. "Individual differences in somatic response patterns." *Journal of Comparative and Physiological Psychology 43* (1950): 338-350.

Lacey, J. I. "Somatic response patterning and stress: Some revisions of activation theory." In *Psychological stress: Issues in research*, ed. M. H. Appley and R. Trumbull, pp. 14–37. New York: Appleton-Century-Crofts, 1967.

Lacey, J. I., Bateman, D. E., and Van Lehn, R. "Autonomic response specificity: An experimental study." *Psychosomatic Medicine 15* (1953): 8–21.

Laird, D. A., and Coye, K. "Psychological measurements of annoyance as related to pitch and loudness." *Journal of the Acoustical Society of America 1* (1929): 158–163.

Langer, J., and Rosenberg, B. G. "Non-verbal representation of verbal referents." *Perceptual and Motor Skills 19* (1964): 363–370.

Langfeld, H. S. "Synesthesia." *Psychological Bulletin 26* (1929): 582–585.

Lawler, C. O., and Lawler, E. E., III. "Color-mood associations in young children." *Journal of Genetic Psychology 107* (1965): 29–32.

Leckart, B. T., and Bakan, P. "Complexity judgments of photographs and looking time." *Perceptual and Motor Skills 21* (1965): 16–18.

Lewis, J., Baddeley, A. D., Bonham, K. G., and Lovett, D. "Traffic pollution and mental efficiency." *Nature 225* (1970): 95–97.

Lindsley, D. B. "Emotion." In *Handbook of experimental psychology*, ed. S. S. Stevens, pp. 473–516. New York: John Wiley & Sons, Inc., 1951.

Lindsley, D. B. "Psychophysiology and motivation." In *Nebraska symposium on motivation*, ed. M. R. Jones, pp. 44-105, Lincoln, Nebraska: University of Nebraska Press, 1957.

Lion, J. S. "The performance of manipulative and inspection tasks under tungsten and fluorescent lighting." *Ergonomics 7* (1964): 51–61.

Lorenz, K. *On aggression.* Translated by M. K. Wilson, New York: Harcourt, Brace & World, Inc., 1966.

Loring, W. C., Jr. "Housing characteristics and social disorganization." *Social Problems 3* (1956): 160–168.

Loveless, N. E., Brebner, J., and Hamilton, P. "Bisensory presentation of information." *Psychological Bulletin 73* (1970): 161–199.

Lovingood, B. W., Blyth, C. S., Peacock, W. H., and Lindsay, R. B. "Effects of d-amphetamine sulfate, caffeine, and high temperature on human performance." *Research Quarterly 38* (1967): 64–71.

Luft, J. "On nonverbal interaction." *Journal of Psychology 63* (1966): 261–268.

Lundholm, H. "The affective tone of lines: Experimental researches." *Psychological Review 28* (1921): 43-60.

Luria, A. R. *The mind of a mnemonist.* New York: Avon Books, 1969.

Lyman, S. M., and Scott, M. B. "Territoriality: A neglected sociological dimension." *Social Problems 14* (1967): 236–249.

Lynch, K., and Rivkin, M. "A walk around the block." *Landscape 8* (1959): 24–34.

McBain, W. N. "Noise, the 'arousal hypothesis,' and monotonous work." *Journal of Applied Psychology 45* (1961): 309–317.

McBride, G., King, M. G., and James, J. W. "Social proximity effects on galvanic skin responses in adult humans." *Journal of Psychology 61* (1965): 153–157.

McCall, R. B. "Stimulus change in light-contingent bar pressing." *Journal of Comparative and Physiological Psychology 59* (1965): 258–262.

McCarroll, J. E., Mitchell, K. M., Carpenter, R. J., and Anderson, J. P. "Analysis of three stimulus-seeking scales." *Psychological Reports 21* (1967): 853–856.

McClelland, D. C., Atkinson, J. W., Clark, R. A., and Lowell, E. L. *The achievement motive.* New York: Appleton-Century-Crofts, 1953.

McCord, C. P., and Witheridge, W. N. *Odors: Physiology and control.* New York: McGraw-Hill Book Company, 1949.

McCormick, E. J. *Human engineering.* New York: McGraw-Hill Book Company, 1957.

MacFarland, R. A., Roughton, F. J. W., Halperin, M. H., and Niven, J. I. "The effects of carbon monoxide and altitude on visual thresholds." *Journal of Aviation Medicine 15* (1944): 381–394.

McGehee, W., and Gardner, J. E. "Music in a complex industrial job." *Personnel Psychology 2* (1949): 405–417.

McMurray, G. A. "A study of 'fittingness' of signs to words by means of the semantic differential." *Journal of Experimental Psychology 56* (1958): 310–312.

Maddi, S. R. "Exploratory behavior and variation-seeking in man." In *Functions of varied experience*, ed. D. W. Fiske and S. R. Maddi, pp. 253–277. Homewood, Illinois: Dorsey Press, 1961.

Maher, B. A. *Principles of psychotherapy: An experimental approach.* New York: McGraw-Hill Book Company, 1966.

Maisonneuve, J., Palmade, G., and Fourment, C. "Selective choices and propinquity." *Sociometry 15* (1952): 135–140.

Malmo, R. B. "Anxiety and behavioral arousal." *Psychological Review 64* (1957): 276–287.

Malmo, R. B. "Activation: A neuro-psychological dimension." *Psychological Review 66* (1959): 367–386.

Maltzman, I. "Individual differences in 'attention': The orienting reflex." In *Learning and individual differences,* ed. R. M. Gagné. Columbus, Ohio: Charles E. Merrill Publishers, 1967.

Mandler, G., and Sarason, S. B. "A study of anxiety and learning." *Journal of Abnormal and Social Psychology 47* (1952): 166–173.

Markus, T. A. "The function of windows–a reappraisal." *Building Science 2* (1967): 97–121.

Martens, R., and Landers, D. M. "Motor performance under stress: A test of the inverted-U hypothesis." *Journal of Personality and Social Psychology 16* (1970): 29–37.

Martin, B. "The assessment of anxiety by physiological behavioral measures." *Psychological Bulletin 58* (1961): 234–255.

Maslow, A. H., and Mintz, N. L. "Effects of esthetic surroundings: I. Initial effects of three esthetic conditions upon perceiving 'energy' and 'well-being' in faces." *Journal of Psychology 41* (1956): 247–254.

Mason, J. W. "The central nervous system regulation of ACTH secretion." In *Reticular formation of the brain,* ed. H. H. Jasper, L. D. Proctor, R. S. Knighton, W. C. Noshay, and R. T. Costello, pp. 645–670. Boston: Little, Brown and Company, 1958.

Mason, J. W. "Visceral functions of the nervous system." *Annual Review of Physiology 21* (1959): 353–380. (a)

Mason, J. W. "Psychological influences on the pituitary-adrenal cortical system." In *Recent progress in hormone research: Proceedings of the Laurentian hormone conference,* Vol. 15, ed. G. Pincus, pp. 345–389. New York: Academic Press, Inc., 1959. (b)

May, R. B. "Running for stimulus change." *Psychonomic Science 13* (1968): 11–12.

Mehrabian, A. *An analysis of personality theories.* Englewood Cliffs, New Jersey: Prentice-Hall, Inc., 1968.

Mehrabian, A. "Significance of posture and position in the communication of attitude and status relationships." *Psychological Bulletin 71* (1969): 359–372.

Mehrabian, A. "A semantic space for nonverbal behavior." *Journal of Consulting and Clinical Psychology 35* (1970): 248–257. (a)

Mehrabian, A. *Tactics of social influence.* Englewood Cliffs, New Jersey: Prentice-Hall, Inc., 1970. (b)

Mehrabian, A. "The development and validation of measures of affiliative tendency and sensitivity to rejection." *Educational and Psychological Measurement 30* (1970): 417-428. (c)

Mehrabian, A. "Some determinants of affiliation and conformity." *Psychological Reports 27* (1970): 19-29. (d)

Mehrabian, A. *Silent messages.* Belmont, California: Wadsworth Publishing Co., Inc., 1971. (a)

Mehrabian, A. "Verbal and nonverbal interaction of strangers in a waiting situation." *Journal of Experimental Research in Personality 5* (1971): 127-138. (b)

Mehrabian, A. "Nonverbal communication." In *Nebraska symposium on motivation, 1971,* ed. J. K. Cole, pp. 107-161. Lincoln Nebraska: University of Nebraska Press, 1972. (a)

Mehrabian, A. *Nonverbal communication.* Chicago: Aldine-Atherton, 1972. (b)

Mehrabian, A., and Diamond, S. G. "Seating arrangement and conversation." *Sociometry 34* (1971): 281-289. (a)

Mehrabian, A., and Diamond, S. G. "The effects of furniture arrangement, props, and personality on social interaction." *Journal of Personality and Social Psychology 20* (1971): 18-30. (b)

Mehrabian, A., and Epstein, N. "A measure of emotional empathy." *Journal of Personality 40* (1972): 525-543.

Mehrabian, A., and Ksionzky, S. "Models for affiliative and conformity behavior." *Psychological Bulletin 74* (1970): 110-126.

Mehrabian, A., and Ksionzky, S. "Categories of social behavior." *Comparative Group Studies 3* (1972): 425-436.

Mehrabian, A., and Ksionzky, S. "A theory of affiliation." Unpublished manuscript, UCLA, 1974.

Mehrabian, A., and Reed, H. "Some determinants of communication accuracy." *Psychological Bulletin 70* (1968): 365-381.

Melzack, R. "Irrational fears in the dog." *Canadian Journal of Psychology 6* (1952): 141-147.

Mendelson, J. H. "Alcohol." In *Principles of psychopharmacology,* ed. W. G. Clark and J. del Giudice, pp. 505-516. New York: Academic Press, Inc., 1970.

Middleton, W. C., Fay, P. J., Kerr, W. A., and Amft, F. "The effect of music on feelings of restfulness-tiredness and pleasantness-unpleasantness." *Journal of Psychology 17* (1944): 299-318.

Milerian, E. A. "Electrical activity of the cerebral cortex during attention to auditory stimuli." *Voprosy Psikhologii 6* (1955): 101–112.

Miller, J. G. "The development of experimental stress-sensitive tests for predicting performance in military tasks." Technical Report No. PBR 1079, 1953, Army Project No. 29562000, Psychological Research Association, Washington, D.C.

Miller, N. E. "Experimental studies of conflict." In *Personality and the behavior disorders*, ed. J. McV. Hunt, pp. 431–465. New York: The Ronald Press Company, 1944.

Miller, N. E. "Some implications of modern behavior theory for personality change and psychotherapy." In *Personality change*, ed. P. Worchel and D. Byrne, pp. 149–175. New York: John Wiley & Sons, Inc., 1964.

Minton, H. L. "A replication of perceptual curiosity as a function of stimulus complexity." *Journal of Experimental Psychology 66* (1963): 522–524.

Mintz, N. L. "Effects of esthetic surroundings: II. Prolonged and repeated experience in a 'beautiful' and an 'ugly' room." *Journal of Psychology 41* (1956): 459–466.

Montgomery, K. C. "Exploratory behavior as a function of 'similarity' of stimulus situations." *Journal of Comparative and Physiological Psychology 46* (1953): 129–133.

Montgomery, K. C. "The role of the exploratory drive in learning." *Journal of Comparative and Physiological Psychology 47* (1954): 60–64.

Montgomery, K. C. "The relation between fear induced by novel stimulation and exploratory behavior." *Journal of Comparative and Physiological Psychology 48* (1955): 254–260.

Montgomery, K. C., and Segall, M. "Discrimination learning based upon the exploratory drive." *Journal of Comparative and Physiological Psychology 48* (1955): 225–228.

Moon, L. E., and Lodahl, T. M. "The reinforcing effect of changes in illumination on lever-pressing in the monkey." *American Journal of Psychology 69* (1956): 288–290.

Mooney, R. L., and Gordon, L. V. *The Mooney Problem Check Lists.* New York: The Psychological Corporation, 1950.

Munsinger, H., and Kessen, W. "Uncertainty, structure, and preference." *Psychological Monographs 78* (1964): (9, Whole No. 586).

Murphy, S. D. "A review of effects on animals of exposure to auto exhaust and some of its components." *Journal of the Air Pollution Control Association 14* (1964): 303–308.

Murphy, S. D., Ulrich, C. E., and Leng, J. K. "Altered function in animals inhaling conjugated nitro-olefins." *Toxicology and Applied Pharmacology 5* (1963): 319–330.

Nakshian, J. S. "The effects of red and green surroundings on behavior." *Journal of General Psychology 70* (1964): 143–161.

Newcomb, T. M. *The acquaintance process.* New York: Holt, Rinehart & Winston, Inc., 1961.

Newhall, S. M. "Warmth and coolness of colors." *Psychological Record 4* (1941): 198–212.

Newman, R. I., Jr., Hunt, D. L., and Rhodes, F. "Effects of music on employee attitude and productivity in a skateboard factory." *Journal of Applied Psychology 50* (1966): 493–496.

Nichols, K. A., and Champness, B. G. "Eye gaze and the GSR." *Journal of Experimental Social Psychology 7* (1971): 623–626.

Norman, R. D., and Scott, W. A. "Color and affect: A review and semantic evaluation." *Journal of General Psychology 46* (1952): 185–223.

Nowlis, V. "Research with the Mood Adjective Check List." In *Affect, cognition, and personality*, ed. S. S. Tomkins and C. E. Izard, pp. 352–389. New York: Springer Publishing Co., Inc., 1965.

Nunnally, J. C., Knott, P. D., Duchnowski, A., and Parker, R. "Pupillary response as a general measure of activation." *Perception and Psychophysics 2* (1967): 149–155.

Odbert, H. S., Karwoski, T. F., and Eckerson, A. B. "Studies in synesthetic thinking: I. Musical and verbal associations of color and mood." *Journal of General Psychology 26* (1942): 153–173.

Oken, D. "The psychophysiology and psychoendocrinology of stress and emotion." In *Psychological stress: Issues in research*, ed. M. H. Appley and R. Trumbull, pp. 43–64. New York: Appleton-Century-Crofts, 1967.

Okuma, T., Fujimori, M., and Hayashi, A. "The effect of environmental temperature on the electrocortical activity of cats immobilized by neuromuscular blocking agents." *Electroencephalography and Clinical Neurophysiology 18* (1965): 392–400.

Olds, J. "Pleasure centers in the brain." *Scientific American 195,* no. 4 (1956): 105–116.

Oltman, P. K. "Field dependence and arousal." *Perceptual and Motor Skills 19* (1964): 441.

Osgood, C. E. "The cross-cultural generality of visual-verbal synesthetic tendencies." *Behavioral Science 5* (1960): 146–169.

Osgood, C. E. "Dimensionality of the semantic space for communication via facial expressions." *Scandinavian Journal of Psychology 7* (1966): 1–30.

Osgood, C. E., Suci, G. J., and Tannenbaum, P. H. *The measurement of meaning.* Urbana: University of Illinois Press, 1957.

Osmond, H. "Function as the basis of psychiatric ward design." *Mental Hospitals 8* (1957): 23–32.

Osmond, H. "The relationship between architect and psychiatrist." In *Psychiatric architecture*, ed. C. Goshen. Washington, D. C.: American Psychiatric Association, 1959.

Osmond, H. "Worlds apart: Some thoughts about the architect, his client and his customer." Unpublished manuscript, Bureau of Research in Neurology and Psychiatry, Princeton, New Jersey, 1969.

Park, J. F., Jr., and Payne, M. C., Jr. "Effects of noise level and difficulty of task in performing division." *Journal of Applied Psychology 47* (1963): 367–368.

Penney, R. K., and McCann, B. "The children's reactive curiosity scale." *Physhological Reports 15* (1964): 323–334.

Penney, R. K., and Reinehr, R. C. "Development of a stimulus-variation seeking scale for adults." *Psychological Reports 18* (1966): 631–638.

Pereboom, A. C. "Systematic-representative study of spontaneous activity in the rat." *Psychological Reports 22* (1968): 717–732.

Perret, E., Grandjean, E., and Lauber, A. "Subjective evaluation of distress created by airplane sounds." *Travail Humain 27* (1964): 53–62.

Persky, H., Hamburg, D. A., Basowitz, H., Grinker, R. R., Sabshin, M., Korchin, S. J., Herz, M., Board, F. A., and Heath, H. A. "Relation of emotional responses and changes in plasma hydrocortisone level after stressful interview." *A.M.A. Archives of Neurology and Psychiatry 79* (1958): 434–447.

Peterson, J. E., and Stewart, R. D. "Absorption and elimination of carbon monoxide by inactive young men." *Archives of Environmental Health 21* (1970): 165–171.

Philipp, R. L., and Wilde, G. J. S. "Stimulation seeking behavior and extraversion." *Acta Psychologica 32* (1970): 269–280.

Pitts, C. E. "Affective arousal as a function of deviations in perceived complexity from an adaptation level." Unpublished doctoral dissertation, Washington University, 1963.

Plutchik, R. "The effects of high intensity intermittent sound on performance, feeling, and physiology." *Psychological Bulletin 56* (1959): 133–151.

Podvin, M. G. "The influence of music on the performance of a work task." *Journal of Music Therapy 4* (1967): 52–56.

Poffenberger, A. T., and Barrows, B. E. "The feeling value of lines." *Journal of Applied Psychology 8* (1924): 187–205.

Pogrund, R. S. "Biologic synergisms in rats produced by carbon monoxide and positive ions." *International Journal of Biometeorology 13* (1969): 123–134.

Premack, D. "Reinforcement theory." In *Nebraska symposium on motivation*, ed. D. Levine, pp. 123–180. Lincoln, Nebraska: University of Nebraska Press, 1965.

Pressey, S. L. "The influence of color upon mental and motor efficiency." *American Journal of Psychology 32* (1921): 326–356.

Price, D. B., Thaler, M., and Mason, J. W. "Preoperative emotional states and adrenal cortical activity: Studies on cardiac and pulmonary surgery patients." *A.M.A. Archives of Neurology and Psychiatry 77* (1957): 646–656.

Proshansky, H. M., Ittelson, W. H., and Rivlin, L. G., eds. *Environmental psychology: Man and his physical setting.* New York: Holt, Rinehart & Winston, Inc., 1970. (a)

Proshansky, H. M., Ittelson, W. H., and Rivlin, L. G. "Freedom of choice and behavior in a physical setting." In *Environmental psychology: Man and his physical setting*, ed. H. M. Proshansky, W. H. Ittelson, and L. G. Rivlin, pp. 173–183. New York: Holt, Rinehart & Winston, Inc., 1970.   (b)

Proshansky, H. M., Ittelson, W. H., and Rivlin, L. G. "The influence of the physical environment on behavior: Some basic assumptions." In *Environmental psychology: Man and his physical setting*, ed. H. M. Proshansky, W. H. Ittelson, and L. G. Rivlin, pp. 27–37. New York: Holt, Rinehart & Winston, Inc., 1970. (c)

Provins, K. A. "Environmental conditions and driving efficiency: A review." *Ergonomics 2* (1958): 97–107.

Provins, K.A. "Environmental heat, body temperature and behavior: An hypothesis." *Australian Journal of Psychology 18* (1966): 118–129.

Radloff, R., and Helmreich, R. *Groups under stress: Psychological research in Sealab II.* New York: Appleton-Century-Crofts, 1968.

Ramsey, J. M. "Oxygen reduction and reaction time in hypoxic and normal drivers." *Archives of Environmental Health 20* (1970): 597–601.

Rand, G. "What psychology asks of urban planning." *American Psychologist 24* (1969): 929–935.

Razran, G. H. S. "Conditioning away social bias by the luncheon technique." *Psychological Bulletin 35* (1938): 693.

Razran, G. H. S. "Conditional response changes in rating and appraising sociopolitical slogans." *Psychological Bulletin 37* (1940): 481.

Rieber, M. "The effect of music on the activity level of children." *Psychonomic Science 3* (1965): 325–326.

Ritter, C. E. *A woman in the polar night.* New York: E. P. Dutton & Co., Inc., 1954.

Rohles, F. H., Jr. "Environmental psychology: A bucket of worms." *Psychology Today 1* (1967): 55–63.

Rosenberg, B. G., and Langer, J. "A study of postural-gestural communication." *Journal of Personality and Social Psychology 2* (1965): 593–597.

Rosenberg, B. G., Langer, J., and Stewart, J. "Nonverbal learning." *American Journal of Psychology 82* (1969): 181–190.

Ross, R. T. "Studies in the psychology of the theater." *Psychological Record 2* (1938): 127–190.

Russo, N. J. "Connotation of seating arrangements." *Cornell Journal of Social Relations 2* (1967): 37–44.

Sabshin, M., Hamburg, D. A., Grinker, R. R., Persky, H., Basowitz, H., Korchin, S. J., and Chevalier, J. A. "Significance of preexperimental studies in the psychosomatic laboratory." *Archives of Neurology and Psychiatry 78* (1957): 207–219.

Sarason, I. G. "Empirical findings and theoretical problems in the use of anxiety scales." *Psychological Bulletin 57* (1960): 403–415.

Schachter, S. *The psychology of affiliation.* Stanford, California: Stanford University Press, 1959.

Schaie, K. W. "A Q-sort study of color-mood association." *Journal of Projective Techniques 25* (1961): 341–346. (a)

Schaie, K. W. "Scaling the association between colors and moodtones." *American Journal of Psychology 74* (1961): 266–273. (b)

Scheerer, M., and Lyons, J. "Line drawings and matching responses to words." *Journal of Personality 25* (1957): 251–273.

Schmitt, R. C. "Implications of density in Hong Kong." *Journal of the American Institute of Planners 29* (1963): 210–217.

Schroder, H. M., Driver, M. J., and Streufert, S. *Human information processing.* New York: Holt, Rinehart & Winston, Inc., 1967.

Schulte, J. H. "Effect of mild carbon monoxide intoxication." *Archives of Environmental Health 7* (1963): 524–530.

Schwartz, A. K. "Effect of white noise on bar-press rate in rats." *Psychonomic Science 8* (1967): 93–94.

Searles, H. F. *The non-human environment in normal development and in schizophrenia.* New York: International Universities Press, 1960.

Seaton, R., ed. *Miscellaneous undergraduate research on spatial behavior: A classified and annotated listing.* Berkeley: Department of Architecture, University of California, Berkeley, 1968.

Selye, H. *The physiology and pathology of exposure to stress.* Montreal: Acta, 1950.

Selye, H. *The story of the adaptation syndrome.* Montreal: Acta, 1952.

Selye, H. *The stress of life.* New York: McGraw-Hill Book Company, 1956.

Selye, H. "Perspectives in stress research." *Perspectives in Biology and Medicine 2* (1959): 403–416.

Sem-Jacobsen, C. W., and Torkildsen, A. "Depth recording and electrical stimulation in the human brain." In *Electrical studies on the unanesthetized brain*, ed. E. R. Ramey and D. S. O'Doherty, pp. 275–290. New York: Hoeber Medical Division, Harper & Row, Publishers, 1960.

Sherif, M., Harvey, O.J., White, B. J., Hood, W. R., and Sherif, C. W. *Intergroup conflict and cooperation: The robbers' cave experiment.* Norman, Oklahoma: University of Oklahoma Press, 1961.

Shock, N. W., and Coombs, C. H. "Changes in skin resistance and affective tone." *American Journal of Psychology 49* (1937): 611–620.

Silverman, R. E. "The manifest anxiety scale as a measure of drive." *Journal of Abnormal Social Psychology 55* (1957): 94–97.

Simon, H. A. "Complexity and the representation of patterned sequences of symbols." *Psychological Review 79* (1972): 369–382.

Simpson, R. H., Quinn, M., and Ausubel, D. P. "Synesthesia in children: Association of colors with pure tone frequencies." *Journal of Genetic Psychology 89* (1956): 95–103.

Skinner, B. F. *Cumulative record.* Enlarged ed. New York: Appleton-Century-Crofts, 1961.

Slater, B. R. "Effects of noise on pupil performance." *Journal of Educational Psychology 59* (1968): 239–243.

Slocum, J. *Sailing alone around the world.* New York: P. F. Collier Books, Inc., 1962.

Smith, H. C. "Music in relation to employee attitudes, piece-work production, and industrial accidents." *Applied Psychology Monographs* (1947) no. 14.

Smith, K. R. "Intermittent loud noise and mental performance." *Science 114* (1951): 132–133.

Smith, P. C., and Curnow, R. " 'Arousal hypothesis' and the effects of music on purchasing behavior." *Journal of Applied Psychology 50* (1966): 255–256.

Smith, W. A. S. "Effects of industrial music in a work situation requiring complex mental activity." *Psychological Reports 8* (1961): 159–162.

Snider, J. G., and Osgood, C. E., eds. *Semantic differential technique.* Chicago: Aldine Publishing Company, 1969.

Sobol, M., and Day, H. I. "The effect of colour on exploratory behaviour and arousal." Paper read at the 28th Annual Meeting of the Canadian Psychological Association, Ottawa, June 1967.

Sokolov, E. N. "Neuronal models and the orienting reflex." In *The central nervous system and behavior*, ed. M. A. B. Brazier, pp. 187–276. New York: The George Macy Companies, Inc., 1960.

Sokolov, E. N. *Perception and the conditioned reflex.* New York: The Macmillan Company, 1963.

Soleri, P. *Arcology: The city in the image of man.* Cambridge, Massachusetts: The M.I.T. Press, 1969.

Solomon, L. N. "A factorial study of the meaning of complex auditory stimuli (passive sonar sounds)." Unpublished doctoral dissertation, University of Illinois, 1954.

Solomon, P., Leiderman, P. H., Mendelson, J., and Wexler, D. "Sensory deprivation: A review." *American Journal of Psychiatry 114* (1957): 357–363.

Sommer, R. *Personal space.* Englewood Cliffs, New Jersey: Prentice-Hall, Inc., 1969.

Spence, W., and Guilford, J. P. "The affective value of combinations of odors." *American Journal of Psychology 45* (1933): 495–501.

Spielberger, C. D., Gorsuch, R. L., and Lushene, R. E. *Manual for the State-Trait Anxiety Inventory.* Palo Alto, California: Consulting Psychologists Press, 1970.

Spielberger, C. D., Lushene, R. E., and McAdoo, W. G. "Theory and measurement of anxiety states." In *Handbook of modern personality theory,* ed. R. B. Cattell. In press.

Spivack, M. "Sensory distortions in tunnels and corridors." *Hospital and Community Psychiatry 18* (1967): 24–30.

Spivack, M. "Psychological implications of mental health center architecture." *Hospitals 43* (1969): 39–44.

Srivastava, R. K., and Good, L. R. *Patterns of group interaction behavior in three architecturally different psychiatric treatment environments.* Topeka, Kansas: Environmental Research Foundation, 1968.

Srivastava, R. K., and Good, L. R. *St. Margaret's Park public housing project, an environmental and behavioral profile.* Topeka, Kansas: Environmental Research Foundation, 1969.

Srivastava, R. K., and Peel, T. S. *Human movement as a function of color stimulation.* Topeka, Kansas: Environmental Research Foundation, 1968.

Steinberg, H. "Effects of nitrous oxide on reactions to stress." *Bulletin of British Psychological Society 23* (1954): 12.

Stennett, R. G. "The relationship of performance level to level of arousal." *Journal of Experimental Psychology 54* (1957): 54–61.

Stevens, S. S., and Harris, J. R. "The scaling of subjective roughness and smoothness." *Journal of Experimental Psychology 64* (1962): 489–494.

Stewart, R. D., Fisher, T. N., Hosko, M. J., Peterson, J. E., Baretta, E. D., and Dodd, H. C. "Experimental human exposure to methylene chloride." *Archives of Environmental Health 25* (1972): 342–348.

Stewart, R. D., Peterson, J. E., Baretta, E. D., Bachand, R. T., Hosko, M. J., and Herrmann, A. A. "Experimental human exposure to carbon monoxide." *Archives of Environmental Health 21* (1970): 154–164.

Stikar, J., and Hlavac, S. "The impact of noise on continued activity." *Ceskoslovenska Psychologie 7* (1963): 246–251.

Stone, L. A. "Subjective roughness and smoothness for individual judges." *Psychonomic Science 9* (1967): 347–348.

Suci, G. J. "An investigation of the similarity between the semantic spaces of five different cultures." Report for the Southwest Project in Comparative Psycholinguistics, 1957.

Teichner, W. H. "The subjective response to the thermal environment." *Human Factors 9* (1967): 497–510.

Teichner, W. H., Arees, E., and Reilly, R. "Noise and human performance, a psychophysiological approach." *Ergonomics 6* (1963): 83-97.

ten Cate, J., Horsten, G. P. M., and Koopman, L. J. "The influence of the body temperature on the EEG of the rat." *Electroencephalography and Clinical Neurophysiology 1* (1949):   231–235.

Terwilliger, R. F. "Pattern complexity and affective arousal." *Perceptual and Motor Skills 17* (1963): 387–395.

Teschan, P., and Gellhorn, E. "Influence of increased temperature on activity of the cerebral cortex." *American Journal of Physiology 159* (1949): 1-5.

Thayer, R. E. "Measurement of activation through self-report." *Psychological Reports 20* (1967): 663–678.

Thayer, R. E. "Activation states as assessed by verbal report and four psychophysiological variables." *Psychophysiology 7* (1970): 86–94.

Tinker, M. A. "Effect of stimulus-texture upon apparent warmth and affective value of colors." *American Journal of Psychology 51* (1938): 532–535.

Toffler, A. *Future Shock*. New York: Random House, Inc., 1970.

Triandis, H. C., and Osgood, C. E. "A comparative factorial analysis of semantic structures in monolingual Greek and American college students." *Journal of Abnormal and Social Psychology 57* (1958): 187–196.

Tucker, W. T. "Experiments in aesthetic communications." Unpublished doctoral dissertation, University of Illinois, 1955.

Uhlich, E. "Synästhesie und Geschlecht" [Synesthesia in the two sexes]. *Zeitschrift für Experimentelle und Angewandte Psychologie 4* (1957): 31–57.

Uhrbrock, R. S. "Music on the job: Its influence on worker morale and production." *Personnel Psychology 14* (1961): 9–38.

United States Department of Health, Education, and Welfare. "Air quality criteria for carbon monoxide." Washington, D.C.: United States Public Health Service, March 1970.

Valentine, C. W. *The experimental psychology of beauty.* London: Barnes and Noble, 1968.

Van der Ryn, S., and Silverstein, M. *Dorms at Berkeley: An environmental analysis.* Berkeley: Center for Planning and Development Research, 1967.

Vernon, J., and Hoffman, J. "Effects of sensory deprivation on learning rate in human beings." *Science 123* (1956): 1074-1075.

Vitz, P. C. "Preferences for rates of information presented by sequences of tones." *Journal of Experimental Psychology 68* (1964): 176-183.

Vitz, P. C. "Preferences for different amounts of visual complexity." *Behavioral Science 11* (1966): 105-114. (a)

Vitz, P. C. "Affect as a function of stimulus variation." *Journal of Experimental Psychology 71* (1966): 74-79. (b)

von Euler, C., and Söderberg, U. "The relation between gamma motor activity and the electroencephalogram." *Experientia 12* (1956): 278-279.

von Euler, C., and Söderberg, U. "The influence of hypothalamic thermoceptive structures on the electroencephalogram and gamma motor activity." *Electroencephalography and Clinical Neurophysiology 9* (1957): 391-408.

von Hornbostel, E. M. "Über Geruchshelligkeit." *Pflüger's Archiv für die gesamte Physiologie des Menschen und der Tiere 227* (1931): 517-538.

Walsh, P. A. S. "The relationship of acoustical environment to the evaluation of perceived loudness of connected discourse." Unpublished doctoral dissertation, Michigan State University, 1966.

Washburn, M. F., Haight, D., and Regensburg, J. "The relation of the pleasantness of color combinations to that of the colors seen singly." *American Journal of Psychology 32* (1921): 145-146.

Wayne, W.S., Wehrle, P. F., and Carroll, R. E. "Oxidant air pollution and athletic performance." *Journal of the American Medical Association 199* (1967): 901-904.

Weinstein, A., and Mackenzie, R. S. "Manual performance and arousal." *Perceptual and Motor Skills 22* (1966): 498.

Weir, P. A., and Hine, C. H. "Effects of various metals on behavior of conditioned goldfish." *Archives of Environmental Health 20* (1970): 45-51.

Weisen, A. "Differential reinforcing effects of onset and offset of stimulation on the operant behavior of normals, neurotics and psychopaths." Unpublished doctoral dissertation, University of Florida, 1965.

Wells, B. W. P. "The psycho-social influence of building environment: Socio-metric findings in large and small office spaces." *Building Science 1* (1965): 153-165. (a)

Wells, B. W. P. "Subjective responses to the lighting installation in a modern office building and their design implications." *Building Science 1* (1965): 57–68. (b)

Wells, B. W. P. "Psychological concepts of office design." In *Second national conference on architectural psychology*, ed. C. W. Taylor, R. Bailey, and C. H. H. Branch, pp. 1–27. Salt Lake City: University of Utah, 1967.

Wexner, L. B. "The degree to which colors (hues) are associated with mood-tones." *Journal of Applied Psychology 38* (1954): 432–435.

Weybrew, B. B. "Psychological problems of prolonged marine submergence." In *Unusual environments and human behavior*, ed. N. M. Burns, R. M. Chambers, and E. Hendler, pp. 87–125. London: Free Press of Glencoe, 1963.

Weybrew, B. B. "Patterns of psychophysiological response to military stress." In *Psychological stress,* ed. M. H. Appley and R. Trumbull, pp. 324–362. New York: Appleton-Century-Crofts, 1967.

Wiener, M., and Mehrabian, A. *Language within language: Immediacy, a channel in verbal communication.* New York: Appleton-Century-Crofts, 1968.

Wikler, A. "Pharmacologic dissociation of behavior and EEG 'sleep patterns' in dogs: Morphine, N-allylnormorphine, and atropine." *Proceedings of the Society of Experimental Biology and Medicine 79* (1952): 261–265.

Willerman, B., and Swanson, L. "An ecological determinant of differential amounts of sociometric choices within college sororities." *Sociometry 15* (1952): 326–329.

Williams, J. E., and Foley, J. W., Jr. "Connotative meanings of color names and color hues." *Perceptual and Motor Skills 26* (1968): 499–502.

Wilner, D. M., Walkley, R. P., and Cook, S. W. *Human relations in interracial housing.* Minneapolis: University of Minnesota Press, 1955.

Wilner, D. M., Walkley, R. P., Pinkerton, T. C., and Tayback, M. *The housing environment and family life: A longitudinal study of the effects of housing on morbidity and mental health.* Baltimore: The Johns Hopkins Press, 1962.

Wilson, G. D. "Arousal properties of red versus green." *Perceptual and Motor Skills 23* (1966): 947–949.

Wingfield, R. C., and Dennis, W. "The dependence of the rat's choice of pathways upon the length of the daily trial series." *Journal of Comparative Psychology 18* (1934): 135–147.

Winick, C., and Holt, H. "Seating position as nonverbal communication in group analysis." *Psychiatry 24* (1961): 171–182.

Winslow, C. A., and Herrington, L. P. "The influence of odor upon appetite." *American Journal of Hygiene 23* (1936): 143–156.

Witkin, H. A., Dyk, R. B., Faterson, H. F., Goodenough, D. R., and Karp, S. A. *Psychological differentiation: Studies in development.* New York: John Wiley & Sons, Inc., 1962.

Wohlwill, J. F. "Amount of stimulus exploration and preference as differential functions of stimulus complexity." *Perception and Psychophysics 4* (1968): 307–312.

Wohlwill, J. F. "The emerging discipline of environmental psychology." *American Psychologist 25* (1970): 303–312.

Woodhead, M. M. "An effect of noise on the distribution of attention." *Journal of Applied Psychology 50* (1966): 296–299.

Works, E. "The prejudice-interaction hypothesis from the point of view of the Negro minority group." *American Journal of Sociology 67* (1961): 47–52.

Wright, B. "The influence of hue, lightness, and saturation on apparent warmth and weight." *American Journal of Psychology 75* (1962): 232–241.

Wright, B., and Rainwater, L. "The meanings of color." *Journal of General Psychology 67* (1962): 89–99.

Yarrow, L. J. "Maternal deprivation: Toward an empirical and conceptual re-evaluation." *Psychological Bulletin 58* (1961): 459–490.

Zajonc, R. B. "Attitudinal effects of mere exposure." *Journal of Personality and Social Psychology 9* (1968): Monogr. Suppl. 2, 1–27.

Zander, A., and Havelin, A. "Social comparison and interpersonal attraction." *Human Relations 13* (1960): 21–32.

Zietz, K. "Gegenseitige Beeinflussung von Farb und Tonerlebnissen" [Mutual influences of color and sound experiences: Studies in experimentally induced synesthesia]. *Zeitschrift für Psychologie 121* (1931): 257–356.

Zimny, G. H., and Weidenfeller, E. W. "Effects of music upon GSR of children." *Child Development 33* (1962): 891–896.

Zimny, G. H., and Weidenfeller, E. W. "Effects of music upon GSR and heart-rate." *American Journal of Psychology 76* (1963): 311–314.

Zubek, J. P. "Effects of prolonged sensory and perceptual deprivation." *British Medical Bulletin 20* (1964): 38–42.

Zubek, J. P., Welch, G., and Saunders, M. G. "Electroencephalographic changes during and after 14 days of perceptual deprivation." *Science 139* (1963): 490–492.

Zuckerman, M., Kolin, E. A., Price, L., and Zoob, I. "Development of a sensation-seeking scale." *Journal of Consulting Psychology 28* (1964): 477–482.

Zuckerman, M., Schultz, D. P., and Hopkins, T. R. "Sensation seeking and volunteering for sensory deprivation and hypnosis experiments." *Journal of Consulting Psychology 31* (1967): 358–363.

Name Index

Subject Index

Acquiescence bias, 21–22
Activity factor of semantic differential, 16, 17, 28, 60, 84
Adaptation level, 62, 105–106
  diseases of, 102
Affiliation, 96, 97, 99, 125–131, 136, 137, 139–144, 148–153, 162, 163–170, 174, 198–199, 203
Affiliative tendency, 41, 45, 134, 162–170, 174–176, 182–188, 200
Afterimages, 11
Aggression, 17, 54–55, 99, 125, 130, 133–134, 174, 205. *See also* Anger; Hostility
Air pollution, 117–124. *See also* Pollution
Alcohol, 54–55, 99, 204
Anger, 22, 99. *See also* Hostility
Anxiety, 4, 17, 29–31, 44–45, 46–50, 99, 102–103, 122, 123, 137, 200
  and affiliation, 150, 163–170
  and approach-avoidance, 138–141, 162–181
  and arousal, 43, 47–50
  and chemical pollutants, 121–122
  correlation with arousal-seeking tendency, 44–45
  defined as pleasure, arousal, and dominance, 46–50
  and drugs, 49, 54–55
  and hostility, 134
  intercorrelations of various measures of trait, 44–45
  and noise, 116–117
  our semantic differential measure of, 33, 44–45
  state versus trait, 29–30, 200
  and task performance, 112–114, 123
Approach-avoidance, 4, 7, 8, 29, 55, 96–195, 198, 221
  and arousal, 99–115, 137
  and crowding, 131–132
  defined, 96
  and dominance, 115
  and pleasure, 18, 96–99, 137
  verbal measures of, 221
Architecture, 1, 4, 6, 68, 126, 128, 136. *See also* Design
Arousal, 4, 7, 8, 10, 14–17, 28, 46–54, 73–76, 178–189, 216–217
  and activity factor of the semantic differential, 16–17

and affiliation, 130–136
and anxiety, 43, 48
and approach-avoidance, 29–30, 96, 99–115, 137, 144–196
autonomic, 15
behavioral, 15
and chemical pollutants, 122
and color, 59–61, 75
defined, 18
and drugs, 49, 54–55
electrocortical, 15
as an environmental descriptor, 27–28
and hostility, 51, 132–134
and information rate, 84–88, 94–95
inverted-U function, 99–115, 130–132, 137–196
and light intensity, 63, 76
and odor, 66–67
optimal level of, 29–30, 53, 99–115, 130–132, 137–196
physiological, 14–16, 18–19, 48–49
psychometric properties, 20–22
reliability of trait, 46
and sound, 65–66, 76
and tactile stimulation, 67
and taste, 66–67
and temperature, 61–62, 76
as a trait, 29–30, 31, 33, 41, 45, 46–51, 112–115
verbal self-reports of, 15–16, 22–28
Arousal-seeking tendency, 29, 200 218–219
  and approach-avoidance, 137, 162–189
  correlations with other scales, 43–46
  defined, 29
  defined as pleasure, arousal, and dominance, 46–48
  and hostility, 134
  reliability, 43
  scale development, 30–45
  sex differences in, 45
  and trait arousal, 45
  validity, 43–46
Art, 16, 82, 107, 108
Ascending reticular activating system (ARAS), 14
Attitudes, 1, 4, 96, 114, 125, 129–130, 203
Attraction, interpersonal, 125. *See also* Affiliation
Auditory stimulation, 11–12, 64, 108,